Winter Brides

Winter Brides

A Year of Weddings Novella Collection

Denise Hunter, Deborah Raney
and Betsy St. Amant

ZONDERVAN

Winter Brides

This title is also available as a Zondervan e-book. Visit www.zondervan.com.
This title is also available as a Zondervan audiobook. Visit www.zondervan.com.

Requests for information should be addressed to:

Zondervan, *Grand Rapids, Michigan 49546*

Library of Congress Cataloging-in-Publication Data

Winter brides : a year of weddings novella collection / Denise Hunter, Betsy St. Amant, Deborah Raney.
pages cm
ISBN 978-0-310-33828-4 (paperback)
1. Christian fiction, American. 2. Love stories, American. 3. Weddings--Fiction. I. Hunter, Denise, 1968- December bride. II. St. Amant, Betsy. January bride. III. Raney, Deborah. February bride.
PS648.C43W56 2014
813'.01083823--dc23
2014031908

Interior design: James A. Phinnney
Printed in the United States of America

---

14 15 16 17 18 19 20 / RRD / 24 23 22 21 20 19 18 17 16 15 14 13 12 11 10 9 8 7 6 5 4 3 2

Contents

A December Bride

Denise Hunter

One

Layla O'Reilly squeezed into a corner of the bustling kitchen of Cappy's Pizzeria and leaned into the receiver.

"No, no, no. You cannot cancel on me now. The wedding's in five hours. *Five hours*, Cooper." She wound the spiral cord around her fist, a sweat breaking out on her forehead.

"Layla, I—"

"Don't even tell me you have to work. I asked you over a month ago. You said you got the night off."

"If you'd just let me talk. I have *strep*, Layla. I'm contagious. I have to be on an antibiotic for at least twenty-four hours before—"

"I'll risk it." She didn't care if he had malaria. She was going to this wedding, and she was going with a date. Nothing said *See, I've moved on* like an attractive man draped on your arm.

"I feel like trash. I have a 102-degree fever and barbed wire in my throat."

Layla took a deep breath, the familiar aromas of garlic and oregano filling her nose. She couldn't believe this was happening. "Now that you mention it, you don't sound so good."

"I'm sorry," he said. "I know tonight's a big deal."

She closed her eyes. "It's not your fault. The strep or the wedding." She banged the receiver against her temple once, twice, three times. "I'll bring you chicken soup tomorrow."

"My sister's already on it; don't worry about it. What are you going to do about tonight?"

"I don't know."

"Just don't go. You don't need them."

"My whole family will be there."

"This isn't about your family and you know it," he said. "This is about you having something to prove."

She knotted her fist around the cord. Nothing stung as long and hard as betrayal. "Shut it, Cooper."

"You know I'm right."

Olivia passed with a tray, nodding her head toward the back. Layla followed the direction of her nod. Cappy's bald head gleamed under the kitchen lights. He gave Layla a pointed look.

"I have to go. I'm in the middle of lunch rush."

She took two orders, working on automatic as her mind filtered through the possibilities. She had to find someone and quick. On her break she made a few calls. No luck.

Think, Layla.

She tidied her long brown ponytail before exiting the

break room. She had two and a half more hours of work, one hour to get ready, and a half-hour drive to Louisville. Feeling desperate, she scanned Cappy's. The new busboy, David, wasn't bad looking, and he was always smiling at her. She hadn't encouraged him because he was four years younger, but no one would know. Besides, desperate times and all that.

A few minutes later she walked away from David even more depressed. He was scheduled till closing. Worse, her invitation had encouraged him.

"You okay?" Olivia asked as she passed.

"Yeah, fine."

"Well, order's up for table four, and a family was just seated at five."

"Thanks." Layla grabbed the order from the heat lamp—a personal Whole Shebang—and headed toward four, her mind in overdrive.

She was tableside before she saw him. Seth Murphy recognized her at the same time. He pocketed his iPhone without taking his blue eyes off her.

"Layla," he said in that deep voice of his.

She tipped her chin up, set the pizza down, and didn't bother serving the first slice. "Murphy."

What was he doing here? At her station? Not that he had any way of knowing that. "Don't you have a wedding to be at?" She clamped her lips shut before anything else leaked out.

He checked his watch, a casual number with a big face and lots of dials. "Few hours." He opened his mouth again, then wisely shut it.

She spun around to table five before he could ask her the same. She felt Murphy's eyes on her back as she took the order, making heat flood the back of her neck. She didn't run into him much—didn't exactly travel in the same circles. But when she did, it was awkward. No one knew better than Murphy how badly Jack had hurt her. And no one, save Jack and Jessica, was more responsible.

She brought table five their drinks and delivered the bill to a couple squeezed into one side of a two-seater booth. She briefly considered ignoring Murphy's empty glass, but her conscience kicked in.

A minute later she set down a fresh Mountain Dew and ripped the bill from the tab. Normally she didn't leave it this early, but Murphy wasn't her normal customer. It was hard to be close to him again. To stay angry at him.

"Can I get you anything else?"

He leaned back against the red vinyl booth. The light from the overhead pendant washed over his features in a flattering way. He'd always reminded her of Ryan Gosling, especially when he wasn't wearing that infernal Murphy's Hardware cap.

He opened his mouth and shut it again. She was so tired of being tiptoed around. By him. By everyone.

She pulled herself to her full five feet six and tossed her ponytail over her shoulder. "Go ahead."

He blinked. "What?"

"Go ahead and ask."

His gaze dropped to the half-eaten slice on his plate. He hadn't shaved yet. The five o'clock shadow only made him more handsome. "Layla . . ."

"Yes, I'm going to the wedding. Yes, I'm over him. And yes, I'm happy for my cousin. That about cover it?"

His eyes drifted to hers again. It was all she could do to hold his gaze. He had a way of looking at her that made her feel like he was seeing all the way inside. She hadn't seen that gaze since the summer they painted sets at the community theater. She'd liked it then. Now, not so much.

"I'm glad," he said. "You deserve . . ." He struggled to fill in the blank.

She didn't need his take on that anyway. She slapped the bill facedown. "Have a nice afternoon, Murphy."

Her heart was beating too fast as she spun away. Her legs trembled as she made her way to the kitchen. If seeing Murphy had this effect, what would tonight be like? Seeing Jack and Jessica exchanging vows, kissing, dancing?

She didn't have time to worry about her feelings. She still needed a date, and the clock was ticking. She'd exhausted her contact list. She scanned the restaurant again as she carried out an order. A group of guys she didn't know had gathered around the pool table in the back room. Married couples and families filled the restaurant. She scanned the kitchen again. Three males. David, Cappy, and a man old enough to be her grandfather.

Come on, God, a little help here.

Her eyes fell on Murphy as she set down a medium pepperoni at the next table and began serving slices.

No. Absolutely not. For reasons too numerous to mention.

She gave a mechanical smile to the couple and went for more refills. Maybe he was single. And yes, attractive. But he was also a friend of Jack's. She was surprised he wasn't in the wedding, but then Jessica had probably insisted that Jack choose her brothers.

She looked out the tinted window to the snowy landscape. Fat snowflakes drifted to the white carpet. It was beautiful, she had to admit. Perfect day for a winter wedding. If things had gone differently, it might have been *her* day.

A loud slurp drew her eyes to Murphy's table. He set his empty cup down and took another bite of his pizza.

Fine. One more refill.

A minute later she set the drink on Murphy's table and turned to go.

"Layla . . ." He touched her arm. "Wait."

His touch sent a jolt of something through her. His fingers still rested lightly there. She turned, raising her brows.

"Do you . . . need a ride? To the wedding? The roads are getting bad."

She stared into his eyes. He had a way of catching her completely off guard. Always had. Even back when they'd been friends, back before she and Jack had gotten together.

"I mean—you probably have a date . . ."

"I did. Two hours ago. Cooper came down with strep."

He scratched his neck. "I'm going alone, so . . ."

"Oh."

Was this the answer? Was God sending her the most unlikely of lifelines?

And the real question: was she really that desperate?

Sadly, she knew the answer to that one.

"So," he said.

She shifted her weight. "Yeah, thanks. A ride would be great."

Something flickered in his eyes, but it was gone before she could guess what it was.

"Pick you up at five thirty?"

"Sure." Layla turned away before she could reconsider. Before she could wonder why her knees were knocking too hard to hold her upright.

Showing up at her ex-fiancé's wedding with Murphy was infinitely better than showing up alone. Wasn't it?

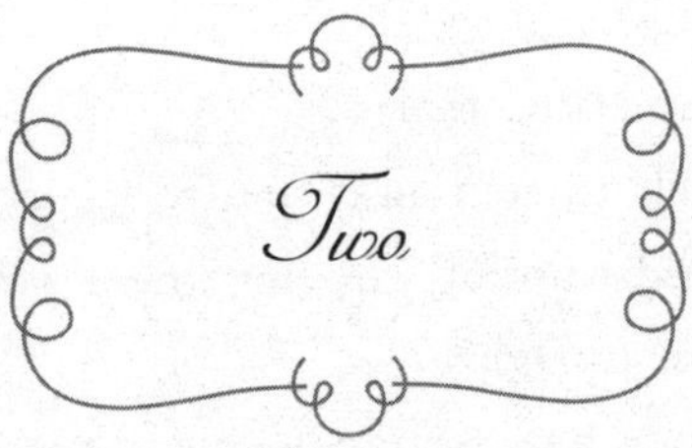

Two

Seth inched forward in the receiving line, glancing covertly at Layla. Her generous lips were set into a brittle smile, her moss-green eyes flashed with some emotion. She hadn't so much as flinched during the ceremony. Maybe she really was over Jack.

When they moved forward again, she stepped closer to him, tucking her hand into the crook of his elbow. He pulled her into his side, his heart shooting warning signals to his brain. *This has nothing to do with you*.

Layla had hardly looked at him since they'd left Chapel Springs except to shoot him disdainful looks. He couldn't seem to say anything right. Even when he'd complimented her appearance—and he'd meant every word—she'd twisted his words.

They moved forward. Jack was now just inches away. Jack, his former best friend. They were still friends, but it wasn't the same. Jack had changed as he'd moved up in the world. The old Jack never would've treated a woman so callously.

"Murphy." Jack reached out for a one-arm hug. "Thanks for coming, man."

"Congratulations, you two."

The groom's eyes drifted to Layla, widening slightly at the sight of her on Seth's arm. He recovered quickly, leaning in for a shoulder hug. "Layla. Thank you for coming."

As Layla pulled away from Jack, her hand tightened to a death grip on Seth's arm.

"Layla!" Jessica greeted her cousin with a plastic smile and leaned in for a kiss that didn't quite meet Layla's cheek.

"Jess. Congratulations." There was no sign of anxiety in her even tone. "You look lovely."

"Thank you! It took *forever* to find this dress." Her eyes swept down Layla and back up again. "Oh my gosh. I used to have a dress just like that. Mom finally gave it to Goodwill, but I just loved it."

Seth inched away, tugging Layla with him. "We should move on. We'll catch you at the reception."

As soon as they rounded the corner, Layla pulled away. Her shoulders set, she walked stiffly, her heels clicking on the hallway tile. There was no sign of distress on her face, save her clenched jaw.

"You're doing great," he said.

She shot him a look as they exited the church and remained quiet on the ride to the reception, which was being held at an elegant hall a few miles away.

After finding a table, Layla made the rounds with her family. Seth had offered to go with her, but got only a hard look in return. There was no question she blamed him for all this. But he'd never meant for it to happen. Would never have hurt Layla intentionally.

It had started when he'd intercepted a call from Jessica, whose car had broken down on the highway. How could he possibly have known when he sent Jack after her where it would lead? And in the coming weeks, when Jack had mentioned Jessica in passing, he'd thought nothing of it. In retrospect Seth could see he'd been a little slow on the uptake. And Layla blamed him for not warning her. Or maybe she blamed him for getting the ball rolling. Probably both.

He watched her now, peeling away from her great-aunts. Even with the fake smile, she was the most beautiful woman in the room, with her long dark hair, flawless skin, and wide green eyes. She was long-legged, with curves in all the right places. But that wasn't why she'd dug so deeply under his skin. No, it was her feisty spirit that drew him most. The way her eyes sparked with emotion. The way she stood up for herself and those she cared about. Layla was flat-out amazing.

And Jessica knew it too. That's why she jabbed at her cousin every chance she got. That comment in the receiving line had made him want to shake the spoiled woman. Watching Layla now, he had a feeling things hadn't gone any better with her aunts.

She was finishing what appeared to be a pleasant conversation with her dad; her brother, Beckett; and Beckett's fiancée, Madison. A moment later Layla passed by him, stopping at the open bar several feet away.

"Mr. Malcolm, good to see you," she said.

Stanley Malcolm extended his hand. "You too, ah . . ."

"Layla O'Reilly. I stopped into your office awhile back."

"Right, right. Nice to see you again."

Layla had recently started staging homes for sale. Seth had heard good things about her decorating skills, but she was still part-time at Cappy's, so he wondered if she was struggling to get her business off the ground.

Layla's body language exuded confidence as she spoke with Stanley. Good for her. Malcolm Realty specialized in the high-end historical homes in their region. Stanley could put her enterprise on the map. Layla handed him a business card, and he stuck it in the pocket of his suit coat.

Daniel Dawson, the very young mayor of Chapel Springs, approached them, extending his hand to Stanley. The broker turned from Layla to give Daniel his full attention.

Layla's smile fell away. Her hands floundered in the air a moment.

"Hello, Seth." Marsha Marquart appeared in front of him, blocking his view.

He stood and shook her hand. "Mrs. Marquart, good to see you."

"You haven't forgotten about Silent Night, have you?"

"Of course not." In a weak moment this summer she'd talked him into participating in the annual tour of homes the weekend before Christmas.

"I can't wait to see what you come up with." She patted his shoulder. "Have a lovely evening."

As she walked away, he wished for the dozenth time he'd turned her down. Decorating his old house was going to bite. He possessed exactly one boxful of Christmas decorations and zero decorating skills.

A commotion sounded at the front of room as the bride and groom made their entry. Layla returned to the table as the couple began their first dance. She said little to Seth through the toasts and dinner, chatting mostly with the others at the table. Beckett and Madison sat at Layla's other side, keeping her engaged.

As soon as the orchestra struck up a tune, Madison dragged Beckett onto the dance floor. Layla continued picking at her food. A curly wisp of hair had come loose from her updo, kissing the side of her face. Seth longed to brush it behind her ear, to feel the silky smoothness of her skin under the pad of his thumb. He clenched his fist before he followed through and got his hand smacked away.

He could only imagine what she was feeling. This must be the longest night of her life. "We can leave anytime you want."

She set her fork down. "We have to stay until they cut the cake."

Must be some kind of rule. The band struck up a new tune. An old Frank Sinatra song. More couples headed to the floor.

"Would you like to dance?"

She arched a delicate brow. "With you?"

He reached for his drink. "I'll take that as a no."

"Feel free to ask someone else, Murphy."

He wasn't leaving her now, even if he wanted to dance with someone else—and he didn't. Jack and Jessica were making the rounds, only one table away now. He could tell Layla had noticed by the way she punished the napkin in her lap.

"You can call me Seth, you know."

She shrugged.

"You used to." She used to do other things with him too. Like laugh and touch and make small talk.

"Jack always called you Murphy. I got used to it."

The other two couples slid away from their table to join the growing throng on the dance floor.

"So your house is in the Tour of Homes?" Layla asked a moment later.

"How'd you—"

"I overheard your conversation with Marsha."

"Ah. Yes, unfortunately, I succumbed to the pressure."

"Why unfortunately?"

He gave her a wry smile. "I'm pretty clueless when it comes to decorating. I don't even have—" An idea occurred. A pretty brilliant one. "You wouldn't be interested in helping me out . . ."

Her lips turned down. Her eyes dimmed as she turned away.

"I could pay you—"

"Hey, cuz!" Jessica sidled up beside them.

The four of them reconnected, their greetings as artificially sweetened as a can of Diet Coke.

"So are you guys, ah, together?" Jack asked.

Jessica swatted his shoulder. "Oh, honey, I'm sure they're not actually *together*. Layla's not his type."

Her implication was clear. Seth would never date a lowlife like Layla. Never mind that her groom had.

Seth reached for Layla's hand, closing it around her clenched fist. "Actually, we are."

"You don't mean dating . . ." The disbelief on Jessica's face made Seth want to shake her again.

His gaze toggled to Layla. "Yes, dating."

Jessica gave an unladylike snort and looked at Seth like he was missing a screw. "Seriously?"

"Jessica . . ." That was Jack's lame attempt to rein in his bride.

Layla's nose flared and her eyes flashed. Her lips parted.

Seth knew that look. "Engaged, actually."

Layla's head spun toward him.

"Just recently," Seth said, leaning in conspiratorially. "We haven't told anyone yet."

A moment of silence was punctuated by the pain of Layla's nails digging into his palm.

Jessica scowled, her eyes toggling between them and resting on Seth. "You are not engaged."

"Wow." A genuine grin spread across Jack's face. "Just . . . wow. Congratulations, guys. What a . . . wow."

"Jack, stop it," Jessica said. "There's no way he's marrying *Layla*."

The way she said Layla's name brought Seth an inch off his chair.

Jessica's eyes narrowed. "When?" Her tone challenged.

"Christmas Eve." Pain radiated from his palm.

"That's so great," Jack said. "Wow."

Jessica's maid of honor approached and said something in her ear before walking away.

"Duty calls," Jessica said, looking between them with a frown marring her perfectly made-up face. Then she seemed to shake it off. "It's cake-cutting time, baby." She planted a kiss on Jack's lips and gave Layla a syrupy smile. "We'll chat later, cuz."

~

Layla jerked her hand from Murphy's. "What. Have you. Done."

Murphy took a swig of his drink. His face gave nothing away. Maybe his eyes would, but he wouldn't look at her. And no wonder. He'd just announced their engagement to her ex-fiancé and the cousin he'd betrayed her with.

"*Murphy.*"

He set his drink down. A shadow flickered across his clean-shaven jaw. He ran his hand over his face. Finally his eyes drifted to hers. "I couldn't help it."

"You couldn't *help* it?"

"She was being awful. And you were about to go off on her, don't tell me you weren't."

"So you told them we're *engaged*?"

He flinched. "I didn't mean for it to go that far."

"Well it did!"

"She didn't believe it."

"Well *he* did!" Hadn't Murphy seen Jack's big ol' smile? Heard the hearty congratulations? She'd never seen him so relieved.

"It'll . . . blow over."

Layla stared at him, speechless. Something like this did not "blow over."

"Stop looking at me like that."

"Like you're crazy?" Layla drew a deep breath. Exhaled. She was vaguely aware of the activity around the cake table. Words being said into a mike. Laughter.

"Look," Murphy said. "It was an impulse. I'm sorry."

"You gave them a wedding date. A wedding date that's less than four weeks away."

"I'm sorry. I'll fix it."

"How?"

"I'll talk to him. I'll pull him aside when he's done up there. Explain."

"Explain that you felt sorry for me and were trying to make me look less pathetic?"

His eyes softened. "Nobody thinks that. I'll tell him the truth. That Jessica set me off with her . . . cosmetically engineered nose stuck up in the air like it always is."

"I don't think that's going to help." She took a sip of her drink. "Though I'd like to see Jack's face when you say it."

He looked at her, those blue eyes like a direct laser. "I'll fix it, Layla. You have my word."

". . . and that's why we'd like to make one more toast this evening," Jack was saying into the mike.

Layla halfheartedly turned her attention to the front of the room and the elaborate cake the bride and groom had just fed each other.

Jack held up his glass, his eyes honing in on Layla and Murphy.

Layla stopped breathing. A niggle of dread wormed up her spine and settled heavily in her throat.

"To my good friends, Murphy and Layla. Happy engagement, you two. We're very happy for both of you."

Three

The rumble of the engine cut through the silence inside the cab. Seth gave the Silverado some gas as he eased onto 65 North. Snow covered the road and traffic had slowed, but he drifted to the left lane and accelerated, the tension in the truck driving him faster.

He was afraid to look at Layla. Could almost feel the steam coming off her. Once he uncapped the bottle, she was going to blow. He hadn't thought he could make things worse between them, but somehow he'd managed.

They'd slipped from the reception hall shortly after the announcement. What else could they do? They had to figure out how to handle this. But so far she was uncharacteristically speechless.

"Layla . . . listen, I know you're mad—"

"You think?"

"—but I'll figure something out. Maybe we can just say it was a misunderstanding and—"

"My whole family was there!"

He let out a breath. "Okay. Let's think this through. Beckett and your dad are the only family who live in town. I'll call them tonight and—"

"Don't forget Jessica. And what about Daniel? The town *mayor*? And Stanley Malcolm and his wife? And William and Francis Wellington? It was a flipping Who's Who of Chapel Springs in there!"

He scrubbed a hand over his face. "I'll call them all tomorrow. I'll . . . tell them it was a mistake. A misunderstanding. My fault."

"Tomorrow's Sunday. Everyone'll be at church, and the gossip will fly."

She was probably right. "Well . . . good news doesn't spread as fast," he offered.

She gave a wry laugh. "Are you kidding? You and *me*? This is the juiciest kind of gossip."

She was so jaded. "I'll call tonight. I'll stay up until I've reached everyone."

"And wake them? That'll make them happy."

"I don't care about them." He cared about her. More than she'd ever know. More than he'd ever admit—what good would it do?

He dared a glance at her in the darkened cab. The glow of a streetlight streaked across her face, lighting her rigid features. There was something in her eyes. More than anger. She crossed her arms over her stomach, a protective gesture, and lifted her chin.

Wasn't it bad enough she was looked down on for reasons

beyond her control? Now she had to face another humiliation because he couldn't control his big mouth. *You're an idiot, Seth.*

Layla white-knuckled the dashboard. "Can you slow down, please?"

"Relax, this isn't your car. It's a—"

"What's *that* supposed to mean?"

He couldn't win with her. He sighed. "It means it's a four-wheel drive, and it handles just fine in the snow. If you could just take that chip off your shoulder for two seconds."

He remembered earlier when Stanley Malcolm had all but snubbed her, and he went a little soft inside. He eased off the gas. "You have a pen and paper?"

"What for?"

"We have a list to make."

Layla was shedding her dress when another text came in. Her brother had already blown up her phone. She hadn't responded yet. Didn't know what to say.

She ignored the text and checked her e-mail instead. A few had come in since she'd left home. Her eyes honed in on one from Stanley Malcolm.

> Layla, congratulations on your engagement! So glad we got the chance to speak about your business tonight. I'd like to meet you for lunch on Monday to continue our conversation. Why don't you bring your fiancé with you?

Layla gaped at the words. He wanted to meet her for lunch! He hadn't seemed interested at the reception—or the other time she'd spoken to him. She'd felt like a nuisance, but maybe he'd given it more thought. Or maybe he was just standoffish by nature.

She reread the e-mail, smiling, then noticed the part about Murphy. Why would he ask her to bring him along? No doubt they ran in the same circles, but—

Layla frowned. Had her supposed engagement to Murphy somehow lifted her in Stanley's eyes? Made her worthy of his attention?

She thought back to the two times she'd stopped into his office. The first time he'd spoken with her briefly, and she'd felt brushed off. The second she'd been told he was in a meeting. Their conversation earlier tonight had been pretty one-sided. He hadn't even glanced at her business card. He'd seemed only too eager to part ways when Daniel Dawson had approached. And now he suddenly wanted to have lunch. Now that she was engaged to the wealthy and reputable Seth Murphy.

She flung her dress onto the bed and jabbed her feet into her pajamas. She should be used to it by now. Still, it wasn't right. Her work should be taken at face value. She was good. She'd worked hard to earn her credentials. Her four clients had sold their homes quickly and had given her excellent references. She'd spent all her free time on her business, every spare dime on props.

But there were always some people who couldn't let it go. Couldn't see her for who she was, only where she'd come from. Never mind that her dad had gone through rehab and come out sober. Never mind that she now lived on the right side of the tracks. Barely.

She picked up her phone and stared at the e-mail, then scowled as she dug her phone book from the junk drawer in the kitchen. Seth couldn't have started making his calls yet. She hoped.

Four

Seth spotted Layla in a darkened corner of the café and made his way to her. He blew on his cold hands as he wove between full tables. The snow had stopped sometime during the night, but the temperatures hadn't made it into the double digits yet this morning.

After Layla's call last night he'd hardly slept. She'd raised more questions than she'd answered. His mind had spun all night with the kind of restless hope that could only lead to heartache. But that didn't stop him from dreaming.

He shrugged from his coat as he neared the booth. Judging by the shadows under Layla's eyes, he guessed she hadn't slept well either.

But her eyes brightened at the sight of him.

It was enough to give a guy a little hope.

"Morning."

"More like afternoon," she said.

"I overslept, missed church."

She squeezed a lemon into her water. "I didn't go at all. Too many questions I'm not ready to answer."

"Speaking of questions . . ."

Her eyes found his. Something he'd never seen flickered in the green depths. Uncertainty? Vulnerability? She looked away before he could decide.

A waitress approached, and they quickly settled on the special.

When she left, Seth tucked the menus behind the condiment caddy. "So what's this all about?" All she'd said last night was not to make those calls just yet.

Layla plucked the saltshaker from the caddy and balanced it on its beveled edge. Her long dark lashes swept down over her olive skin. She bit the inside of her lip, making it pucker. What he'd give for just one taste of those lips.

He longed for the summer they'd worked together on the play. Back when she talked to him. Back when she laughed with him and touched him, however fleetingly. Back before his best friend had beaten him to the punch.

Layla moved the shaker in circles. "I need a favor."

"What is it?"

Her eyes bounced off him, then focused on the saltshaker. "I got a text from Stanley Malcolm last night. He wants to meet me for lunch tomorrow to discuss doing some work for him."

"That's great, Layla. Your networking paid off." He couldn't help feeling a little proud of her.

"He, uh, wondered if you might like to come along."

"To your business lunch?" He lifted a shoulder. "You want me to?"

The saltshaker thwacked the table as it fell on its side. Grains of salt scattered.

Layla set the shaker in the caddy and brushed the salt into a tidy pile with her long, slender fingers. "Here's the thing. I, uh, think his interest in Superior Staging hinges on something else."

"Like . . ."

She nailed him with those big green eyes. When she looked at him like that, he'd do anything for her. Lunch. Yard work. Armed robbery . . .

"Like our being a couple."

The server set down his OJ and bustled away, but Seth couldn't take his eyes off Layla's face. Off the color blooming on her cheeks.

"Come again?"

Her fingers flittered around the salt pile, taking all her attention. "I've been thinking about it all night. He didn't give me the time of day until our . . . engagement was announced. I think he sees our association, such as it is, like some kind of endorsement. If I'm good enough for you, I'm good enough for him, I guess." Her chin notched up.

He didn't even like *her* thinking that way, much less anyone else. He frowned. "That's ridiculous."

She lifted a shoulder. "Well, it's the truth. Otherwise, why the sudden change?"

"He probably just wants to keep it friendly. Comfortable for you." But Seth was never going to change Layla's mind. And why should he? Another hour with her was another hour. "Sure, I'll go. No problem."

"That's not all." She swallowed hard. Turned a sheepish

look on him. "I might need you to, uh . . . hold off on breaking our engagement."

He turned his head to the side, eyeing her. "Hold off . . ."

"Just until I . . ." She swept the salt off the table and curled her arms over her stomach. "Look, I need to get my business off the ground. I need a realty group to hire me, and there's none more prestigious than Malcolm's. He specializes in the big stuff—the fancy historical homes and riverside estates."

"I bought my home two years ago from one of his agents."

"So you know what I'm talking about."

"But how's this going to work? People will think we're—"

"Just for a little while. If the lunch goes well, and he hires me, I'll be able to show him what I can do. Once he sees my work, he'll be satisfied."

There was nothing he'd like more than an extended fake engagement. Unless it was a real one. How much time would this give him? He remembered the hardened look on her face when she'd first spotted him in Cappy's yesterday.

Not nearly long enough, Seth.

"Maybe only a few days," Layla said. "I mean, once he gives me an assignment, I'll get right on it. He'll give me a contract, and *poof*—engagement over."

Nice. A few days wouldn't buy him nearly enough time. A few years was probably pushing it. And after the lunch there'd be no need for her to come around.

He needed to leverage this somehow. This was his chance to make things right, earn her trust, maybe even see if someday she could feel the same for him.

Layla's eyes darkened. Her arms shifted, crossing higher, over her chest. She leaned into the table, her eyes sparking. "Look. You got us into this mess. The least you can do is this tiny little favor."

Favor.

An idea formed in his head. One that would keep Layla around awhile. Maybe long enough to shift things between them. Only sheer willpower kept a triumphant smile from forming on his lips.

"Okay then," he said. "I'll make you a deal."

She pressed her lips together, narrowed her eyes. Her trust in him was overwhelming. "What kind of deal?"

"Remember when we talked about the Tour of Homes last night? I really could use your help."

"How much help?"

He shrugged. "I'll do the heavy lifting . . ."

"In other words, all of it. Do you have any idea how many hours a project like that takes? I think you're forgetting that you already owe me."

She didn't have to spell out all the reasons why. "Think of your portfolio. Decorating a home for the tour is prestigious. People come from all over the region, and they'd see your work." He was making this up as he went, loving that it was a win-win.

She leaned back, considering.

"You can even put up signage and leave business cards. No telling how much work you could get off this alone."

She took a sip of her water. Rearranged her silverware. "Do you have the decorations? I don't have any Christmas props."

He wasn't going to mention the mildewed cardboard box in his attic. "I'll buy whatever you need."

"You have any idea how much that's going to cost?"

"I own a hardware store—I'll get everything wholesale. What do you say?"

She cocked her head, regarding him. "You don't have a girlfriend who's going to pitch a fit about this?"

He lifted his shoulders. "Free as a bird."

"And you'll hang with me, even if it takes more than a few days."

"As long as it takes."

She regarded him steadily, quietly. For so long that Seth was about to explode before she finally extended her hand across the table.

"Fine. It's a deal."

Five

Stanley Malcolm was somewhere in his fifties, slender, with thinning gray hair. His winter-white skin creased around his eyes when he managed a smile, calling attention to his hazel eyes.

Layla bit into her club sandwich, barely tasting it as she listened to Stanley's monologue on the housing market. In the background a soothing rendition of "White Christmas" played over the restaurant's speakers, mingling with the clinking of silverware and the buzz of idle chatter.

Her nerves were already shot, and they hadn't even discussed her working with Malcolm Realty. Stanley was leading up to it in a slow, methodical way that was about to send her over the edge.

Beside her in the booth, Murphy finished off his BLT. He'd been quiet once the greetings and congratulations were out of the way. His jean-clad thigh pressed against hers, making her too warm. She wished she could ditch the suit coat, but the sleeves of her blouse were frayed.

"So you're new to the staging business, Layla?" Stanley pushed his salad plate back. The server removed it before he could lean back in the booth.

"Technically I opened in October, but I staged a few homes before that." They'd been friends' homes, and payment had been pizza and chocolate, but he didn't need to know that. "The four homes I've done since opening have sold within two months."

He gave her a nod. "That's impressive in this market."

She presented him with the statistics on staged homes, adding that it increased the value by three to four thousand, in effect paying for itself.

After viewing the chart, he handed it back to her. "I'm intrigued. Have you a portfolio I can see?"

"Actually, I have photos with me."

She pulled her iPad from her bag. The expenditure for the tablet had been painful, but now she was thinking it was worth every penny. She opened the photos and slid the iPad toward him, making an effort to breathe deeply.

Stanley swiped through the photos, nodding appreciatively at a couple. She wished the homes had been nicer. They were nowhere near the price range of most Malcolm homes.

"You're so talented, baby." Murphy edged closer, wrapping an arm around her.

She barely refrained from elbowing him in the gut.

"Thank you, Murph." She blinked innocently, using the nickname he hated.

Layla sipped her water, trying to hide her trembling fingers. Never mind that Stanley held her future in his hands. Never mind that he could make or break her business with the next words he uttered.

His business would keep her busy year-round. No more scrimping. No more Cappy's. No more cheapest apartment on the good side of town. She could buy a house of her own. She could do what she loved full-time. She could finally make a good name for herself.

A few minutes later Stanley handed the tablet back, his thin lips turned up in an almost-smile. "I like what I see here, Layla."

Yes. Her heart felt like it buzzed with caffeine. "Thank you." *Come on, Stanley. Make me an offer.* She was so close. "I'd love to work together."

A frown puckered between his brows. She wondered if he was thinking of her father. Of her lack of a college degree.

"I'm a hard worker, and I'm dependable. I can get you references if you'd like. My clients were more than satisfied."

The server came and removed the remainder of their plates. After they refused dessert, he left the bill.

Stanley set down his credit card, and an instant later it was removed. "My only qualm at this point is your lack of experience. Are you prepared to stage larger homes? Historicals? They require a different touch."

"I understand. Historicals have a certain authentic appeal. My strategy is to enhance the natural character of older homes. In fact, I'm starting work on a historical this week. I'm staging Murphy's home for the Silent Night Tour of Homes."

His eyebrows ticked up. "Very nice."

Murphy squeezed her shoulder. "Only the best."

Layla called upon her theater skills, trading a loving smile with Murphy.

"That'll give me the perfect opportunity to see what you can do," Stanley said.

See what she could do? The tour was almost three weeks away. She couldn't keep up this engagement that long. It had been all she could do to avoid her brother for a day and a half.

Layla worked to keep the smile on her face. "I'd be happy to give you a free sample with one of your existing homes."

"That won't be necessary." Stanley signed the credit card slip and tucked the credit card back in his wallet. "I'm sure you'll have your hands full with Seth's home." He took his coat and slid from the booth. "I'm afraid I have a one o'clock, so I have to run."

Layla shook his hand. "Thank you so much for lunch. And for the opportunity."

"I look forward to seeing what you can do, Layla." He took Murphy's hand. "Always good to see you, Seth. We should set up a tee time once all this winter muck clears away. I sure miss playing with your father. He was a heck of a golfer."

"That he was. Let's do it."

Only when Stanley had slipped out the door did Layla let the smile fall from her face. She tried to tell herself it had gone well. He liked her portfolio. He was going to give her a chance. But she'd hoped to walk away with a contract.

How could she maintain this engagement charade for

almost three weeks? Word had already spread. She'd hoped to get this squared away today. She had a dozen unanswered texts and four missed calls; she couldn't avoid them forever.

Murphy squeezed her shoulder. "Come on now, it went well."

She shrugged his hand away. "This hinges on the tour now, Murphy."

"You'll knock it out of the park and get the contract."

She nailed him with a look. "It also hinges on our engagement."

He shrugged. "So we ride it out a little while."

"We're supposed to be getting married in three weeks. It's going to look pretty suspicious when the invitations don't go out and no gets asked to be in the wedding party."

"I'm fine with a small wedding."

She jabbed him in the ribs, her elbow meeting a set of taut muscles. He let out a grunt. Why wasn't he the least bit concerned? She was glad her mom's side of the family was far away in Louisville. And she didn't have to worry about Jack and Jessica until they returned from their honeymoon.

There was another pleasant thought. Jessica would stir it all up. She wasn't happy unless she was making trouble. Wasn't it enough that she'd stolen Layla's fiancé?

And what was Layla going to tell Beckett? This wasn't going to work.

"I can't lie to my brother." They'd been through too much together. She didn't want to lie to her friends either. And she couldn't tell them the truth for fear it would get back to Stanley. If he found out they'd faked the engagement, he'd never hire her.

"Hey . . ." Murphy hooked a finger under her chin and turned her head until her eyes caught in his. "It's going to be fine. It's just a few weeks. Tell your brother the truth. He won't say anything. As for everyone else, it'll mostly just be putting up with a bunch of congratulations. Say thanks and move on. Mostly you'll be holed up at my place stringing lights and draping green stuff."

"Garlands," she said absently. That was true. She'd be busy. Maybe she could even cut her hours at Cappy's so she could focus on Murphy's house, not to mention avoid the general public. Financially it would be a challenge, but she knew how to stretch a dime.

She looked into his blue eyes, noticing subtle flecks of silver. They were nice eyes. Really nice. He had a fringe of dark lashes that would make most women jealous. "You think so?"

When he tweaked her chin, she wasn't even tempted to swat his hand away. "Piece of cake."

Six

Layla opened her front door to find her brother scowling on the stoop. She should've called him after lunch, but she'd wanted to scope out Murphy's house and start a list of supplies.

"I can explain," she said by way of greeting.

"By all means." Beckett edged past her into the living room. At least he hadn't brought Madison. This was embarrassing enough. She just hoped he could keep it to himself.

He followed her a few steps into her galley kitchen, where she gave the boiling pasta a stir.

"Have you eaten?" she asked.

"I'm going to Madison's for dinner. What's this about you and Seth Murphy, Layla?"

She really didn't want to start there. "I'll explain in a minute, but first I have good news."

Beckett leaned against the counter and crossed his bulky arms, frowning.

"So you know it's been an uphill battle, getting my business off the ground. Well, I've been able to make some inroads with Stanley Malcolm. He's the man who—"

"I know who he is. He approached me about building a boat a few weeks ago."

"Oh, nice. Well, anyway, we talked at the reception Saturday and had lunch again today. He really liked my portfolio. There's a good chance he'll hire me to stage his homes." She injected enthusiasm into her voice. "You know what that means?"

Beckett's frown relaxed. "That's great, little girl."

"I'll be able to quit Cappy's. Not only would I get to stage full-time, but I'd be doing some of the area's most upscale homes. Can you believe it?"

One corner of Beckett's mouth tipped up. "Yeah, I can." He wasn't much on words, but Beckett had always been there for her, believed in her.

He stirred the spaghetti sauce. "Want me to ask Madison's dad to put in a good word for you?"

"Mr. McKinley?"

"They're good friends. Stanley goes to our church."

Layla bit the inside of her lip. This was too close for comfort. If she told Beckett the engagement wasn't real, and he told Madison . . . Was it even fair to ask him to keep secrets from his fiancée? He hated secrets. One had nearly come between him and Madison. He wouldn't keep another from her, not after that.

And if Madison knew the truth, how long before the other McKinleys knew, before her father found out? Before it made its way back to Stanley?

"So," Beckett said. "You and Seth . . ."

Layla gave the spaghetti another stir. *Think, Layla.* Could she afford to tell the whole truth? "We met at the theater two summers ago, remember? I helped do the sets for *Nightingale*."

"I remember. I also remember you started going out with Seth's best friend, and I have a vague recollection of another engagement in there somewhere." He lifted the big spoon to his mouth, tasting the sauce.

She swatted his arm and snatched the spoon. "Thanks for the refresher. I was getting to all that if you'd just be patient." And give her time to figure this out.

"You've pretty much exhausted my patience over the past two days."

She fished in the cabinet for a strainer. "So, *anyway*. We kind of connected at the theater. He made me laugh, was easy to talk to, and he treated me, I don't know, as an equal." All true.

"You are an equal."

"You know what I mean." She came up with the strainer and set it in the sink. "I was, you know, attracted to him." Unfortunately, also true. "But then Jack asked me out. It was when I was working at the Quick Spin, and he'd come in weekly for his dry cleaning and flirt a little." She shrugged. "When he asked me out, I said yes. I didn't know he and Murphy were best friends."

"And once you went out with Jack, Seth backed off."

"Of course. Then there was the engagement—"

"And Jessica came between you—with a little help from Seth."

Layla snapped up tall. "A *little* help? He practically threw her in Jack's lap."

Beckett arched a brow. Okay, so she was a little bitter. Better rein it in a little. He was her fiancé now, after all.

Layla poured the cooked spaghetti into the strainer. "Water under the bridge. I've forgiven him." She flinched under the steam at the untruth.

Beckett gave the sauce a stir. "Glad to hear it. I always thought the blame was a little misplaced."

Layla bit the inside of her lip. Hard.

"I guess your relationship with Seth was a little sensitive, with Jack and all. Still, why didn't you tell me? I'm your brother."

Layla turned off the heat and looked up at Beckett. Strong, sturdy Beckett who'd always been there for her. While their father had been out finding his next buzz, her brother had attended her volleyball games and cheered her on at track meets. He was the one person she could always count on.

"I can't do this," she said.

"Can't do what?"

"It's not real. The engagement's a farce."

Beckett frowned. "What are you talking about?"

She explained the situation with Stanley and how the engagement, which really wasn't an engagement at all, had become a game changer. She tried her best to talk him over to her side, but the longer she talked, the deeper his scowl grew.

"I know, I know," she blurted before he said anything. "But it's just for a little while." She shot him a pleading look. "You think you could not mention any of this to Madison?"

He crossed his arms. "I'm not keeping secrets from my fiancée."

Layla slouched. She'd figured as much. "All right, I get it. But can you at least swear her to secrecy? If this gets back to Stanley, I'll be working at Cappy's until I retire."

His scowl let up a smidge. "Fine. But this isn't going to be as easy as you think. Dad's wanting us all to get together Friday. He wants to make sure Seth's good enough for you."

"Now he decides to be a dad." She sighed. Since her father had gone through rehab, he was like a different man. But she never knew what to expect from him. She'd distrusted him for too many years to take a chance like that.

"Better late than never."

"Fine. I'll check with Murphy. But you can't tell Dad."

"All right. But I hope you know what you're doing."

"Me too," she said as she gave the sauce another stir.

"Where do you want these?" Seth shifted the boxes of white Christmas lights in his arms.

Layla looked small standing in front of the grand fireplace in her fitted jeans and fuzzy red sweater. He could get used to seeing her in his home.

"Just set them anywhere," she said without turning.

He set the boxes by the mounds of fresh greenery in the middle of the room. The place already smelled like Christmas. She'd given him a list last night, saying she'd like to start in the morning. He'd never seen anyone in such a hurry to break an engagement.

"Do you have some Christmas catalogs I can look at?" she asked.

"Sure, back at the store."

She turned to him, her dark hair tumbling over her shoulder. "What kind of budget are we on?"

"Spend what you need to. I'm not worried about it."

"This could get expensive."

He wasn't going to let a few dollars come between her and her dream job. "This is your time to shine. Besides, I'll probably get suckered into doing the tour again next year."

Her eyes sparkled with excitement. She glanced around the room. She may not have wanted this job, but she was in her element now. Seemed almost giddy at the work in front of her.

"It's in great shape," she said.

"I refurbished it after I moved in." He'd painted the walls in the rich tones popular for the era. Removing the layers of paint from the trim and chair rail had taken months, but now the oak gleamed with a honey-colored stain. The wood floors had been another time-consuming challenge, but worth the work. Especially now.

"I'm glad you used authentic colors. I love the high ceilings and molded tiles. And the draperies are perfect."

"They came with the house."

"Even the furnishings are perfect. Antique but still masculine. I didn't know what I'd have to work with."

"Most of it came from Grandma's Attic." He hadn't sacrificed the modern amenities, though. The sofas were new. They blended with the style but were built with comfort in mind. He also had a sweet audiovisual system hidden away in the vintage entertainment center.

"I know it's kind of bare. I'm not much on the . . . doodads. And you might have to move stuff around to make it look better."

She shrugged. "That's fine. It's part of what I do. Take something ordinary and make it special."

He let his gaze roam over her. "It's already pretty special."

She looked away, a blush blooming on her cheeks.

The floorboards gave a squeak as she moved across the room. "I'm just glad I'll be able to use the theme I wanted."

"Which is . . . ?"

"An old-fashioned Christmas. I want the decorations to be simple, organic." She meandered over to the built-in bay that faced the street. "The tree will go here. Maybe eight foot, decorated with strung popcorn, old-fashioned ornaments, and candles. Not too big, though. It's not the focal point."

"What is, then?"

She turned. "The fireplace."

Floor-to-ceiling, it was unarguably the room's main event.

"I'm going to put an old sled up there." She pointed over the mantel. "A pair of skates draped here, some greenery to dress it up. A nice fat garland running across the mantel with candles, and homemade stockings hanging down. A cozy fire crackling—" She turned to him. "It's a working fireplace?"

"Yeah." He would've paid to see the smile that lit her face.

"Perfect." And then the smile slid away as she seemed to remember who she was talking to. She looked away, kneeling on the rug, and began picking through the boxes from the store.

"I have a couple empty rooms upstairs . . ."

"I saw them. I thought I'd ask Madison's mom if I can borrow some things from Grandma's Attic."

"Good idea."

She picked up her iPad and made some notes. Seth shifted on his feet. "Guess I should get back to work. No reason for me to hang around. Is there?"

"No, I'm good," she said without looking up from her tablet.

He remembered the way it used to be between them. The way conversation had flowed like the river. The way she'd touch him on the arm as she laughed. Now there was a cold shoulder wedged between them.

She set down the pad and sorted through the fresh evergreens, stirring up smells of Christmas past.

Maybe he should address the elephant in the room. Otherwise it was going to be a long three weeks. Besides, how could he hope to win her over unless she forgave him?

He cleared his throat. "Layla . . . I'm really sorry about my part in what happened between you and Jack."

Her hands stopped, the garland draped between her arms. He watched her face for some signal, but got nothing.

"I never saw Jessica as a potential threat," he said.

"I don't want to talk about it." She tossed her hair over her shoulder, set the greenery aside, and began picking at the berries on a wreath.

"She was your cousin. Why would he want her when he had *you*?"

She fixed him with a look. "I said I don't want to talk about it."

Why couldn't she see he hadn't meant any harm? That if Jack couldn't see what he'd lost, he wasn't worth the tears? Seth just wanted her forgiveness, but he could see that wasn't going to happen.

"We're going to be together a lot the next few weeks. Can we at least call a truce?"

Her lips pressed together. She went back to the wreath, her slender fingers working the sprigs of evergreen and the pinecones.

"Maybe you're not ready to forgive me. Okay. But can we put the past aside for a while? If memory serves, we got along pretty well before all this happened."

Her hands paused. Her eyes dropped to the floor. He knew she was remembering those long nights working on the sets. Laughing, teasing, flirting.

Man, he missed those days. For the hundredth time he wanted to slap himself for waiting too long.

"Fine. We'll put it aside."

He let out the breath he didn't know he'd been holding. "Thanks. That'll make this a lot more pleasant for the both of us." A text came in from an employee. Seth replied and pocketed his phone. "Have you told your brother yet?"

"Yeah. And he's going to tell Madison." She explained about Mr. McKinley's connection with Stanley and her fear that it would get back to him. "Beckett, Madison, and my dad want to get together Friday for dinner or something."

"Sounds good."

Two tiny crescents appeared between her brows. "You know what that means. Going out in public together. A whole evening of pretending. My dad'll probably give you the third degree. No, I'm going to put it off."

"We're supposed to get married in three weeks, right after the Tour of Homes. He's not going to put it off."

"Well, what do you suggest?"

"Let's invite them here for dinner. I'll cook. Keep it private, at least."

"I won't be anywhere near done by then. The house'll be a mess."

He shrugged. "Your call. But I make a mean lasagna. It's your favorite, right?"

She bit her lips, her eyes drifting around the room before settling on him again. "All right. But don't say I didn't warn you."

Seven

"How did we get sucked into this?" Layla finished lacing her ice skate and tied a bow. Beckett and Madison were already gliding around the frozen pond in the center of the town square. Dad was bumbling around the edge of the ice.

"What?" Murphy said. "It'll be fun. I can't remember the last time I went ice skating."

She picked at the knot on her other skate. Fat flakes of snow drifted down, settling on her hair and on the backs of her bare hands, making them stiff and clumsy. And the stupid knot wouldn't budge.

"I'm freezing, Murphy. I can't even work out this knot."

"Here, let me." He knelt in front of her. She was tempted to refuse his help, but what the heck. Let him do it. Her nerves were frayed from the long dinner, from the third degree—and she hadn't even been the recipient. It was a side of her dad she hadn't seen before.

She watched Madison and Beckett skating hand in hand. Madison lost her footing. Beckett caught her by the elbow, and they spun awkwardly until they came to a standstill, laughing. Nearby, Dad's arms windmilled before he steadied himself.

"You think he suspects anything?" Layla asked.

Murphy had loosened the knot and had her boot halfway laced. "Nope. Layla, you need to relax. Let's just go out there and have fun, okay?" A second later he tied a bow and patted her skate.

The music was nice—an upbeat Christmas tune. White lights twinkled from nearby pine trees, dancing in the breeze. And though it was snowing, it wasn't all that cold. He held out her gloves, and she stuffed her hands inside them.

He gave her a hand up. "Come on."

They skated side by side around the rink with a couple dozen others, mostly strangers. Layla was glad for that. The fewer people they knew, the better.

Awhile later Beckett and Madison joined them. They talked about her progress on the house. Dad skated up to them, a little steadier now that he'd practiced.

"How are the wedding plans going?" he asked Layla. "I don't know how you're finding time, what with staging the house and working at Cappy's."

"Sometimes wedding planning seems like a full-time job," Madison said.

Guilt pricked Layla. She couldn't wait for this night to end. "We're keeping it very simple."

"And I'm helping with whatever she needs," Murphy said.

"Hey, man," Beckett said. "You're making me look bad."

Madison elbowed her fiancé, trading a mock scowl. "Yes, *some* people can't make a simple phone call."

"I keep getting voice mail," Beckett said.

"Are you sure Christmas Eve's a good idea?" Dad asked. "A lot of people have family plans."

"We want to keep it small anyway," Layla said. So small no one would be there.

"You don't have a ring yet?" Dad must've noticed over dinner.

Murphy turned backward and skated in front of Layla. He took her gloved hands, holding eye contact. "We haven't found the right one yet, have we, baby?"

Murphy's cheeks were flushed, the tip of his nose red. Fog plumed in front of his face with each breath, and his blue eyes sparkled under the lighting. A fat flake landed on his eyelashes.

Layla unconsciously reached out and wiped it away with her gloved thumb. The look in his eyes shifted. She couldn't break away from his gaze. His hand tightened around hers. Suddenly she felt warm. Too many layers. She needed to ditch the scarf. Maybe the coat. What was wrong with her?

"You guys are cute together," Madison said.

Layla tore her eyes from Murphy. Her cheeks went warm under his stare.

"When did you realize you loved my girl, Seth?" Dad asked.

Layla stiffened. *Change the subject.* Her thoughts spun for a topic and came up empty. Her eyes flew to Murphy.

"It was at Cappy's, actually," Murphy said.

Layla frowned at him. What was he doing?

"At Cappy's?" Madison said.

"I was watching her work. She was waiting on the table next to mine, and the customer said something that made her laugh." His eyes held her hostage. "I thought, I could listen to that sound for the rest of my life."

Layla's breath caught. His breath plumed between them on an exhale. He'd been wasting his time on the sets. The guy should've had the lead role.

"That's sweet," Madison said. Layla could feel her eyes on them.

How was he doing this? Making stuff up off the cuff like that? Looking at her like she held his world in her hands? Wasn't this getting to him at all? Dad was eating it all up, and it was lies—all of it.

She had to get away from this—from them. "I . . . need a break. My ankles . . ." Layla pulled her hands from Murphy's and skated toward the bench. She was shaking and wasn't sure why. The stress of pretending? The look in Murphy's eyes? So disconcerting.

She wanted this night to be over. She wanted to flop into bed and pull the quilt over her head and pretend none of this was happening. But they'd only been here fifteen minutes.

On the shore, she passed the first bench and headed toward the one farther back in the shadows, shuffling along the frozen ground.

Her heart pounded and her limbs quaked. She just wanted to hide for a while. She didn't want to face Dad and his questions. Or Beckett and Madison and their knowing eyes.

She couldn't sit, even when she reached the bench. Even though her ankles throbbed. She perched on the seat back, facing away from the ice, glad for the cover of darkness.

The strains of "Santa Baby" floated through the air, suddenly cooler in the shadows of the night. Overhead, skeletal branches stretched across the darkened sky like icy fingers. In the distance someone laughed, and she remembered what Murphy had said. About realizing he loved her, about wanting to hear her laughter for the rest of his life.

"You okay?"

She jumped at the sound of his voice, so close.

"No, I'm not okay."

He stood in front of her, his face too shadowed to read.

"I can't stand this anymore. I'm lying to my father, and our friends think we're planning a wedding but we aren't, and someone's going to figure that out, and even if they don't, how are we going to get out of this when it's over?" Her voice rose as she went.

He set his hands on her shoulders. "Come on, baby, you've got to pull it together."

She shrugged his hands off. "What's with the baby stuff?" She didn't like it. And she didn't want to think too hard about why.

"Just hang in there awhile longer. We can't quit now. There's too much at stake."

Like her whole career. If they called off the engagement now, Stanley Malcolm would probably drop her like a hot potato even if she staged Murphy's home like the Biltmore Mansion.

"How can you stand this? How can you field questions and look all . . . swoony, and do it with a straight face?"

He stilled. And didn't speak for so long she was ready to shake the answer out of him. She regretted the shadows now because she couldn't see his eyes and didn't have a clue what he was thinking. But she could feel his tension in the rigid way he held himself. Could hear the stress of his shallow breaths.

"It's easy," he said so softly she strained to hear.

The last notes of the song rang out, fading into the night. Only her heartbeat, thumping hard and heavy, punctuated the silence.

"I just tell the truth," he whispered.

A soft, soulful tune began. The strains of the violins wove around them, casting a sweet spell. Layla couldn't breathe. Couldn't move.

Murphy turned and walked away, leaving her to stare after him.

Eight

Layla took the porch steps, careful of the slippery spots. Murphy's neighborhood was quiet on this Saturday morning. A dusting of snow covered the ground, and the chill in the air burned her lungs.

She stifled a yawn as she slid the key into the lock. She'd stared at the darkened ceiling half the night wondering about what Murphy had said. Turning the comment every which way. And every way she turned it, she ended up with the same view: Murphy had feelings for her.

She couldn't believe he might love her—though his answer to Dad's question suggested otherwise. And she definitely wasn't about to address the subject with him. Last night had been awkward enough.

Today she anticipated a much-needed break from him. He'd be at the hardware store, and she'd be off to work at Cappy's before he returned. The thought of a pleasant morning doing what she loved put a spring in her step as she entered the quiet house. She closed the door, shutting out the cold, and loosened her scarf.

Murphy emerged from the kitchen.

Layla jumped, palming her heart. Her eyes took stock. Pajama bottoms, dark skin, rippling muscles. There was a mug of coffee involved somewhere.

She spun around under the guise of hanging her coat. "Why aren't you at work?"

"I don't work Saturdays. What are you doing here?"

She tossed a look over her shoulder. "I *do*."

Even facing the other way, she could still see him. She closed her eyes against the picture. She was kidding herself. She'd never erase that image from her brain. Broad shoulders, sculpted chest, muscular arms. Nope. It was there for good.

"It's Saturday," he said. "I didn't think you'd be here so early."

"I have to be at Cappy's at two."

"Ahh . . . cup of coffee?"

"Sure. Thanks." Anything to get him out of the room. A set of clothes wouldn't hurt either. Who knew he was hiding all that under those flannel shirts?

A few minutes later he returned with a mug. She kept her eyes on the brew, caramel colored, just the way she liked it. "Thanks. You have a ladder somewhere?"

"In the garage. I'll get it before I hop in the shower."

"No hurry. Take your shower first."

She was in the library when he returned with the ladder. "Where do you want it?"

"Right there." She pointed to the strip of oak paneling

between the tall bookshelves, then put the finishing touches on the wreath.

"Can I help?"

"Hold this." She handed him the wreath as she climbed the ladder. It wobbled on the hardwood floor. "I guess the floor's not level."

"Part of the old house charm."

At the top she stretched high, reaching for the bottom of the picture hanging on the wall, then handed it down to him. The ladder wobbled as they swapped pieces.

She grabbed onto the sides, but it wobbled again. When she looked down at Murphy, he wore a roguish smile, and his eyes held a mischievous sparkle.

"Stop that," she said.

"What?"

"It was you."

"I don't know what you're talking about."

She spared him a look and climbed to the highest safe rung, hoping he had the good sense not to fool with the ladder anymore. The wreath wasn't heavy, but it was awkward. She tried to hook it on the nail that had held the picture. Missed. She rose on her toes. Just out of reach.

She breathed a laugh. "Sheesh." After another try, she lowered her arms for a rest.

The ladder moved. "Stop it."

She steadied herself, then realized the ladder wasn't wobbling. It was vibrating as Murphy climbed up behind her.

"What are you doing?"

"Helping."

She tightened her grip. "Get down. It isn't safe."

"This is the heaviest-duty ladder I sell. Since neither of us weighs three hundred pounds, it'll be fine."

He stopped behind her, the ladder stilling. The warmth of his chest pressed against her back. The clean, musky scent of his soap teased her nose. Her throat went dry. Her heart flittered around her chest like flurries in a snowstorm.

He took the wreath, leaning closer, reaching higher. His thighs pressed against hers. His breath stirred the hairs at her temple. A shiver skated down her spine.

Her legs trembled, and she braced a hand against the wall. *This is Murphy, Layla. Remember? The guy who practically threw Jessica at Jack? The guy who didn't bother mentioning that your fiancé was hooking up with your cousin?*

Even as the thought surfaced, Beckett's words came back to her. Had she blown Murphy's role out of proportion? Her thoughts tangled into a snarly knot.

Murphy settled the wreath against the wall and leaned back infinitesimally. "That where you want it?" His lips were inches from her ear. If she turned her head just a bit—

What the heck, Layla?

She gave the wreath a cursory glance. "Yeah." She didn't care if it was upside down, backward, and flourishing with a moldy infestation. "Can you get down already?"

"You seem a little tense." His tone teased. Did he know the effect he was having on her?

"You're shaking the ladder, and your weight is straining the capacity." Her fingers pressed against the wall, going white against the oak paneling.

"Have it your way." He leaned in, his lips close enough to brush her hair. "Let me know if you need any more help."

~

Layla was exhausted by the time dinner rush ended. It had been a busy night. A caroling group had stopped in, taking the whole back room, and the restaurant was short staffed. Earlier, during the slow hours, she'd experimented with the tables, moving them around to allow for better flow. She loved the new look. Cappy hated it, though, so she'd had to move it all back.

Now her station had cleared out, and she helped David by busing a couple of tables. On her way past the door, she saw Cooper by the hostess stand, brushing the snow from his brown curls. She hadn't seen him since he'd weaseled out of the wedding. And look where that had gotten her.

Be nice. It's not his fault. "Hey there. Feeling better?"

"Not as good as you, apparently." His crooked smile and brown eyes teased.

So he'd heard about the engagement. She reconsidered her plan, giving him a pointed look. "Table for one?"

"Yep."

She led him to a window booth, wondering how she was going to explain why she'd had a date planned with Cooper on the same night she'd turned up engaged.

Cooper slid into the booth, stretched out his long legs, and leveled his gaze at her. "So you gonna explain yourself, young lady?"

Layla notched up her chin. "Nope. Pepsi?"

He leveled a look at her. "That'll do. For now."

She took her time with the drink, hoping he wouldn't press hard. She could always just refuse to answer. They were friends, but not the spill-your-guts type. Layla didn't have any friends of that sort. Having been raised with a father, a grandfather, and a brother, she'd grown up accustomed to men and their ways.

She returned to Cooper's table with the Pepsi. "Decide what you want?"

Cooper cocked his head, gave her a half grin. "I want to know how a last-minute date turns into a spontaneous engagement."

She gave him a sassy look. "Yeah, well, I want a high salary and a mansion on Main Street, but we can't all have what we want, can we."

"So you're not gonna talk, huh?"

"Only about pizza."

"You know everyone else is talking about it."

Her stomach tightened at his words, but she kept a nonchalant smile. "About pizza?"

He chuckled, tugging the hem of her polo. "Fine. Be mysterious. I'll get it out of you eventually."

"Good luck with that."

"I don't need luck." He wiggled his fingers. "I got magic hands."

She gave in and laughed. "Which aren't coming anywhere near me, buddy." She raised her order pad, pen poised. "Did you just come to annoy me, or are you actually going to order something?"

"All right, all right." He frowned down at the menu. "Women," he muttered.

After taking his order, Layla headed toward the kitchen, spotting Murphy at a booth on the other side of the room. She couldn't miss his scowl.

Great. She hung the order, and when she spun around, he was right behind her. She stopped just short of slamming into his chest.

His hands curled around her upper arms. "Can I talk to you?"

"I'm working," she said quietly, aware of the eyes on them.

He was blocking her path. He didn't seem inclined to let go. His eyes impaled hers.

She huffed. "Fine." She led him down the darkened hall toward the restrooms and break room. She'd talked to Cappy so many times about taking the paneling down. The whole place needed brightening.

When they reached the end she turned, raising her eyebrows expectantly.

He planted his feet and crossed his arms. "You shouldn't be flirting with other guys."

"What? I wasn't, I was just—"

"Talking and laughing and tossing your hair—otherwise known as flirting."

Of all the nerve. "I was not— Who do you think you are?"

He leaned in, driving his point home. "Your fiancé."

She lowered her voice. "In case it got past your radar, we're not actually engaged."

His mouth tightened. A shadow flickered across his jaw. "But everyone thinks we are, and if they see you flirting with every Y chromosome that struts by, nobody's going to—"

"He's a *friend*, Murphy. I have lots of male friends, and I do not flirt with them. And even if I did—none of your business, pal, fake engagement or no. Now, if you want a pizza, I suggest you find your table. We close in thirty minutes."

Seth watched Layla sashay away, his blood pounding in his ears. He wanted to grab Cooper from his booth by his shirt collar and toss him to the curb.

He ran a hand over his mouth, making an effort to calm down. Fact was, Layla was right. They weren't actually engaged. He had no real claim to her, no right to be jealous.

But that didn't change the fact that he was. Or the fact that she was so deep under his skin now, he was never going to get her out. He pounded the paneled wall with his closed fist. A black-and-white picture of a younger Cappy tossing pizza dough wobbled against the wall.

His emotions were wagging him from one side to the other. Earlier today, with Layla pressed against him on the ladder, he'd been content, hopeful. It was clear his nearness had rattled her. Maybe it was only physical attraction, but it was a start. He could work with that.

Now he wanted to put his fist through the wall. The woman was driving him crazy. And time was ticking. He had two weeks to make this happen, and he was starting to think he was in major need of a Christmas miracle.

Nine

Layla rooted through the bag of supplies. Where was the burlap? She'd seen it a few days ago, and now it was nowhere to be found. She tossed the bag to the ground, suppressing a growl.

Nothing had gone right today. The nursery furniture for the spare room had arrived. Everything had to be taken apart and put back together to get through the door. It had taken almost two hours.

She'd broken Murphy's foyer chandelier while hanging evergreen boughs, and she was pretty sure the piece was irreplaceable.

The garden center sent white poinsettias instead of the red ones she'd ordered, and they weren't sure how long it would take to get the right ones.

At least things were better with Murphy. He'd apologized the day after their confrontation at Cappy's. The memory of his sheepish look was almost enough to put a smile on her face. Almost.

The tour opened December 20. In eleven days Stanley would walk through the house and decide whether or not she was good enough for Malcolm Realty.

And now she couldn't find the flipping burlap. A growl escaped as she threw a bag of pinecones to the library floor.

"Whoa. Bad day?"

Layla jumped. "You scared me." The man walked like a ballerina. And was it that late already? She checked her watch. Five o'clock. She hadn't gotten squat done today.

"What's wrong?"

She tossed aside another bag. "I can't find the burlap. Have you seen it?"

"Sorry, I haven't."

Did he have to stand over her shoulder like that? She rooted through a bag of ornaments, the cellophane rattling. "It was here, in one these bags, I'm sure of it."

He squatted beside her, grabbing her hand. "Come on. We're getting out of here."

She huffed. "I can't."

"You've been at it since six a.m. Did you even stop for lunch?"

She gestured wildly. "Look at this place. I have eleven days. There's a lot riding on this, Murphy. For you, it's one home show. For me, it's my job. My future." She grabbed another bag.

He captured her shoulders. "Layla."

She slowed down enough to look at him.

"Put the bag down. You have to get a tree, right?"

"Yes."

"So we'll grab a quick bite and head over to the Christmas tree farm."

She looked into his calm eyes. She could use a little of that. Maybe a lot.

"If you don't get one soon, it'll be slim pickings, and you'll end up with a Charlie Brown tree. You don't want that, do you?"

He knew the right buttons to push. She couldn't settle for anything less than perfection. She pulled in a breath. Maybe she did need a break. She was starting to see dancing Christmas lights when she closed her eyes.

He jerked his chin toward the door. "Come on. Let's go get a tree."

The Christmas tree farm was on the west side of Chapel Springs, in the gently rolling hills by the state park. The private lane used to be a popular spot for teenagers to make out, but Layla had never been past the white wooden sign that proclaimed the farm's name and hours.

She scanned the landscape as they rode down the long gravel drive. A soft blanket of snow pillowed the ground. Pine trees in varying sizes lined up alongside the lane. In the distance the sun squatted low on the horizon, giving off the day's last light.

"We don't have much time." She tossed her wrapper into the Burger Barn bag and drained the last of her soda.

"It won't take long—unless you're going to hold out for the perfect tree."

She smiled wide, blinking innocently, and he groaned.

A few minutes later they were out of the truck and walking toward the barn. The fresh scent of pine hung heavily in the crisp air. There weren't many customers, she was glad to note. Just a few families here and there.

Outside the barn, a sign explained the variety and costs of trees. Tree wagons were lined up against the barn's red exterior, and a teenaged employee shoved a tree through a machine. It came out the other side netted and ready for a waiting couple.

"Okay, so how does this work?" she asked.

"You've never been here?"

She shrugged. "We always got our trees at Walmart." When they got one at all. Sometimes money was just too tight. Some Christmases had passed with hardly a mention, though Beckett and her grandpa had always made sure she had something to open. These days a small artificial tree sufficed. It didn't always make it out of the box, though.

"First we grab one of these." Beckett took the handle of a tree carrier. "Grab a saw. What were you thinking—blue spruce, Frasier fir?"

"Um . . . let me look." She stopped in front of the sign and read about needles, fragrance, and cost. "They're expensive." No wonder they hadn't always bought a tree. It was more than they'd spent on gifts.

"Get what you want."

She settled on Scotch pine, and they headed toward the appropriate section. She pulled up her hood against the bite of the wind.

Murphy tugged his cap lower, his ears and the tip of his nose already pink. "The needles are going to be prickly with a Scotch."

She shrugged. "I'll wear gloves."

They walked side by side over the packed snow trail that was lined with evergreens. Layla scanned the fields. Hundreds and hundreds of trees. She tucked her gloved hand into her pocket, balling it into a fist for warmth.

"We used to come here every year," Murphy said. "Dad would point to about a hundred trees before Mom finally agreed to one. Then she'd supervise as Dad and I took turns with the saw. She got us hot chocolate while we waited for them to get our tree ready, and we sipped it while she proclaimed this year's tree the best ever."

Layla's heart tugged. His parents had died several years ago in a small plane crash while they'd been out west on vacation. His father, who'd started the hardware store, had retired the year before.

"Sounds nice," she said.

"It was. The holidays have been a little lonely since they died."

She wondered if that was why he didn't seem to have any Christmas decorations.

"What about you?" he asked. "What were Christmases like growing up?" His breath fogged in front of him. The tree wagon bumped along behind him.

"They were great." Guilt pinched her, and she bit the inside of her lip. He'd been honest about his memories, painful as they probably were. She shrugged. "Maybe not so great."

She felt his appraisal, but he didn't press her. Maybe that's why she felt safe to continue.

"I don't remember much before my mom left." Before her dad became a drunk and life had fallen apart. "We put up a tree and had presents. She used to make us gingerbread cookies. That smell still takes me back. That's a happy memory. But after she left, things changed. Sometimes Dad was in jail, and it was just Grandpa and Beckett and me. Other times Dad was drunk. We didn't make a big deal of it. Grandpa always took us to church, but the tree and decorations . . . that didn't always happen."

They walked in silence for a minute, the only sounds their footsteps on the packed snow and the creak of the wagon wheels.

"So Christmastime doesn't bring back good memories."

"Not especially, no." Now Grandpa was in the nursing home with Alzheimer's, and Beckett was joining the McKinley family. There was just Dad, and she knew better than to count on him. She supposed she was about to be as alone as Murphy.

"You can always make new memories."

She thought of her tiny apartment with its treeless living room. "Sure."

When they reached the Scotch pines, he veered off the path, trudging through fresh snow. "Have you decided where we're going on our honeymoon?"

"What?"

"I've always wanted to go to Hawaii for Christmas."

She nudged his arm. "You seem to be forgetting there isn't going to be a wedding."

"I could get into a warm, sandy Christmas. Although now that I think about it, Maui would be better. Less touristy, more private."

"You're delusional."

His gaze bounced off hers, wearing a disarming half smile. He stared off into the distance. "A guy can dream," he muttered into the wind, and Layla wondered if she'd heard right.

~

An hour later Layla stood back, surveying the naked tree. The Scotch stood eight feet tall in the alcove of the built-in bay, thick, dark, and lush. Perfect.

"You're worse than Mom ever was," Murphy said from under the tree.

"I told you, my future's riding on this."

He poured a pitcher full of water into the reservoir, his backside sticking out. "That's a lot of pressure to put on a tree."

She trimmed another branch. "I think he's up for the challenge."

Murphy backed out and looked up from his spot on the wood floor. "He?"

She shrugged. "Christmas trees are male. Everyone knows that."

"And you think *I'm* delusional." He softened the words with a smile, sitting back on his haunches. "Should we decorate tonight, or are you beat?"

She looked at her watch. "Yes and yes."

"Okay, let's do this right, then."

Twenty minutes later there was a fire crackling in the fireplace and Christmas music playing from his state-of-the-art sound system. They were carefully placing strands of candles. It was a challenge to make each one straight.

She realized halfway through that they wouldn't be able to go much further without the popcorn strands. She'd hired a teenager from her old neighborhood to make them.

Layla moved the ladder around the tree next to Murphy and stepped onto it. It wobbled, throwing her off balance, and she tightened her hold.

"Murphy . . . !" she said.

He grabbed her waist, steadying her. The ladder stilled. His hands were warm through her thin sweater.

"I didn't do it," he said.

She gave him a look over her shoulder.

"Scout's honor."

She had her doubts he was ever a scout, but let it pass since he looked so sincere. She followed his gaze to the floor where a trimmed bough rested under the foot of the ladder.

"Oh," she said. "Sorry."

She started to step down, but he hadn't moved. His hands still rested on her waist. They felt nice. Strong and sure. The step evened their heights, bringing them eye to eye. Calling attention to the silver flecks flashing in a sea of blue. To the perfectly sculpted nose trailing down to a nice set of lips. Bowed on top, generous on bottom.

His thumbs moved at her waist, sending a shiver up her spine. Her eyes swung back to his and locked there. His words from earlier came back to her. *A guy can dream.*

Did he really have feelings for her? The look in his eyes said he did. They said that and so much more.

His gaze dropped to her mouth.

Layla's lips tingled with want. Her hands tightened on

the metal rung. No, she couldn't want Murphy after what he'd done to her and Jack.

He leaned in. The movement sent panic flooding through her. She stepped down, slipping past him. "I think I'm about done for the night." She couldn't hide the tremor in her voice.

~

Seth grabbed the ladder rung with both hands. The space where Layla had just stood was empty now. His head dipped forward as she scrambled for her coat behind him. *Stupid!* What was he thinking?

"See you in the morning," she said.

He turned, mouth open for a reply, but she was slipping out the door. The door slammed, and a cold gush of wind drifted across the room. A minute later the sound of her engine cut through the night. Headlights chased across the wall as she backed from the drive, and then she was gone.

He ran a hand over his face. *Idiot! The engagement is fake, Murphy.*

As much as he might lie to himself, tell himself it was real, it wasn't. All the public displays in the world didn't give him the right to kiss her or hold her or even touch her. Her response made that clear enough.

And yet, he'd thought he'd seen something in her eyes. Something promising. Something hopeful. Maybe Layla's feelings were starting to change. Maybe she'd be willing to give him another chance.

Or maybe it was only wishful thinking.

Ten

Layla set the white votive inside the Mason jar and slid it down the table to Murphy.

He caught the jar and cut a length of twine. "I swear they're going to revoke my man card."

Layla scooped sugar into the next jar and arranged red berries around the votive. "You own a hardware store; I think your manhood is intact."

He scowled. "I'm tying bows on glass knickknacks. Don't you need some wood chopped or something?"

"What I need is thirty of these to line the walkway, so butch up and tie the bow."

It had taken a couple days for the awkwardness of Tuesday's incident to pass. Layla spent the time convincing herself Murphy hadn't really intended to kiss her. Had he actually leaned in? Maybe she'd only lost her balance and swayed a bit.

No sense dwelling on that when there was so much to do.

The main floor was almost complete, but she still had the upstairs and the exterior. And only one week to go.

The fire crackled in the fireplace. Her gaze swept over the mantel where a pine swag draped lazily between three old-fashioned stockings. On the hearth a set of wooden milking buckets overflowed with boughs and pinecones. The sled above the mantel had turned out nice too.

"I saw the sewing room. Great idea."

"Thanks. I saw that sewing table at Grandma's Attic and got inspired." She'd bought a length of red cotton batiste to drape over the table. "I'm going to put a dress form in the corner and cover it with a Victorian morning dress." She was borrowing the dress from an antique collector in town.

"That'll look great. Have you heard from Stanley?"

"I touched base with him yesterday. I was hoping he'd come over on Friday before the tour starts, but he's got plans that night. He's coming over on Saturday."

"A week from tomorrow?"

She nodded. Which meant they'd have to drag out their engagement until a few days before their supposed wedding. How was that going to work? She was already tired of fielding questions at Cappy's and hearing complaints about their Christmas Eve wedding date. She could hardly wait to deal with the fallout.

"How are we going to handle all this?" She slid the jar to him, her eyes flickering to his.

"All what?"

"You know, the end of our pretend engagement."

His mouth tightened as he focused on the twine, his thick fingers making awkward work of the bow. "I don't know."

Last time she'd brought it up, he'd changed the subject, but it had to be discussed. They were racing toward the deadline, and she needed a plan in place.

"It's going to fall awfully close to our pretend wedding."

He frowned. "I know that."

"Well . . . someone's going to practically get jilted at the altar," she said lightly, hoping to draw a smile.

Her efforts failed.

"Don't worry, I'll take the fall. I got us into this, I'll get us out of it." He didn't seem too happy about that.

She'd already been through one broken engagement. This one would be a breeze, though. No feelings involved.

No feelings? You sure about that, Layla?

She thought of Tuesday's incident, of the stirring in her stomach at his nearness. Of the way she anticipated his return each evening. She told herself she was eager for help, but was that really true? Or was she only kidding herself?

She gazed at him from beneath her lashes. Watched his sturdy hands work at the tedious task. It was Friday night, and instead of being out with friends, he was tying bows on Ball jars. For her. Maybe he'd gotten them into this, but it was her fault that they'd followed through. He didn't owe her anything.

Unless you count the thing with Jack and Jessica. The newlyweds were arriving home tonight. Layla wasn't looking forward to seeing them.

But she didn't want to think about that right now. She followed her string of thoughts back one thread to Murphy and their situation. She couldn't deny that her—affection—for him had grown. He'd weaseled his way into her heart a little with his quiet sincerity and teasing ways. With his crooked smile and his sea-blue eyes and his old worn cap.

All the reasons he'd appealed to her two summers ago were still there. The stomach flutterings and noodle knees were there too. What would've happened if Murphy had asked her out before Jack? Would she be settled into this house with him, warm and snug, a wedding band circling her finger?

The thought made her ache inside. *Is that what was supposed to happen, God? Was I supposed to go out with Murphy and not Jack? Did we somehow mess up Your plans?*

Maybe she'd never know. Maybe she'd lost her chance at happiness and was destined to be alone the rest of her life.

They worked in tandem, the fire popping and sizzling nearby. The musky scent of his cologne wafted over as he reached for a jar.

"Why didn't you ask me out?" Layla blurted, suddenly needing to know. She bit the inside of her lip, cursing her impulsive tongue. Her heart beat erratically, thumping hard against her ribs. "Two summers ago when we volunteered at the theater? I kept thinking you might."

His hands paused on a spool of twine as he looked at her, his eyes somber. "I wanted to. But I was coming off a difficult relationship—I needed some time." Regret laced his voice.

"Chloe Peterson."

He nodded.

She'd seen them around town for about a year. The grapevine claimed she'd cheated on him with Chris Geiger, but who knew?

"I was about to ask you out," he said. "But before I could . . ."

"Jack."

His eyes skimmed over her face. "You have no idea how many times I've regretted waiting."

Her face warmed under his perusal. Her pulse skittered. "Wonder what would've happened."

One corner of his lips tipped up as a look of serenity passed over his face, displacing the regret. "Who knows. Maybe we'd be engaged for real."

Maybe, she thought. But she couldn't bring herself to say it out loud. Instead, before she got caught in his eyes, she placed another votive and slid the jar to Murphy while her mind toyed with the notion.

The next afternoon Layla let herself into Murphy's house. They'd kept at it until midnight, and this morning she'd had the earliest shift at Cappy's, coming in for lunch prep. They'd been busy with Christmas parties through lunch, and Layla had been on edge, wondering if Jessica would make an appearance. After work she'd gone to see her grandpa at the nursing home, feeling guilty for missing the previous week. He didn't remember her today.

She was ready for the quiet reprieve of Murphy's house. She shrugged from her coat, a familiar smell making her draw another breath. It smelled like Christmas, but it wasn't the piney scent of the tree or the woodsmoke from last night's fire.

She followed the smell toward the kitchen. Dirty mixing bowls sat in the sink, filled with water and assorted utensils.

Flour dusted the island, and on it sat a baking sheet full of cookies.

Layla moved closer, her lips parting as she neared the island. Gingerbread men. Her eyes skated over the misshapen forms. White eyes of varying sizes stared back. Fat buttons lined the fronts. The icing that outlined the cookies was sparse in places and globby in others.

A laugh bubbled up at the pathetic sight of them. But it got stuck in her throat, held by the growing knot. The gesture caught her in the gut, like a sucker punch, leaving her breathless and teary-eyed. What Murphy lacked in artistic ability he made up for in heart. She pulled in a breath, the scent of ginger filling her nose, and thought it might just be the best thing she'd ever smelled.

Eleven

Seth talked Layla into attending his church on Sunday. Not only would it be odd for them to go separate ways so close to their nuptials, but it would also give Layla a chance to chat with Stanley.

Seth sat tall in the pew, loving the feel of Layla pressed against his side. She wore a red dress that fell just short of her knees, and it was taking all kinds of willpower to keep his mind on the message. They'd slipped in late at her request, but now, as they stood for the last song, he could feel her muscles going taut, her spine lengthening.

Jessica and Jack were three rows up, tanned and glowing with happiness. There'd be no avoiding them afterward. Them or anyone else. Seth didn't care. He was proud to be with Layla, and his feelings were as real as the hymnbook he held in his hands.

After church he fended off congratulatory wishes in the vestibule while Layla chatted with Stanley and his wife. Next time he checked on her, Jack was talking to her. Seth excused himself from Daniel Dawson, the young mayor, and hurried to Layla's side, not liking the familiar way Jack set his hand on her arm.

"Welcome back." Seth shook Jack's hand. "Looks like you got plenty of sun."

"Stepping off the plane was a rude awakening, let me tell you. We had a great time, though. I was just telling Layla that Jess and I'd like to have you two over Thursday for dinner."

Seth looked at Layla, not missing the panic behind her plastic smile. "Oh, well, that's her last night before the tour opens. She's staging my house."

"She told me." He smiled fondly at Layla. "I'm really proud of her."

Something twisted inside Seth at the proprietary words. He set his hand at the curve of Layla's waist and pulled her closer. "You should see the house. She's amazing."

A delicious shade of pink rushed into Layla's cheeks, and he could hardly tear his eyes away.

Layla cleared her throat, glancing at him.

Jessica sidled up to Jack and nestled into his side. "So are we on for Thursday? I'm making my lamb, and believe me, you don't want to miss it." Her eyelashes fluttered at Seth.

Jack smiled down at her. "She's a great cook."

Seth wanted to smack Jack. How could they have ever been such close friends?

"I'm afraid Thursday's no good for us, is it, baby?" Seth said. "We'll be too busy with final touches on the house." He addressed Jessica. "Layla's staging my house for the Tour of Homes."

"Oh, how cute! Well, you still have to eat. Plus, I invited my mom and Aunt Lorraine already, and they're expecting you. We're not taking no for an answer." She waved her manicured fingers at someone over Seth's shoulder.

Seth tightened his hand on Layla. "I don't think—"

Jessica touched Layla's arm, wincing. "Oh, sweetie, is it still too hard?"

Seth fisted his free hand as he drew Layla into his side. "She's engaged to me now, Jessica."

"You know what?" Layla said. "It's fine. I'm sure I'll be finished by then. We can come over for a couple hours."

"Perfect! See you at seven." Jessica parted with an air kiss to Layla's cheek and tugged Jack off to talk with someone else.

Seth and Layla made their way to his truck, his stomach churning. He didn't want to sit through a meal with Jack and Jessica any more than Layla possibly could. It made him physically ache to see Jack and Layla together, even if he was married now. Thinking of his hands on Layla, his lips on hers, made Murphy want to punch a brick wall.

He put the truck in drive and pulled from the lot. Once they were on the street, Layla dropped her head against the window, her hair falling over her face.

He lifted his hand to brush the hair away. But she wouldn't welcome his touch. They weren't in public anymore. He turned up the heat instead. "You didn't have to do that. We could've put it off."

"And let her think I'm still hung up on Jack?"

He sighed. He didn't want to put Layla through this dinner. Shoot, he didn't want to put himself through it.

Seth turned the truck and angled up the hill. The sun glinted brightly off the snowy street. "I can call him later and cancel."

She sat up straight, squaring her shoulders. "No. I have to get used to it sooner or later."

His stomach clenched. "To what? Seeing them together?"

"We live in the same town. I can't avoid them forever."

He hated the brittle sound of her voice. His heart worked as hard as the Chevy's engine as it climbed the hill. The thought of her pining for Jack soured his stomach.

"Is it hard?"

"Is that your way of asking if I still love him?"

He kept forgetting he had no right. No right to ask things like that. No right to brush her hair from her eyes. "You don't have to say."

Maybe he didn't want to know anyway. Maybe it'd be another sucker punch to the gut. He wasn't a glutton for punishment. Or never had been until Layla.

"I don't love him anymore," she said softly.

Her words sent a flood of relief through him. Maybe there was hope. Maybe he hadn't imagined the way she'd looked at him on the ladder last week. Or the softening in her eyes when she'd thanked him for the cookies last night.

He couldn't resist a look. Her face had relaxed, her eyes staring into the distance. In memory? In sadness? He couldn't tell.

"The only thing I feel in regard to Jack is humiliated." She tossed him a wry grin. "I don't know what that says about me, but I'm pretty sure it's nothing good."

The engine shifted gears as the road leveled. Seth let off

the gas and turned onto his street. "Anyone would feel the same. It only added insult to injury that she's your cousin—and not a very nice person, I might add."

A minute later he pulled into his drive, aware of the tension that threaded through the cab. *You had to go and remind her about your part in it. You're making great headway here, Seth, and with exactly five and a half days left.*

He shut off the engine and reached for the door.

Layla grabbed his arm. "Wait."

Her green eyes flittered to his, then away again, looking uncharacteristically vulnerable. When they swung back to him again, piercing him with their sincerity, he wanted to pull her into his arms and hold her tight. He clenched his hands against the seat before he could act on the notion.

"I was wrong before." She tucked her hair behind her ear. "It wasn't your fault, what happened with Jack and Jessica." She looked down at her purse straps, twined around her hand. "I just needed somebody to blame, and you were convenient. I'm sorry."

The words healed a broken place inside him. He let it soak in for a minute. "I know what betrayal feels like. If I'd realized what was happening between them, I would've told you."

"I know."

"I'd never hurt you on purpose, Layla."

She swallowed, nodded. "I know that too."

That was something, wasn't it? Trust was a good place to start. Especially after the kind of betrayal she'd been through. It made him want to prove he was the kind of man she deserved. The kind of man who'd love her for better or worse. The kind who was faithful and true.

"For what it's worth," he said, "I think he's the biggest fool on the planet."

Her eyes came back to him, as if needing not only to hear the words but to see the authenticity on his face. Her lips curled up a fraction. "Thanks, Seth."

His heart squeezed at the sound of his name. Every inch of him wanted to touch her. Wanted to pull her into his arms and claim her lips, her heart. Wanted to hear his name escape on a sigh. But he sensed she needed space. Time to sort through her feelings. And he'd give her that. He'd give her whatever she needed.

He reached for the door handle. "You said something about needing a sixteen-foot ladder—I'm afraid to ask what for."

She cocked a brow as she opened the door.

He loved seeing the strength return to her face. That sassy side he loved about her.

"Hope you're not afraid of heights." She glanced back over her shoulder with a mischievous smile as she slipped from the cab.

~

The moment in the truck had eased something between them. Layla wasn't sure if it was her admission that she no longer loved Jack or her apology.

But the tension gave way to a lighthearted afternoon. Despite the hard work and pressure of a deadline, she was having fun. With Seth of all people. He knew when to buckle down and when to play a practical joke to break the monotony.

Outside now, she stepped down from the ladder and

moved back to survey her work. There would be plenty of lights by the time they were done. The roofline remained untouched. Layla had teased him about heights, but truth was, she wasn't too fond of them herself.

The wreath on the front door was large and beautiful, as was the fat swag Seth was hanging now above the gorgeous leaded door. Wreaths hung from every window, the lit Mason jars would line the walkway, every tree would twinkle with white lights.

She tucked her gloved hands into her pockets and scanned the snowy yard, frowning. Something was missing. She couldn't put her finger on it.

"What's wrong?"

"I don't know." The small yard stretched to the snow-packed street, sloping down just before the sidewalk. Its barrenness bothered her, but she couldn't exactly throw up a plastic Santa or standard yard ornaments like candy canes and peppermints.

"It's going to be great. Just wait till it's finished and lit."

That would help, but that wasn't what was bugging her. A few well-made snowmen would fill the space, but who knew what the weather would do between now and Saturday. It wasn't the right look anyway.

"Something's missing," she said.

Seth stepped from the ladder and walked to the edge of the porch, hands low on his hips. His breath plumed in front of his face.

She surveyed the yard again. Something big and old-fashioned. Artificial deer? She shook her head even as a new thought occurred.

Of course.

She swung her head toward Murphy, a smile breaking loose. "A sleigh."

His brows popped up. "A sleigh?"

"An old-fashioned sleigh. It'll be perfect." She trudged through the few inches of snow and stood in the middle of the yard. "Right here, facing this way. Lit with white lights, a garland draped around the edges, and big fat presents piled in the backseat." Unable to contain her excitement, she clapped her hands.

Seth's lips twitched. "And where do you think you're going to find a sleigh at this late date, little miss?"

Her smile fell. "You're right. It's too late." Even she could hear the defeat in her voice.

It wasn't something she could run down to the hardware store for. It wasn't even something Grandma's Attic carried. And she didn't know anyone who had one. She might be able to find one online or at an antique store somewhere, but get it here in time? In five days? Besides, she didn't have time to hunt one down.

It would've been perfect. Unique.

Seth came down the porch steps. "Well, hang on, maybe we can find one."

"You know of someone who has one?"

"No, but that doesn't mean there isn't one sitting around a barn somewhere."

"I don't have time to refurbish some broken-down thing. My schedule's full this week as it is. It would have to be hauled out here and cleaned up. The big presents would have to be made, the lights and garlands strung . . . I really needed it a week ago."

"I'll find you a nice one. And I'll find it today. *And* I'll help you get it ready."

She gave him a look. "You *are* delusional. It's already four o'clock, and the antique stores are closed on Sundays."

He crossed his arms, aiming a cocky grin her way. "You underestimate me, Layla. I'll make it happen."

She gave him a wary look. "How?"

"I'm not giving away my secrets." His eyes lit mischievously. "But I'm willing to bet on it: suitable sleigh, right here, by midnight tonight."

Now she was suspicious. "You know someone who has one."

"No, I don't. Scout's honor. Now are you taking the bet or not?"

She turned her face from him, her eyes narrowing on him. "What kind of bet?"

"Name your price."

She stared at the house, thinking. "If you don't find one, you have to . . ." Her gaze climbed to the roof. "Do the roofline." She smiled big.

He looked up, squinting against the light, then back to her. "Fine. I'm not losing anyway."

He pulled his keys from his coat pocket. "Time's a wasting." With one last smile over his shoulder he headed for his truck.

"Wait, what about you?"

He turned in the snow, giving her a strange look. Then

he slowly started toward her. It took all her willpower to keep her boots planted as he came within inches of her.

"If I win . . . ," he said, those blue eyes warming her clear down to her toes, "I get to kiss you." His lips twitched as his eyes slid down to her mouth and back up where they held her hostage.

Layla swallowed hard.

With a final look, he traced his steps to his truck, only turning once he reached the door. "And, Layla . . . ," he said with a smug grin, "I *will* win."

Five hours later the work was going slow. Layla had lost her helper and had moved inside when darkness had fallen. It would be worth the reduced production if only Seth found a sleigh. But as badly as she wanted one, the stakes he'd put on it made her stomach knot. Would he really collect on the kiss?

Did she want him to? Things had changed since last week on the ladder. They'd spent hours working and talking and sharing. She'd forgiven him for his minor role in the Jack and Jessica fiasco. Then there were those gingerbread cookies.

And, let's face it, you're attracted to the man.

She still saw him shirtless when she closed her eyes at night. Still saw the rippling muscles of his arms, the sturdy set of his shoulders. She thought of the protective way he'd slipped his arm around her when they'd stood with Jack and Jessica. Despite priding herself on independence, she'd liked the way it felt. Liked the way he made her skin tingle, made her heart shiver.

Yes, if he brought home a sleigh, she'd let him kiss her. And she'd enjoy it, she had no doubt about that. But every car that roared outside the windows passed on by. And every time her phone buzzed, it was a text from Cooper or one of her other friends.

Layla picked up the sprigs of pine and berries for the kitchen counter. *Come on, girl, you've got work to do.*

By the time she finished the arrangements, her hands ached from twisting and cutting. She was placing the pieces strategically when she heard a commotion out front. *Please let it be a sleigh.*

She rushed to the front door and opened it. Seth and another man were squeezed into the front seat of a sleigh. A horse-drawn sleigh. The house's exterior lights shone down on the beautiful animal as he pulled the sleigh across the sidewalk, up the slope, and came to a stop at the precise spot she'd pointed out.

Layla slipped on her boots and stepped onto the porch, crossing her arms against the cold.

Seth turned to her, smiling. "This about right?" he called.

Her eyes ran over the sleigh as she took the porch steps. It was an antique red two-seater, with a sloped back and curved runners. She clasped her hands to her chest. "Seth, it's perfect!"

He introduced her to Mr. Stephens, a customer of his who lived outside Chapel Springs. They chatted while he unhitched the horse. Layla admired the condition of the sleigh. Plush red velvet covered the benches, dotted with matching upholstery buttons. The sleigh's exterior was smooth and shiny with gold detailing.

A few minutes later Layla thanked Mr. Stephens as he mounted the horse and said good night. Then he was trotting down the street, the horse's hooves clip-clopping on the packed snow.

"So it meets with your approval?" Seth asked.

"It's beautiful. How'd you find it?"

Seth climbed down and began covering it with a tarp. "I called about a hundred friends and customers."

She arched a brow as she moved forward to help. "A hundred?"

"A slight exaggeration. Eventually someone pointed me toward Mr. Stephens. He was in my store awhile back, and I helped him out with a furnace problem. Saved him some money. He was happy to return the favor."

When they finished, a cold wind tousled her hair, and Layla tucked her hands into her jean pockets, shivering. "Well, thanks, it's just what I'd imagined. And in great shape."

"Let's get you inside, it's cold."

She wasn't going to argue. The temperature had dropped since sunset. She kicked off her boots by the closet and moved closer to the fire. She heard the door shut behind her, heard the sound of Seth shrugging from his coat and boots. Then all went quiet except the pop and sizzle of the simmering fire. She wondered what he was doing back there.

She tossed on another log and warmed her hands. They were shaking. Unable to bear the silence, she looked over her shoulder. Seth was leaning against the door, arms crossed, watching her, an enigmatic smile on his face. The golden glow of the lamplight washed over his face, highlighting his five o'clock shadow.

She was suddenly aware that her hair had come loose from her ponytail. That her worn jeans and T-shirt were probably smudged with who-knew-what. This wasn't how she'd imagined looking when Seth kissed her. Why hadn't she done something with herself while he was gone? But judging by the look on his face, he didn't care about any of that.

No longer needing the fire's warmth, she moved away, lifting her chin and tossing her ponytail over her shoulder. "What?"

"I won," he said quietly.

"Won what?" Did he hear the tremor in her voice?

His lips twitched. "Our deal . . . sleigh by midnight . . . the kiss . . . Ring any bells?"

She bit the inside of her lip, fishing for courage. "Looks like we both won, then."

He cocked his head sideways, narrowing his eyes. "Because you got your sleigh?"

There was her chance to save face. But what fun would that be? She arched a brow instead. "That too." She drove her point home with a smile, ignoring the way she trembled from the inside out.

His eyes darkened as his head tipped back. His cocky half smile fell. Oh yeah, he got it. He straightened against the door as his hands fell to his sides. He took a step toward her, then another.

"You're in so much trouble." His voice was as thick as honey. "You know that, right?"

He advanced with a slowness that intimidated and excited her.

"Promises, promises." Her breath left on a shudder.

Unable to hold her ground, she stepped back once, then again. Her back hit the wall. No getting away now. And honest truth? She didn't want to. Even though her insides quaked like an epicenter, even though fear trickled through her veins.

And still he came. His eyes held her captive. Her heart thrashed like a caged bird's wings. And yet . . . she didn't want to be anywhere else but locked up in Murphy's arms.

He didn't stop until they were toe-to-toe. As if remembering the way she'd bolted last time, he braced his hands against the wall on either side of her. Two weeks ago the move would've left her feeling trapped. Now her only complaint was that he was too far away.

His eyes dipped to her lips, and every cell in her yearned to strain forward. But she held still, contented herself with the way his face softened, the way his eyes whispered over her face, as tangible as a caress. A shiver ran down her arms.

He lowered his head. Their lips met, a mere brush. Her legs trembled, her pulse raced, her heart cracked open. How could the softest of brushes undo her so completely?

He came back for more, and warmth curled through her. She strained toward him, loving the manly smell of him, the taste of him on her lips. She tightened her fingers, nails biting into her palms.

His thumb found the curve of her cheek, touching her with a reverence that melted her. It was just a kiss, yet it was so much more. She felt his tenderness toward her, his care.

She remembered his words earlier, his promise that he'd never hurt her on purpose. She'd feared she'd never find a trustworthy man, but Seth made her want to try. Made her wonder if she'd already found him.

He pressed closer, his body warm and solid against her. His hands slid around her waist, pulling her closer, splaying against the small of her back.

Layla's fingers unfurled, sliding up his arms, winding around his neck, weaving into the hair at his nape. It was feather soft and chilly from the cold night air. She imagined coming home every night to a kiss like this one. To the security of his arms, to the passion he kindled inside her.

When they parted, she was short of breath and weak of knees. He set his forehead against hers, and she closed her eyes, inhaling the smell of him. Musk and snow and woodsmoke.

"Confession," he whispered a moment later. "I would've gotten you the sleigh without the kiss."

She opened her eyes, smiling at his words, soaking in the warmth of his gaze. "I would've given you the kiss without the sleigh."

His eyes lit. He nuzzled her nose. "Then you won't mind giving me another," he said.

"Not so much," she whispered just before he pressed his lips to hers again.

Twelve

It's perfect." Seth wrapped his arms around her, pulling her back into his chest. "I'll bet you win the People's Choice Award."

Layla scanned the living room, hoping he was right. She'd worked long hours this week on the exterior and upstairs. She'd put the finishing touches on the main floor, adding snowshoes on the wall above the sofa and black-and-white photos here and there.

True to his word, Seth had finished the sleigh, and it looked just as she'd imagined. In the evenings there'd been lots of talking and a kissing break or two to break the monotony.

An old record player sat on the sofa table, stocked with old Christmas records, and a spicy apple cider mixture was ready to go on the stove. There was nothing else to be done.

"I hope Stanley likes it."

"He's going to love it." Seth's arms tightened around her. His breath stirred the hair at her temple.

As busy as the week had been, she'd savored every moment

with him. Once she'd let him into her heart, he'd quickly filled every nook and cranny. Sometimes it felt as if he'd been there all along. Maybe he had been.

"You know you're amazing at what you do, right?" he said. "And I'm not just saying that because I like kissing you."

She smiled, letting his compliment soak in. It was hard to believe in herself. Sometimes she didn't feel good enough to stage such beautiful homes. Sometimes she didn't feel like she belonged in his world.

"What's wrong?"

"Nothing."

He turned her in his arms, tilting his head, his eyes shadowed under the brim of the cap. "Tell me."

She'd told him plenty this week about lots of stuff, including her childhood. He'd listened without judging. He was a safe place for honesty. She loved that about him. That and so much more.

"I don't know, sometimes I just . . . don't feel like I'm good enough for this."

He frowned. "What do you mean?"

She shook her head. "It's just . . . leftover stuff from childhood, I guess. Little girl from the wrong side of the tracks . . . disreputable family . . . all that. Sometimes I wonder if that's why I connect with staging, you know? I take something that's messed up"—she gave a wry grin—"dress it up, and make it look special."

He cradled her face in his palms, looking her in the eye. "Hey. You don't need dressing up. You're already special."

Her eyes stung at his words. At the sincerity in his eyes. "Thanks."

"Your identity doesn't come from your address."

"I know."

"Or your parents."

"I know that too." She did. But sometimes the knowledge failed to make the twelve-inch journey to her heart.

His thumbs moved over her cheek, sending shivers dancing down her spine. "God made you special, Layla, inside and out. And He gifted you with an amazing talent."

It was easier to believe when Seth said it. When he was looking at her like he adored her. She wanted to fall into the swirling waters of his sea-blue eyes.

"You know I'm crazy about you," he said.

She bit her lip, half afraid her own confession would come tumbling out. Half afraid it wouldn't. She *was* crazy about him. She was falling so hard and fast, she was dizzy with it.

"You don't have to say a word," he said. "It's all right there in your eyes."

"Think so?"

"Know so." A teasing light entered his eyes. "And I'm always right, you know."

She gave a wry smile. "One of those, are you?"

"Know what else I'm right about?"

"I can hardly wait to find out."

He brushed his lips across hers, drawing back with a tender smile. "Jack's going to eat his heart out tonight when he has to sit across the table and know what he missed out on."

"Ugh, you had to go and remind me about dinner."

"Well, it's in an hour, so you weren't likely to forget."

She sighed. "I need a shower."

"I'll pick you up at ten till," he said, and then he kissed

her again, long and sweet, until desire spread slow and thick through her veins.

~

Jack and Jessica lived in a contemporary home situated on a knoll overlooking the river. All that college had paid off for Jack, landing him a job with Nolan, Wells & Ebb. Apparently that was paying pretty well these days.

"I should've asked to bring something," Layla said as they climbed the brick porch steps. She fussed with the neckline of her black dress, second-guessing her choice. A cold wind caught the hemline of the skirt, pebbling her legs with gooseflesh.

"She would've said no," Seth said.

"I still should've asked."

He rang the bell beside the double doors and took her cold hand, bringing it to his lips. "Have I told you how beautiful you look?"

She looked into his eyes, released a breath she didn't know she'd held. She smiled. "Twice." He had a way of calming her. Just by being there. Thank God he was with her tonight. Between this dinner and Stanley's upcoming decision, she was a wreck.

"You look pretty handsome yourself."

"I know. Some foxy lady told me my shirt matches my eyes."

Her lips twitched. "Who says foxy?"

The double doors swung open, Jessica at one and Jack at the other. The gap widened, light flooding out, and then . . .

"Surprise!" a chorus of people shouted.

Layla scanned the group crowded into the bright, two-story atrium. Faces came into focus. A friend of Seth's, Beckett, Madison, her family, Mayor Dawson, Layla's father, her aunts, Stanley Malcolm . . .

Seth tightened his grasp on her hand. "What's all this?" His smile seemed genuine, but his voice was strained.

Layla remembered belatedly to smile.

Jack ushered them in. "Jessica and I thought you needed an engagement party. Hope you don't mind."

"Thanks so much, guys." Seth squeezed Layla's hand.

"Yes, thank you. Everyone," she said, encompassing the group.

"Are you surprised?" Aunt Lorraine asked.

"Totally," Layla said. Now there was an honest statement if ever there was one.

Her coat was taken from her shoulders, and she was relieved of her bag.

"Dinner's in half an hour," Jessica said. "Now go mingle!" She tugged them into the crowd as everyone dispersed into the sitting room. Music played from a stereo somewhere. Iridescent white and silver balloons clustered here and there. One had floated up to the cathedral ceiling and clung to a massive beam, its white ribbon hanging stagnant. Layla wished she could float away too.

A crowd gathered around them, buzzing with congratulations, asking about wedding plans. Layla worked to keep her smile in place as Seth pulled her tight into his side and fielded most of the questions. He seemed to be slowly moving them toward the back of the room where a set of French doors, leading to a balcony, promised freedom.

Across the room she caught her brother's frown aimed her way. *Why didn't you tell me?* she telegraphed with her eyes.

He shrugged helplessly, and she remembered the phone calls she'd ignored this afternoon in her haste to finish the house.

She smiled and nodded as her aunts fussed over them. How had this happened? It was supposed to be an intimate family dinner party—bad enough—but this . . .

When her aunts excused themselves, Seth's store manager and his wife took their places. He was droning on about his own wedding, his wife correcting him every two sentences.

The room was loud with music and laughter and idle chatter. All the bodies that crowded into the house made the temperature stifling. Layla tried to push up her heavy sleeves and found them stiff and unyielding.

Across the way, Stanley Malcolm worked the room in his Armani suit. His wife waved at someone, her diamonds flashing on her fingers like a million stars. When the manager's wife asked a question, Layla turned her attention back to the couple, but Murphy gracefully answered.

Mingling was hard enough, but sooner or later, the focus would turn to them, the happy couple, and she'd have to look into a sea of family and friends and lie. Her throat closed around her windpipe, her fingers grabbed a fistful of Seth's suit coat at his back.

Seth leaned close. "You okay?"

She nodded. Across the room she caught her dad's eye. He raised his glass and saluted her with his cola. She tried for a smile. She caught a glimmer of pride in his eyes. How many years had she waited for that?

And it was all a lie. Why, oh why had she started down this ridiculous path? Seth broke free of the couple, and they managed a few steps before Madison's parents, Mr. and Mrs. McKinley, stopped them.

"You look flushed, dear," Mrs. McKinley said after a few minutes of wedding chatter. "It is a bit warm in here."

"I was just taking her out back for some fresh air." Seth tugged her hand. "We'll catch up with you later."

Layla smiled her gratitude as the couple shooed them toward the balcony. They made it as far at the threshold between the sitting room and dining room before they were stopped again, this time by her father.

Her dad hugged her and shook Seth's hand. "You make a fine couple."

Beckett and Madison joined them. "Look, you're under the mistletoe," Madison said, eyes sparkling playfully.

Jessica appeared at their side. "Hey, everyone," she called over the clamor. "The lovebirds are under the mistletoe."

Voices hushed, and expectant faces turned their way. Her family backed out of the spotlight, leaving her and Seth alone.

He tugged her close and smiled down at her. "Happy to oblige," he whispered just before his lips settled on hers for the briefest of touches.

A polite smattering of applause sounded along with a few good-natured boos. Layla offered a strained smile, then turned toward the French doors.

She'd taken two steps when someone clinked their glass. "Speech!"

More clinking sounded, more beckons for a speech. She stopped, shooting a panicked look at Seth. Swallowing hard, she looked over the eager faces of their guests, here to celebrate their engagement. Their fake engagement.

Stanley Malcolm and his wife, the mayor, business owners. But that wasn't who got to her. What got to her was her family. Her friends. Her dad, her brother. Madison and her family, gazing adoringly at the phony bride and groom. At *them*.

As if sensing her rising panic, Seth pulled her into his side. But it wasn't enough this time. Not even close.

Her throat closed. Her mouth dried. A trickle of sweat ran down her back. She looked into the warmth of his eyes. "I can't do this anymore. We have to end it."

He put his back to the crowd, blocking Layla from their sight. His lips parted. She could see the denial on his face. Then something seemed to shift as he stared into her eyes.

"Okay. I get it. I do. But it doesn't have to be that way, Layla. Just listen and everything will be—"

"Don't you dare say it's going to be fine," she said through a smile. "It's not fine! All these people think we're getting married on Tuesday. They came here to celebrate us. We're lying to our friends and family for a *job*."

Before he could stop her, she moved around him, stepping back toward the living room and addressed the crowd. "I have an announcement to make."

Before they could hush, Seth turned her around, his mouth coming down on hers, confident and possessive. She set a hand on his chest with every intention of pushing him away. But then his lips softened, and her resistance melted.

The crowd cheered. Someone let out a catcall, the last thing she heard. The last rational thought she had. A moment later, when she was shaky and breathless, he drew away.

"You gotta stop standing under the mistletoe," he said softly.

She closed her eyes, drawing a steadying breath as the crowd hushed again. His kiss had wiped the slate of her mind clean. She needed a moment, just two seconds to gather her thoughts.

"What Layla's trying to say," Seth said, staring into her eyes, "is there's been a slight change in plans . . ."

What was he doing? She looked at him questioningly.

He squeezed her hand, reassured her with his eyes. "We're moving the wedding back a bit."

"Seth . . . ," she whispered.

He palmed her cheek, his eyes skating over her face, and lowered his voice. "You know you want to go to Hawaii. Come on, Layla. I love you. I have for a long time. Let's make this real."

She blinked. He wanted to marry her? For real? *Think, Layla*. "I . . . I thought you preferred Maui."

"You're stalling." His eyes turned somber. "Do you love me?"

"Everyone's staring."

"Do you love me, Layla?"

She swallowed against the burning in her eyes and whispered the truth that had been lingering in her heart for days. "Yes."

His lips turned up, silver flecks danced in his eyes. "Marry me for real. If you want to wait till spring or summer, we will. I'll wait as long as you want."

"Ahem!" someone said. "You were making an announcement . . . ?" Chuckles sounded.

"What do you say?" Seth whispered.

What could she say with him looking at her like that, eyes full of love, heart full of hope?

She cleared her throat, her gaze never leaving his, and addressed the crowd. "What Seth's trying to say . . . is that we're putting off the wedding . . . until New Year's Eve. So all of you can come."

Cheers sounded as a smile broke out on Seth's face, his sweet lips stretching wide. "I can wait that long."

"An extra seven days?" she teased. "Are you sure?"

Someone announced dinner, and the crowd flooded toward the kitchen, some stopping to express their approval.

Stanley set a hand on her shoulder as he passed. "Looking forward to seeing the house tomorrow. I've heard great things about it."

"What did I tell you?" Seth said when Stanley was gone. "He's going to love it." He tugged her toward the kitchen.

Someone had opened the French doors. A cold breeze fluttered the filmy curtains and swept over her heated flesh, making her shiver. Outside fat flakes had begun to fall from an onyx sky. They swirled and danced in the wind before melting into the rippling river.

Layla curled into Seth's side for warmth as they passed. "I hope you were serious about Hawaii."

He pressed a kiss to her head. "I'd never joke about a honeymoon."

Epilogue

Layla slid into a chair in the darkened corner of the town hall and slipped off her heels. The McKinley family had transformed the hall into a wonderland of silver and ice blue. Circular tables dotted the room, covered with white cloths and featuring small flower arrangements. People milled in groups, chatting, laughing, dancing.

She settled into the chair, twisting the rings on her finger, admiring the antique set. When Seth had presented his grandmother's rings, she'd known it was the set she'd wear the rest of her life. The platinum band featured a round brilliant-cut diamond. A curved row of channel-set diamonds filled out the other band, curling intricately around the larger diamond.

One of her favorite country tunes began, and Layla considered another turn on the dance floor, but her aching feet said no.

The past several days had been a whirlwind. The Silent

Night Tour of Houses had been a raging success. Seth's home had taken the People's Choice Award, and Layla had walked away with a contract from Malcolm Realty.

She took a moment to breathe a prayer of thanks. She was going to be very busy in the coming weeks. Busy doing what she loved. Busy starting her new life with Seth.

After the tour ended, Madison had taken her dress shopping. They'd found a simple but beautiful dress at a boutique in Louisville. Madison said she was stunning in it, and if the look on Seth's face as she came down the aisle was any indication, he agreed.

Her eyes scanned the crowd for her groom, and she found him walking toward her, his eyes fixed on her. He looked so handsome in his crisp white shirt and bowtie—he'd ditched the suit coat shortly after arriving at the reception.

She watched him approach, taking in his broad shoulders, narrow hips, and long legs. His dark hair, free for once from his baseball cap, curled enticingly at the collar of his shirt. His eyes sparkled under the lights, and his lips curved in that adorable half smile of his.

All mine.

And she couldn't wait to get him alone. They were spending their wedding night at his place. Tomorrow they were off to Maui. A whole week of sand, sunshine, and Seth. She couldn't help the giddy smile that formed as he neared.

He dropped into the seat beside her and leaned in close, his thigh pressing against hers. "What put that pretty smile on your face?"

"You."

He rewarded her with a long look and followed up with

a lingering kiss. The kind that made her wish the evening was over. He palmed her face, deepening the kiss. His fingers threaded into the loose hair at her nape, sending shivers down her arms.

The song wound to a close, and the microphone squealed.

"All right, everyone," Mr. McKinley said over the intercom. "I'm told it's time to see the couple off. Gather out front, please."

Seth drew away. "I hope it's okay. I told him we were ready."

She gave him a final kiss. "You read my mind."

Seth tugged her to her feet.

"My shoes!" she said, scrambling for them.

He helped her slip them on, and they made their way toward the door where the crowd was gathering out front. She gave last-minute hugs to her family.

Madison appeared, slipping Layla's coat around her shoulders. "You're going to need this."

"Did someone pull the car around?" Layla asked Seth as they stepped outside into the crowd. Birdseed rained down on them. She squealed and ducked her head against the onslaught.

Seth grabbed her hand, pulling her through the tunnel of well-wishers. They emerged unscathed at the sidewalk, laughing and brushing the birdseed from their hair and clothes.

When Layla raised her head, she paused at the sight on the street. A horse-drawn sleigh waited curbside. In the front seat Mr. Stephens, holding the reins, winked at her.

"Come on, wife," Seth said. "Your ride awaits."

She gave Seth a huge smile as he helped her into the backseat. The sleigh teetered as he entered behind her. He set a blanket over their laps, then they waved to the cheering crowd as the sleigh pulled away.

A few moments later only the clip-clop of the horse's hooves and the shush of the runners broke the silence of the night.

Seth adjusted the blanket and tucked Layla close. "Warm enough?"

"Yes." Though the air was chilly, she felt snug under the thick blanket, curled into her husband's side. "I can't believe you did this."

He leaned close, his warm breath stirring the hair at her temple. "It's going to cost you."

She stifled a smile, remembering their bet and the subsequent payout.

"And I'm not settling for a kiss this time," he said.

"Oh yeah?"

"Yeah." He leaned in and feathered her lips with a kiss. "But we'll start there and see where it goes."

Her smile quickly faded as he kissed her again, and soon all she heard was the beating of her own heart.

1. Who is your favorite character and why?
2. Layla went to a lot of extremes to reach her goal of working with Stanley Malcolm. Have you ever gone overboard in trying to reach your goals? What was the outcome?
3. Layla worried too much about how others perceived her. How did this affect her decisions? Do you worry too much about what others think of you?
4. Layla blamed Seth for her breakup with Jack because she needed someone to blame. Have you ever found yourself in a similar situation? How did it work out?
5. How is Layla's profession a reflection of how she views herself?

I'm so grateful for the fabulous team at HarperCollins Christian Fiction, led by publisher Daisy Hutton: Ansley Boatman, Katie Bond, Amanda Bostic, Sue Brower, Ruthie Dean, Laura Dickerson, Jodi Hughes, Ami McConnell, Becky Monds, Becky Philpot, Kerri Potts, and Kristen Vasgaard. Thank you for giving me the honor of launching this novella series.

Thanks especially to my editor, Ami McConnell. Woman, you are a wonder! I'm constantly astounded by your gift of insight. I don't know of a more talented line editor than LB Norton. You make me look much better than I am!

Author Colleen Coble is my first reader. Thank you, friend! I wouldn't want to do this writing thing without my buds and fellow authors, Colleen Coble, Diann Hunt, and Kristin Billerbeck. Love you, girls!

I'm grateful to my agent, Karen Solem, who is able to

somehow make sense of the legal garble of contracts and, even more amazing, help me understand it.

To my family: Kevin, Justin, Chad, and Trevor. You make life an adventure! Love you all!

Lastly, thank you, friend, for letting me share this story with you. If you enjoy *A December Bride*, be sure and check out *Barefoot Summer* to read Madison and Beckett's story!

I've enjoyed connecting with readers like you through my Facebook page. Visit my website at the link www.DeniseHunterBooks.com or just drop me a note at Denise@DeniseHunterBooks.com. I'd love to hear from you!

PHOTO BY AMBER ZIMMERMAN

Denise Hunter is the bestselling author of many novels, including *The Trouble with Cowboys* and *Barefoot Summer*. She lives in Indiana with her husband, Kevin, and their three sons.

A January Bride

Deborah Raney

For Ken, love of my life

One

Glancing at the chaos around her, Madeleine Houser set her coffee mug on the dining room table and shoved another packing carton out of her path. It didn't budge. She bent over and attempted to read the smudged label. *Kitchen—good china.* Oh. Good thing she'd resisted the temptation to kick the box.

Maddie looked into the kitchen where cupboards gaped open, hinges naked. The cabinet doors were lined up against the wall in the empty breakfast nook. Even after four days, the smell of wet enamel stung her nostrils. The flooring couldn't be laid until the electrician fixed the mess he'd made of the wiring. And she didn't dare put her china in the cupboards until all that was finished.

What had her sister gotten her into? Kate's husband had been transferred to Ohio, but with their mother in the nursing home here in Clayburn, Kate had begged her to leave her beloved New York loft and move into Kate and Jed's house on Harper Street while it was being refurbished to sell. "You can write anywhere, Maddie," Kate had pled in her best big-sister voice. "Besides, you can sublet the loft, and just think what you'll save on the rent."

So here she was in Clayburn, Kansas—the middle of nowhere—proving quite soundly that one could not write just *anywhere*.

Lugging the carton of china out of the way, she wove her way through the maze of boxes and poured another cup of coffee. She blew a long strand of dishwater-blond hair out of her eyes and slid into a dining room chair. In the midst of the piles of books and boxes and unsorted mail strewn across the table, her laptop computer glared accusingly at her.

Ignoring the disorder, she pulled the computer close, pushed her glasses up on her nose, and tried to remember where she'd left off. Ah, yes. The heartless landlord had just evicted the young widow. *Oh, brother, Houser, how cliché can you get?* Well, too bad. She didn't have time to change the whole plot now. She'd managed to write almost two thousand words this morning, but given her track record lately, she'd be lucky if fifty of them were worth keeping.

What had she been thinking to let her editor talk her into a January 1 deadline in the midst of this cross-country move? It was nearly October! "You can do it, Madeleine," Janice had crooned in her conniving editor's voice. "If we can get this book on the shelves before next Christmas, the first print run will sell out in a month. Come on. Say you'll do it. Houser fans are clamoring for your next book."

Over the six years Janice Hudson had been Maddie's

editor, they'd become dear friends. But right now Maddie wanted to strangle her.

She edited the sentence in front of the blinking cursor and forced herself to return to the nineteenth century and the plight of Anne Caraway, her suffering heroine. Poor Anne. She'd lost her beloved William and been evicted from her home, alone with a small child to care for. Now, Maddie was about to throw Anne Caraway onto the mean streets of Chicago. It was the bane of an author's existence—this need to make her beloved characters suffer. To put them in the furnace and turn up the fire. But without conflict, there was no story, and conflict often equaled sorrow. So, onto the streets Anne Caraway and little Charlie must go. She typed furiously.

The faint echo of dripping water pierced her concentration. She glanced up from her laptop and tilted her head, listening. Was it raining? Who could tell with the heavy drapes covering the room's high windows? Those would have to go. But first she must finish this book. Brushing off the temptation to get up and check outside, she turned back to the keyboard. She typed twenty words before the *drip, drip, drip* became demanding.

She pushed her chair back and navigated the labyrinth of cardboard boxes. The sound seemed to be coming from the kitchen, but nothing was leaking there as far as she could tell. Dodging sawhorses the contractors had left, she crossed to the basement door. As a rule, basements gave her the creeps, but in this tornado alley on the Kansas prairie, it was a rare house that didn't have one. She'd been relieved to find Kate and Jed's charming Tudor had only a closet-sized cellar.

Just enough space to provide refuge from a cyclone, but not enough to have dank corners where . . . well, where whatever it was she was afraid of could hide.

She opened the door—and gasped. The wooden treads at the bottom of the flight glistened with moisture, and from the far end of the cellar, she could hear the unmistakable sound of water trickling into more water. A naked lightbulb hung over the stairs. *Rats!* The string attached to the pull chain was caught on one of the splintered rafters overhead. Maddie straddled the steps, one foot on the top landing, the other on the thin ledge that ran the length of the stairwell. Grabbing the door handle for support, she scooted along the ledge, grasping blindly for the string.

Next thing she knew, she was teetering on the ledge. She reached for something to steady herself. Unfortunately, what she found was the door, which slammed shut behind her.

The stairwell went dark. Miraculously she found the string with the next random swing of her arm. Not so miraculously when she pulled on the chain, the light flickered, then sparked. She heard the ominous sound of every electric device in the house powering down.

Had she remembered to save her manuscript? The old laptop barely held a charge anymore; it would be dead before the auto-save kicked in. She felt herself slipping and gasped when she hit the stairs. Hard. A sharp pain sliced through her left ankle, and she bumped down half the flight of stairs.

When the stairwell quit spinning, she crawled back up to the kitchen and pulled herself to her feet, testing. *Ouch!* Her ankle had already swollen to the size of a small grapefruit.

Damp and aching, she hobbled to the cordless phone on the kitchen wall. Dead. And her cell phone was upstairs in the guest room charging. Thankfully the landline in the dining room had a dial tone. She rummaged through the desk drawer until she found the thin phone book and flipped to the number of her neighbor, Ginny Ross. Ginny answered on the second ring.

"Ginny? Hi, it's Madeleine Houser next door. Is your electricity out?"

"No. Well, at least I don't believe so. Just a minute . . ."

Maddie heard an oven door creak open and then what sounded like the ding of a microwave. "No. Everything's still on over here."

"Rats! I think I've blown another fuse. And there's water in the—ouch!"

"Madeleine? What's happened? Are you all right?"

Maddie cringed as she eased into the desk chair. "I'm fine. I fell down the stairs and sprained my ankle."

"You scared me. I thought you'd electrocuted yourself."

Maddie gave a humorless laugh. "Nothing so dramatic, I'm afraid. Sorry to bother you. I just didn't want to call the electrician again if it was only—"

"I'll be right over."

The phone went dead, and Maddie sat staring at the receiver for a few seconds, until she realized Ginny meant her words literally. Maddie had met her neighbor only two weeks ago, but already she'd grown to love the woman. At eighty-four and widowed for a quarter of a century, Ginny epitomized the word *spry*. She was as independent as any of Maddie's thirty-something New York friends. With her own mother's mind ravaged by Alzheimer's disease, it was good to have a wise older woman to talk to.

"Yoo-hoo!" Ginny's cheery voice floated in from the mudroom.

"Come on in, Ginny. But watch your step."

Ginny bustled into the kitchen, weaving her way through sawhorses and stepladders. "Now what did you do to yourself?" She bent to inspect Maddie's swollen ankle. "Oh, my! Are you sure it's not broken?"

"I don't think so." She rubbed the tender area around the swelling.

Ginny scooted another chair close and helped Maddie elevate her foot. Then she went to the freezer and rummaged inside until she unearthed a package of frozen peas. "Here we go." She wrapped the icy bag in a dishcloth and draped it over Maddie's ankle. She glanced around the kitchen, taking in the renovation chaos. "How are you ever going to finish that book in this mess?"

Maddie couldn't help it. Tears that had been pent up for weeks overflowed. "Oh, Ginny, I'm already so far behind I can't imagine how I'll make my deadline. And without electricity, I'm sunk."

"Well, of course you are." Ginny made sympathetic clucking noises with her tongue and surveyed the kitchen again. "This will never do. I'd offer to let you write at my house, but I'm afraid my beginning piano students would make this wreck seem like a haven of peace."

Maddie swiped at a tear and forced a smile. "I appreciate that, Ginny. But it's not your problem. I'll figure something out. Maybe I can just go to the library. . . ."

"Are you kidding? You'd have a constant stream of onlookers gawking and pestering you with questions." Ginny snapped her fingers and turned to Maddie with a triumphant gleam in her eyes. "I know just the place. My friend Arthur Tyler has that monstrous house sitting empty ever since his Annabeth died. They had a booming bed-and-breakfast until Annabeth got so bad. Arthur rarely has guests at the inn now, so I know he wouldn't mind if you went there to write. You probably wouldn't want to stay overnight, but you could use one of the rooms for an office. Arthur is a professor at the university. Keeps saying he's going to retire, but he never does."

Maddie hesitated. "Where is this place, Ginny?" She felt awkward about the whole idea, but she had to do something. She sure wasn't going to get her book finished here.

"It's just a couple miles east of town. Out on Hampton Road. Pretty little place. Peaceful. Annabeth's parents ran the inn for years. Named it after her, of course. Grover and I stayed there for our fortieth anniversary. Seemed kind of silly to stay overnight two miles from home, but it was nice. Kind of romantic . . ." A faraway look came to Ginny's eyes, and an ever-so-faint blush touched her powdered cheeks. "Let me give Arthur a call. You just get the plumber and electrician here. I'll take care of everything else."

Two

Maddie stood in the doorway of the inn and inhaled. Sunlight splashed saffron patches on the shiny wood floors and caused the jewel tones in the window coverings and upholstery to glow. In spite of her injured ankle, she felt better already, standing in the spacious parlor and looking into tidy rooms free of packing crates.

"Arthur said to make yourself at home." Ginny dropped a key ring into the pocket of her bulky sweater and ran a hand over the oak mantel. Her fingertips left a trail in the film of dust. She cluck-clucked and shook her gray head. "Annabeth always kept this place spotless. Even after she got so sick. Poor Arthur . . ."

"Was Annabeth a friend of yours?"

"She was. A dear friend. She and Arthur both. It was a terrible thing, her dying." Ginny lifted a heavy pewter candlestick and wiped the dust away with the sleeve of her sweater.

"I'm so sorry . . ."

Ginny nodded, then gave a resolute bob of her chin and brightened. "I'd show you the rest of the house, but I don't think your ankle would appreciate that steep staircase yet. Arthur said you could set up shop in one of the guest rooms. He lives in the apartment on the lower level—doesn't use any of the house proper—so I'm sure you'd be welcome to use the main living area here if you prefer. Or you could hole up in this bedroom." Ginny opened the wide French doors off the living room to reveal a guest room beautifully decorated with dark, Old English antiques. "It's the only guest room on the main floor. And by the way, the only bathroom on the first floor is in here."

Maddie poked her head into the room and took in the modern pedestal sink on the far wall just outside a door that apparently concealed the bath.

Ginny pulled the doors closed and led the way through a wide arched doorway into the dining room. To the left, an open staircase led down to the apartment where the proprietor lived, Maddie presumed. The steep stairway was defended by an oak railing, and in the middle of the dining room sat a huge, round, antique oak table on an oriental rug. The walls wore old-fashioned wallpaper in shades of plum and burnished gold. A fine antique buffet held a silver tea service and baskets of teas and jams. Beyond that, an open doorway led to a small galley kitchen, where an array of dishes and baskets and jars of canned goods were displayed on open shelving.

"You're sure Mr. Tyler won't care if I set up right here?" Maddie tipped her head toward the dining room table.

"I'd say this is perfect," Ginny said, obviously pleased with herself. "I'll leave now so you can get to work."

"Oh, Ginny, it *is* perfect. How can I ever thank you?"

Ginny winked. "Just finish that book, sweetie. I've only about three chapters before I finish my last Houser novel, and then I'm fresh out of reading material."

Ginny bustled out the front door, and Maddie was left in the blessed quiet of the old house. She took her laptop from its case and set it on the table, positioning her chair for a lovely view through the arched doorway all the way to the front hall. She connected the power adapter and plugged it in. When she was satisfied with the arrangement, she unpacked her sack lunch and hobbled into the kitchen to put it away.

The refrigerator shelves were empty save for a few cans of soda and a package of ground coffee. Maddie put her lunch on the middle shelf, feeling strangely as though she were trespassing. But Ginny had said Arthur Tyler insisted she have free run of the place, including full use of the kitchen.

She dumped the dark sludge from the coffeemaker's carafe and found fresh filters in a drawer under the counter. Once the coffee was brewing, Maddie went back to the dining room to finish setting up shop. She unloaded her bag, placing her dictionary and several reference books to her left, notebook and pen to her right.

She popped a Mozart CD into her computer. Classical music filled the room, and Maddie sighed as she sank into the brocade padded chair, slipped off her shoes, and propped her swollen ankle on the seat of a neighboring chair. The timeless melody, the rich aroma of fresh coffee, and her

Victorian surroundings transported her back in time. And when she put her fingers to the keyboard, the words flowed as they hadn't in months. *I don't know you, Arthur Tyler, but God bless your generous old heart.*

For the next two hours, Maddie typed, getting up only to refill her coffee mug. Her plot was moving along nicely when a polite *meow* made her look up from her computer.

A monstrous gray-and-white cat stuck its head through the stairway balusters and peered at her. Coming up the last steps, the cat sashayed over to Maddie, arched its back, and rubbed against her ankle before plopping down on her right foot.

Maddie took off her glasses and laid them on the table. "Well, hello there, kitty." She reached down to stroke the leonine head. "They didn't tell me about you."

The cat purred in response and nestled closer to Maddie. Though the house didn't have the chill she'd expected of a high-ceilinged Victorian, the cat's warmth was welcome. The old schoolhouse clock on the wall over the stairwell ticked a reassuring cadence, and she wrote for another hour while the cat napped.

The clock's muffled chime and the growl of her own stomach brought Maddie out of Anne Caraway's world and back to the present. Wiggling her toes and lowering her left foot from its elevated position on the other chair, she nudged the cat. "Sorry, kitty, but I need to get up and stretch a bit."

The cat yawned, bowed his back, and gave a short, friendly *mew* before following her into the kitchen. Maddie took her lunch from the refrigerator and ate it, leaning against the kitchen counter, her mind still on her story. Though her ankle throbbed, it felt good to stand up and flex her muscles a bit. After she finished her sandwich, she filled the sink with warm, sudsy water and washed the dishes, putting them to drain on the old-fashioned wire dish rack. She'd forgotten how nice it was to be in an operational kitchen, and she spent a few extra minutes tidying the kitchen before she went back to her computer.

Her feline friend had disappeared. The clock chimed the half hour and she looked up, surprised to find it was two-thirty already. Checking her word count, she was thrilled to discover she'd written almost three thousand words. A few more days like this and she might actually believe she could make her deadline. She saved the file, closed her laptop, and began gathering her belongings.

Before she left, she scratched out a note for the inn's owner.

Dear Mr. Tyler,

Thank you so much for allowing me to work from your lovely home. It was such a peaceful day, and I accomplished more than I'd hoped. I so appreciate your generosity, and if you're certain it's not too much of an inconvenience, I'll plan to come back tomorrow.

Madeleine Houser

P.S. Your cat was a wonderful companion. He kept my feet toasty warm while I worked. What is his name? He is a "he," isn't he?

The following morning, the plumber and the electrician arrived on the doorstep at eight o'clock sharp. Maddie left them instructions, then hauled her laptop and research books out to her Mazda and drove the eight blocks to the nursing home to check in on her mother before heading to the inn.

A nurse at the front desk greeted her when she came in. "You're Mildred Houser's daughter, aren't you?"

Maddie nodded. "How's she doing this morning?"

"About the same, I guess." The nurse gave her a look that spoke volumes.

With a heavy heart, Maddie trudged down the hall. Her mother was slumped in a chair in her room, staring out the window with that vacant look Maddie had come to despise. It struck her that at sixty-eight, her mother looked older and far more frail than Ginny Ross did at eighty-four.

She took a thin hand in hers. "Good morning, Mom."

No response.

"Your hands are cold. Do you want your sweater?"

Without looking at Maddie, her mother stretched out her arm and with birdlike motions brushed at something invisible on the windowsill.

"It's a beautiful day, Mom. September's almost over. Maybe we can go for a walk when I come back this evening."

She might as well have talked to the wall. Sighing, she went to the closet and picked out a lightweight sweater. As she started to close the sliding door, she noticed something leaning against a far corner of the closet—several old canes she and Kate had bought for their mother when Mom first started losing her balance. On impulse, Maddie chose one of the canes and tested it. It did ease the pressure on her ankle. "I'm going to borrow this for a couple days, Mom, okay?"

No reply. She closed the closet door and went to drape the sweater over her mother's shoulders. She patted Mom's frail hand. "I need to run, but I'll check in on you before dinner tonight, okay?"

Her mother turned slowly from the window and looked from the cane to Maddie's face. For one brief moment, Maddie thought she saw a spark of recognition in the rheumy eyes. But as quickly as it had come, it was gone, and Maddie was left with a familiar dull ache in her heart. *Oh, Mom. I miss you so much.*

Maddie arrived at the inn before nine o'clock. She hadn't noticed before what a beautiful setting the charming house occupied. With a shelter belt of Osage orange trees to the east and a stand of cottonwoods far to the south, the three-story house stood sentinel on the Kansas plains. A late September cool spell had left the trees and shrubs tinged with a hint of the autumn-to-come, but pink- and peach-colored roses were still in bloom, climbing the trellis by the front porch.

Maddie got out of her car and breathed in the country air. Attempting to use her mother's cane, she slung her computer bag and purse over one shoulder and tucked the sack lunch she'd brought under her arm. She hobbled up the steps to the wide wraparound porch, found the key in the mailbox beside the door, and let herself in.

On the dining room table was a message penned in a tidy masculine script on the back of the note she'd written the day before.

Dear Ms. Houser,

I'm delighted you enjoyed the time you spent here yesterday. I apologize for the dust and cobwebs. The inn has been a bit neglected since my wife's death. But I'm glad you were able to make use of it. Please do continue to come for as long as you like.

And thank you for washing up the dishes. I'm sorry to have left the kitchen in such a mess. I rarely have guests at the inn during the week, but I did have someone drop in Tuesday night and didn't get a chance to clean up before I left to teach my eight o'clock class. I shall try to do better in the future.

Arthur Tyler

P.S. The cat's name is Alex. And yes, "he" is a he. I hope he hasn't been a pest. As you probably discovered, he has no claws so is banned from the great outdoors, but please feel free to shoo him downstairs if he becomes a pest. Ginny tells me you have a horrendous deadline, and I'd hate to be responsible—even by proxy—for you not meeting it. (And I confess I haven't read any of your writing yet, but if Ginny has her way, that shall be remedied very quickly.)

Tucking the note into her computer bag, Maddie smiled. What a charming old gentleman Ginny's friend was! Ginny had said Arthur Tyler was retired but still taught English at one of the colleges in Wichita. She wondered if his lengthy missive was due to the English professor in him or merely to loneliness. A little of both, she suspected.

She set up her laptop and started a pot of coffee. While it brewed, she tidied up the kitchen. She found a dust cloth and furniture polish under the sink and polished the dining room table and buffet. She hated cleaning her own house, but it was different here. Besides, it was the least she could do if the proprietor wouldn't let her pay for the time she was spending here.

When the luscious aroma of Irish cream café reached her nostrils, Maddie filled a large mug and placed it beside her laptop. But before she opened the computer file that contained her novel, she penned another note to Mr. Tyler.

Dear Mr. Tyler,

Alex is not a pest at all! I've thoroughly enjoyed his company. I had a cat once myself, when I was a little girl. But since I began writing, I haven't had time to take care of one.

Please don't think another minute about the "dust and cobwebs." I didn't even notice.

She read the last line again. Not exactly the truth. She scratched out a word and changed the sentence to read: *I barely even noticed*. She signed the note, then put her fingers on the keyboard and delved happily into Anne Caraway's world.

Arthur Tyler pulled into the driveway with a weary sigh. The cheerful-looking sign in front of the house read, "Welcome to Annabeth's Inn," but it would never again feel like a welcoming place to him. Not without his Annie.

If this was what thirty-nine felt like, Art couldn't imagine living to be as old as his friend Ginny. Ginny Ross had been Annie's friend first, but as the cancer had sucked away Annabeth's young life, the older woman had taken Art under her wing. As if she and Annie were co-conspirators, Ginny's friendship had gradually been transferred to him. It was Annie's last gift to him, and he was grateful.

Annie had been gone for two and a half years now. Sometimes it seemed forever, and Art struggled to remember how the music of her voice had sounded, how her skin had felt beneath his touch. Other times it seemed as though she would come bounding up the stairs any minute, wearing her pixie smile and the shimmer in her eyes that spoke of how much she loved him.

He parked outside the garage, slammed the door of his pickup, and walked back down the drive to the mailbox. The first day of October had blown in on a chill wind, and he turned up the collar of his overcoat. He pulled down the arched door of the mailbox. Junk. A couple of Christmas catalogs, and the gas bill, which would be outrageously high—even higher next month, now that he was leaving the heat on during the day for Ginny's writer friend. But what did he care? He had nothing else to spend his money on.

Be still and know that I am God. The words floated through his brain, scolding him for his attitude. "Sorry, Lord," he whispered, his footsteps crunching on the gravel drive. He walked around the house and turned the key in the side door that led to his basement apartment. He stepped into the empty foyer. A *thump, thump, thump* on the steps brought a slight smile to his face. Alex. Another gift from Annie. He'd hated cats—or thought he did—until Annie had coaxed this mangy stray off the highway and into his heart. Now Alex greeted him with a comical cross between a purr and a meow, arched his back, and rubbed up tight against Art's pant leg.

Art stooped to scratch the cat under his chin. "Hey, Alex. What's for supper?" He put the mail on the bar in the kitchenette and hung up his coat in the bedroom closet. Alex trotted after him as he climbed the stairs to the inn to make sure Ginny's friend hadn't left the door unlocked or the coffeemaker on. He was glad the woman was able to use the house as a getaway. It would have made Annie happy to think of having a real author staying in the house—*writing* here. Annie had read all of Madeleine Houser's books. Ginny had seen to that, giving her the most recent release each year for Christmas.

He'd never paid much attention to them, leaning as he did toward the classics. He taught Tolstoy, Dostoevsky, Dickens, Jane Austen at the university. With passion. And he'd always teased Annie about the fluffy romance novels she read. He assumed that was what Madeleine Houser wrote, though it was beyond him how someone Ginny's age could even remember what romance was. A wry smile touched his lips. *Who are you to talk, Tyler? Do* you *remember?*

Oh, but he did. That was the problem. He brushed away the memories as if they were cobwebs.

As he came up the steps to the inn's dining room, his gaze landed on something under the table. He went to investigate and found a smooth wooden cane with an ornately carved handle. Apparently the author had dropped it and been unable to reach it beneath the table. Funny she hadn't mentioned it. He pictured the doddering woman trying to navigate his porch steps without her cane and shuddered. The last thing he needed was a lawsuit. But glancing around the room, he noticed the furniture gleamed in the afternoon sun. Madeleine Houser's dust rag had struck again. The woman had come to the inn four weekdays in a row now, and each day he came home to a tidier house than the day before. She must not be *too* infirm.

On the table, he spied a sheet of stationery filled with handwriting that was now familiar. They'd gotten in the habit of writing little notes back and forth concerning the details of their arrangement. Art had rather enjoyed their brief correspondence. Ha! What did it say about him that he received such pleasure exchanging notes with an old woman he'd never set eyes on?

He picked up her note and read.

Dear Mr. Tyler,

Once again, thank you for opening your home to me. The plumber finally got the water problems solved, but the electrical work is taking longer than expected and the man who was to lay the flooring called this morning to say he's a week behind schedule with his other jobs. I'm so sorry. I certainly don't mean to burden you with my problems. I only mention them to explain why I continue to take advantage of your kind offer. Please, if this becomes a burden for you, I hope you'll say something. I could easily go to the library to write if this is not working out for you.

Also, I don't mean to pry, but I noticed Alex seemed a bit listless this morning. I wondered if you'd noticed? I didn't see him at all this afternoon. I hope he's okay. I've grown quite fond of my little foot-warmer.

Thank you again,
Madeleine Houser

Arthur set the note down and stooped to pick up Alex. "Are you feeling okay, buddy?" The cat looked perfectly healthy purring away in his arms. Art gave the furry chin a good scratching. "Maybe Ms. Houser just doesn't realize how old you're getting to be."

He put Alex on the floor and sat down at the table to

reply to the note. Turning over Madeleine Houser's stationery, he wrote on the back:

Dear Ms. Houser,

First of all, please do not apologize again. I am delighted to have you here, especially as it seems that every evening when I come home, one less dirty dish sits in the sink and one more piece of furniture is free of dust. Housekeeping services were certainly not part of the agreement we made, but I confess I don't want to complain too loudly. In all seriousness, I appreciate the tidying up you've done more than you can know.

Second, please call me Art. I hear Mr. Tyler a hundred times a day from my students, and though you and I have never met, I'd like to think we could be on a first-name basis by now.

Third matter of business: As you've probably discovered, you forgot your cane here today. I found it under the table. I've left it for you in the kitchen. Hope you haven't missed it too much.

And finally: As for Alex, I'll keep an eye on him, but I haven't noticed anything out of the ordinary. He's a bit of a couch potato, and like the rest of us, I suppose, he is getting along in years. But thank you for your concern. I'll tell him you asked after him.

He smiled at his little joke, scrawled a happy face beside it, and signed his name. He hoped the old woman was getting as much enjoyment from their note swapping as he was. His step a bit lighter, he went down to his apartment to fix a sandwich and grade the essays his advanced English students had turned in.

Four

By the end of the following week, Maddie had settled into a comfortable routine. She consulted with the workmen before leaving the house, made a quick visit to the nursing home, and usually reached her makeshift desk in the inn's dining room by nine a.m.

On Friday morning, Maddie let the electrician in and headed out, loaded down with packages to mail. Miracle of miracles, she had ten more chapters of her manuscript ready to ship off to Peggy Barton, the woman who proofread her first drafts. Her editors didn't expect her to turn in a perfect manuscript, but Maddie cringed at the thought of her professional editors seeing her rough first draft. She'd always hired someone to proof her work before she sent it off.

Kate had asked Maddie to get some things out of storage, so she had those boxes ready to mail to her sister as well.

She parked in front of the quaint post office and went around to the passenger side for the packages. Though she still favored her left leg a bit, her ankle was much better, and she'd returned her mother's cane the day after retrieving it from the inn. Piling the parcels in her arms, she gave the car door a shove with one hip and started up the sidewalk.

As she approached the double doors of the quaint post office building, a dark-haired man exited and held the door open for her.

"Thanks so much." She smiled at him over her tower of packages.

"No problem." The smile he flashed in return did funny things to her insides.

Forget it, Houser, she warned herself, catching the man's departing reflection in the glass. *He's probably married. Besides, you've given up on men, remember?*

The man greeted another patron by name, then stopped on the sidewalk outside to talk to an elderly couple. Ah, small-town life. Clayburn was possibly one of the last towns in America without home delivery, so the post office was a social hub. She liked the fact that everybody seemed to know everybody else. In her New York neighborhood, no one bothered to exchange more than polite nods.

She dropped off her packages, picked up three days' worth of mail, and drove out to Annabeth's Inn. After two weeks of writing there each day, pulling into the inn's driveway had begun to feel like home. She wasn't sure she'd be able to write in the house on Harper Street once it was livable again, and she was beginning to wish she hadn't prayed so hard for the plumber and electrician to hurry.

She carried her things into the house, then set up her laptop on the dining room table before going through her mail. A wedding invitation and two baby announcements. *Great*. It seemed all her friends back in New York were either getting married or having babies. At least being in Kansas gave her a good excuse to miss those celebrations that only served to remind her that she was alone.

She pushed the thought away and quickly got the coffeepot going, a dust rag flying, while Mozart provided background music for it all. The smell of fresh coffee wafted into the front parlor where Maddie was cleaning, and her spirits lifted. She put away the dust rag, filled a large mug, and set to work on her novel.

By the time the clock chimed eleven thirty, Maddie had almost two thousand words to show for her diligence—along with a stiff spine. She saved the file to her computer and stood to stretch. Her gaze traveled down the hallway to the ornate staircase that led to the upstairs guest rooms. She'd been dying to explore the rest of the house, but had been afraid to try the stairs on her sprained ankle. Gingerly she rotated her foot a few times and bent to rub it. The swelling was almost gone, the pain barely noticeable anymore. She'd dusted the entire first floor twice over the course of two weeks. Maybe it was time to see what kind of shape the second floor was in.

Thickly carpeted steps creaked under her weight, and she felt unaccountably guilty, as if she were snooping. But Mr. Tyler had said she was free to use any room in the house, so surely he wouldn't mind if she took a look around.

She was halfway up the stairs when the doorbell broke the silence and set Maddie's heart pounding. She crept back down the steps and peeked through the curtain at the windowed front door. Ginny Ross's Volkswagen sat in the driveway, and Ginny stood on the porch.

Maddie opened the door, feeling like a child caught snooping under the Christmas tree.

Ginny held out a white bag that bore the golden arches of McDonald's. "I hope you haven't had lunch yet. I brought cheeseburgers."

"Bless your heart! Let's go eat. I hadn't thought about it till now, but I'm starved, and all I brought was peanut butter."

"I can't stay too long. You have work to do, and I have a piano student coming early."

Maddie led the way to the dining room. She swept her books and papers to one side while Ginny opened the paper sack and took out two fat, wrapped burgers and a large order of fries. The savory scent filled Maddie's nostrils and made her stomach growl in protest. She went to the kitchen for paper napkins and glasses of ice water, gratefully tossing the dry sandwich from her lunch bag into the trash.

Maddie joined Ginny at the table, and the older woman bowed her head and blessed their food, ending with, "And please help Madeleine meet her deadline."

"Thank you, Ginny," Maddie said, deeply touched.

"So how *is* the book coming along?"

"Very well, I think. It's sometimes hard for me to tell. I get too close to my work to be objective. But I do know that if it weren't for this wonderful writing retreat you found for me, I'd still be limping along."

Ginny nodded. "Speaking of limping, your ankle seems to be better."

"Much better, thank you."

"And your sister's house? Are they making progress?"

"Slow, but sure," Maddie said over a mouthful of cheeseburger. She swallowed and wiped a spot of ketchup from the corner of her mouth. "To tell you the truth, Ginny, I'm almost dreading the day they finish."

"Why ever would you say that?"

"Because then I won't have an excuse to come to this lovely place anymore. There's just something . . . special about this house." She sobered. "But I know I'm imposing on Mr. Tyler. I don't want to overstay my welcome."

"Nonsense," Ginny said. "You're as welcome as you can be. Why just the other day Arthur was telling me how you've been doing the housekeeping. I think he's the one who's feeling guilty."

"It's nothing really. I just do a little dusting or sweeping each morning while I'm waiting for the coffee to brew."

"The way Arthur talks, it's a lot more than that. He wanted me to tell you that you are welcome to come for as many weeks as you need."

"Mr. Tyler sounds like the sweetest man. I wish I could meet him sometime. I'd like to thank him in person."

A strange twinkle came to Ginny's eyes. "Well, maybe we can arrange that one of these days."

Watching her neighbor, it struck Maddie that perhaps there was more than mere friendship between Ginny Ross and Arthur Tyler. How delightful to think of the lively Ginny having a romance. She'd never given the love lives of octogenarians much thought, but knowing Ginny the way she'd come to, suddenly she could picture it quite clearly. And if Ginny—at eighty-something—could find love again, maybe there was hope for Madeleine Houser somewhere down the road.

She banished the thought as quickly as it had come. Five years ago, after Rob Clevenger broke up with her, she'd decided once and for all that romance was much more trouble than it was worth.

Unfortunately Rob hadn't been the first to break her heart. It seemed marriage simply wasn't something God intended for her. She'd been blessed in many ways—with the warm relationship she had with her sister and her two nieces. With a successful career as a writer, and opportunities to travel all over the world. And now with Ginny's friendship. No, she should be satisfied and fulfilled with those things. Besides, she had Mom to take care of now. She didn't have time for romance.

"Don't you think so, Madeleine?" Ginny's voice interrupted her thoughts.

She had the decency to blush. "I'm sorry, Ginny. My mind drifted. What was that?"

Her neighbor leaned back and studied her for a moment. "I was just wondering if Arthur wouldn't be better off selling this house—the inn."

"I suppose it is an awful lot of work to keep the place up."

"Oh, it's not that. It's Annabeth. The memories must be thick here. They lived here their entire marriage, you know."

"No, I didn't know."

"Well, I, for one, think it's time he moved on. The man has a lot of good years left, and he's wasting them pining away for that woman. She was a dear woman—a dear friend—but she's gone, and he needs to accept it."

Maddie smiled to herself. She wondered if Ginny realized how transparent she was being.

After Ginny left, Maddie pondered the things the older woman had said, and an idea began to take root. Perhaps if Maddie met Arthur Tyler—got to know him a bit—she could spur things along between him and Ginny Ross. If Mr. Tyler was as obtuse in the ways of romance as the men she'd dated, he probably didn't have a clue Ginny had feelings for him. Hmm . . . Maybe there was the seed of a new novel in this. Her mind whirled with lovely possibilities that wove in and out of Anne Caraway's tale.

She scarcely looked up from her computer until the distant buzz of a lawn mower broke her concentration. She pushed back her chair and went to look out the parlor window. A husky, spike-haired teen in a baggy sweatshirt pushed a lawn mower back and forth across the front lawn. Maddie remembered Mr. Tyler mentioning in one of his notes that a high school student would be working in the yard on Fridays.

She went back to her keyboard and wrote steadily until the clock in the hallway chimed four. She packed up her things and wrote a little note to Mr. Tyler. She still wasn't quite comfortable calling the old gentleman Art, as he'd requested. She opted for *Arthur* instead.

Dear Arthur,

My thank-yous surely fall on deaf ears by now.

Goodness, she hoped the man wasn't hard of hearing. She hadn't meant that literally. Ah, well, he was an English professor. Surely he could decipher her intent.

But I simply cannot leave this wonderful house each day until I've properly thanked my unseen host.

Once again, I had a most productive day writing. Sometimes the peace and quiet here are so perfect I almost forget to take a break for lunch. Fortunately our dear, mutual friend remedied that today. Ginny Ross brought lunch out to the inn, and we had a wonderful visit. It made me realize I've been at my house so seldom over the past few days, I've missed the pleasure of having Ginny for a neighbor. I'm not sure I've ever met such a sweet, selfless woman—and so energetic! She runs circles around me.

Maddie reread her note. She hoped her endorsement of Ginny wasn't too obvious. But then could one ever *be* too obvious with men? With a wry smile, she picked up the pen again.

Ginny says you've given permission for me to come back next week. If you're certain that's not an imposition, I will happily take you up on the offer. The workers have made some progress on my house, but it's all going much slower than I imagined. At any rate, with the solitude I've found here at your inn, I'm finally beginning to believe I might make my deadline on this book after all. Thank you again, kind sir.

Have a nice weekend,
Madeleine Houser

~

On the way home from the inn the following Monday, Maddie stopped by the post office to collect her mail. She'd had the mail from her New York apartment forwarded to Kansas, but it was slow in coming. Her mailbox had been depressingly empty recently. She bent and peered in the little windowed door. She had mail. She dug in her purse for the key. Her box yielded a bill from Mason Electric and a postcard saying she had mail too large for the box.

She took the card to the counter and handed it to the clerk. The man went back into the bowels of the building and returned a minute later with a manuscript-sized envelope sent with next-day postage. What was this? Surely Peggy hadn't finished proofreading the last batch she'd sent already. She took the package out to the car and sliced it open with a nail file from her glove compartment.

Inside was the portion of her manuscript she'd sent to Peggy, ominously absent of red ink. A brief note lay on top under the wide rubber band that held the pages together:

> So sorry to return this, Madeleine, but I've taken a full-time job and will no longer be able to proofread for you. I tried to contact you before you mailed the manuscript, but I never got an answer at the number you gave me, and my e-mails aren't going through to you. I do hope this doesn't cause a problem.

The implications of Peggy's note registered, and Maddie smacked the steering wheel with the flat of her hand. Electrical failures and water leaks and proofreaders quitting had conspired to keep her from turning this book in on time. She tossed the manuscript onto the pile of books and magazines in the passenger seat and put the key in the ignition. She really needed to go see her mother before she went home, but she wasn't sure she could handle one more depressing thing.

Tears came suddenly, and she wiped at them with the back of her hand. "Lord, I don't think I can take much more. Please just help me to get–"

A tapping sound on her car window broke through her prayer. She gave a little gasp, grabbed a tissue from the box on the floor, and dipped her head to dab discreetly at her cheeks before turning to roll down the window.

She didn't know the man bent beside her car, wearing an expression of deep concern. Wait. No, it was the handsome man who'd held the door for her at the post office last week.

"I'm sorry to bother you, but"—he gave an apologetic smile—"I couldn't help but notice you were upset. Is everything okay?"

Embarrassed as she was to have been caught crying, she was touched by the thoughtful gesture of this stranger–and a gorgeous stranger at that. Such intense blue eyes. He seemed familiar somehow. "I–I'm okay." She forced a smile. "I just got some bad news in the mail."

"Oh? I'm sorry. I hope it's nothing too serious . . ."

"Oh, no." She shook her head and affected a chuckle. "It's one of those things I'll probably laugh about in a few weeks, but right now it was just . . . too much. Thank you for asking, though. It was very thoughtful of you." She reached for the keys in the ignition, anxious to escape the man's sweet scrutiny.

He shrugged and ducked his head. "Sorry to have bothered you. I hope . . . I hope everything turns out okay."

"Don't worry. I'm sure it will."

He held up a hand in farewell and hurried across the street. In her rearview mirror, she watched him climb into an old Chevy pickup. She shook her head in wonder at the friendliness of these Midwesterners. No wonder Kate and Jed had loved raising their girls here in Clayburn.

Feeling oddly energized, Maddie drove to the nursing home and sat with her mother in the dining room while Mom picked at the bland food they served her. Her mother was quiet, but the vacant stare seemed less pronounced, and she even flashed Maddie a conspiratorial look of disgust when Mr. Bender slopped his coffee on the white linen tablecloth. Maddie headed for home feeling hopeful again.

When she unlocked the kitchen door and flipped on the light, she was delighted to see the cupboard doors back on their hinges and the floor cleaned off in preparation for laying the tile.

"Thank You, Lord." Maddie's whispered prayer echoed hollowly in the empty room.

As she walked through the house, she stopped in the living room in front of the old upright piano her nieces had practiced on. She leaned over the keyboard and played a tentative chord. The piano was sadly out of tune, but she scooted the bench out and sat down. Her rusty fingers explored the keys and soon found a simple melody she'd learned as a child. She hadn't brought her piano or any of her music with her from New York—not that she read music well anyway. She mostly played by ear. Now she plinked out the song, enjoying the mindless activity. The piano had always been good therapy for her.

Maddie played for half an hour, losing herself in the music. As her mind replayed the day, she smiled to herself, thinking of her neighbor's crush on Arthur Tyler, and scheming of ways to get Ginny Ross and the innkeeper together.

But the handsome face of the kind stranger at the post office kept intruding on her scheming.

Five

It was dark by the time Art finished his errands, and he stopped to grab a burger and fries to take home for supper. It'd been a long day—and it was only Monday. He'd been telling himself for a year now that he was going to retire from his teaching job. The commute was getting old, and with winter coming, it would be worse. But if he did retire, what on earth would he do with his time?

He could always start advertising the inn again and get it running back at full capacity. But since Annie's death, he hadn't had the heart for it. Still, it would beat driving an hour each way to work every day. He actually enjoyed the maintenance and odd jobs of keeping the inn up. He even rather liked cooking simple breakfasts for weekend guests. It was the little touches he'd never been good with. Those had been Annie's department—fresh flowers and scented candles, and clean linens on the beds in each room.

Ms. Houser had inadvertently made it clear to him that

he had no clue what it took to keep up with the simple housekeeping of the place. What a difference it made simply to have the cobwebs swept away and the tabletops polished. If he had enough paying guests, he could hire someone to do those things.

The truth was, he could afford to hire someone now. Even after setting college funds aside for Annie's nieces, the inheritance she'd received when her parents died had made it possible for him to retire whenever he wanted.

But that was the trouble. He wasn't sure *what* he wanted.

Life had lost its sunshine, its certainty, when Annie left his world. It had been a long time since he'd felt passionate about anything. His friend Dave Sanders had suggested more than once that perhaps a change of place would provide the impetus he needed to jump-start his life. Maybe he did need to sell the inn and move away. But it was hard to imagine how leaving Clayburn—and his church, and the people he and Annie had come to love—could make his life more fulfilling.

He thought of Madeleine Houser. According to Ginny, the author had left her home in New York and moved to Kansas to be near her mother. If Art thought it would be difficult at his age, what must it be like for someone as . . . well as settled as Ms. Houser must have been in her life? Maybe he'd ask her about it. Their correspondence had deepened over the weeks she'd been coming to the inn to write, and the back-and-forth notes provided a bright spot in his otherwise mundane days.

Alex met him at the door, pawing at his legs, begging for a bit of hamburger. While Art and Alex shared supper, he tried to explain his dilemma in a note to the author.

Dear Ms. Houser,

I have been contemplating something, and it struck me today that you might provide some insight on the topic.

Quite frankly, I have felt rather "stuck" since the death of my wife. Though I can hardly picture it, friends have suggested it might be wise to sell the inn and move away from Clayburn and all the memories it holds for me. Since you've just made the kind of move my friends are advising, I wonder how you feel about their suggestion. I don't want to burden you with the task of giving a floundering soul advice, but if you have any quick thoughts on the subject, I'd certainly be more than grateful for the input.

I trust the writing is still going well. Again, I deeply appreciate all the housekeeping you've done. The inn is wearing a much brighter face these days. And if there is anything I can do to make your stay here more comfortable or conducive to meeting your deadline, by all means, please let me know.

Happy writing,
Art

He reread his note and had to smile at the formal tone he affected whenever he wrote to Madeleine Houser. Quite different from the terse, hip notes he scribbled on his students' essays. Perhaps it was only natural to pander to the sensibilities of one's audience, but reading this brief note reminded him of the long letters he'd written to Grandmother Tyler after he'd gone off to college.

He'd often asked his grandmother's advice—even, sometimes, when he'd already made up his mind about something.

Like marrying Annie. It had been nice to have Grandmother confirm his decisions. On the rare occasion when Opal Tyler offered a dissenting opinion, Art had always given it careful consideration. His heart swelled at the memory.

He left the note lying on the table in the dining room where Ms. Houser would find it in the morning. It might be nice to meet Ginny's friend someday. Tell her how much Annie had enjoyed her books. Maybe he should read one of the woman's novels himself. According to Ginny, Madeleine Houser was quite well known in her genre.

There might even be a marketing angle to it—*Madeleine Houser wrote here.*—should he ever decide to advertise the inn again—provided, of course, Ms. Houser didn't mind him dropping her name in his brochures.

He doubted she would, though. Didn't most authors crave any publicity they could get?

~

Maddie read the note again, already composing a reply in her mind. She thought it rather odd that Mr. Tyler would ask advice of her, but she was glad for an opportunity to offer the inn's owner her opinion. Rubbing her chin thoughtfully, she picked up her pen.

Dear Arthur,

First of all, if we're going to be on a first-name basis, it must be mutual. Please call me Madeleine.

I admit I feel a bit strange trying to offer you advice. Surely you are much wiser and more qualified than I to make such a decision. But I suppose I do have my own experience to share (and I'll try not to write a novel—ha!). Perhaps you'll find a nugget of help in hearing what I've gone through.

I was perfectly happy living in New York. But my sister's husband was transferred out of state, and my mother lives at the nursing home here in Clayburn. My sister convinced me that I could write anywhere . . . well, you know *that* story! At any rate, I made the move somewhat against my will and with an attitude that was less than Christian. For a while I let that attitude fester, and as you can imagine, things only got worse.

Once I finally started assuming God had a hand in this whole thing, I began to recognize many good things about the move. It caused me to step out of a box that had become a little too comfortable. Most of all, I'm happy to be near my mother during her final years. Even though Mom is in the latter stages of Alzheimer's and doesn't know me anymore, it's been a blessing to spend time with her. And then, of course, God put dear, dear Ginny in my life.

But enough about me. Since I don't know you or the reasons your friends are recommending this move, it's hard for me to give advice. I don't know where you stand in terms of faith, but I do know that Ginny has a deep respect for you, so perhaps you'll understand my perspective on this. I believe if you seek God about this matter, He will guide you to the right decision. It may not *seem* right at first. It may be difficult and lonely for a while, as my adjustment has been. But I have lived long enough to know that God can take a noxious weed patch and turn it into a sweet-smelling rose garden.

Maddie started to sign off, tickled she'd found a way to campaign for Ginny again. But suddenly an idea came to her. She wondered why she hadn't thought of this before. She picked up the pen.

Since you felt free enough to ask for my input, might I take the liberty of asking for yours? Last week I received the unfortunate news that I've lost my proofreader. I understand you teach English, and I wonder if you might know of someone among your associates who would be willing to do that sort of work for me. I have a wonderful editor at my publishing house, but what I need is someone to give my manuscript a once-over, checking for simple typographical and grammatical errors, inconsistencies in the story line . . . that sort of thing. It could even be a conscientious college student. If you know of someone who'd be willing to take on the task on rather short notice, I would be most appreciative. I have a January deadline that is beginning to terrify me! (Of course, I would expect to pay the going rate for the service.)

I'll be thinking of you as you mull over the decision facing you. And thank you in advance for any help you can provide regarding a proofreader.

Your friend,
Madeleine Houser

Six

The following Monday Art locked the door to his office at the university and walked out to his parking space. His cell phone lay on the dusty seat of the truck, displaying a message notification. Dustin. He put the key in the ignition and listened to the message.

Dustin Brevits, the high school kid who took care of the inn's lawn, was already overdue with the mowing. Now he'd gotten himself an after-school detention and was backing out on the responsibility again. Art punched the keypad and lobbed the phone onto the passenger seat. He had guests scheduled at the inn for Friday and Saturday nights. The recent rains and balmy weather had the grass growing as if it were summer again, and by the weekend it was going to look like a jungle.

He sighed. He'd just have to mow it himself. Not that he really minded the job, but it got dark so early these days he usually watched the sun set on the drive home. Maybe he could rearrange some office appointments and get home early enough on Friday afternoon to at least mow the main lawns. The flowers would have to go without a much-needed deadheading.

He could see why Ms. Houser had been so frustrated over her lost proofreader. Nothing was more irritating than people who were not dependable. But—

Art slapped the ball of his hand to his forehead. He'd meant to post something on the job board in the English department about the proofreader job. Talk about unreliable!

But wait a minute. He'd been wanting to read one of Ms. Houser's novels anyway. Why didn't he offer to proofread it himself? Judging by her neatly penned notes, he doubted there would be much to mark on one of her manuscripts. Not to mention that he was beginning to feel rather guilty about the amount of housekeeping the woman was doing for him.

He'd walked through the house last night and rejoiced at how spotless it was. He wouldn't have to do a thing to the main floor before the guests arrived. He would, however, need to clean the third-floor guest room they'd reserved. Ms. Houser's cane undoubtedly had not allowed her to brave the steep stairway to the attic room.

With one hand on the steering wheel and one eye on the traffic, he rummaged in his briefcase for a notepad and pen, then jotted down some cryptic reminders to himself.

He pulled off of Hampton Road to the inn just as a beautiful Kansas sunset splashed across the western horizon. He parked the pickup, jumped out, and walked back to the mailbox, marveling at shades of pink and turquoise and tangerine he'd never seen any artist reproduce successfully. Walking back to the entrance to his basement apartment, the crunch of gravel beneath his feet echoed in the still fall air. How could he ever leave this place? Dave was crazy.

He threw his briefcase and jacket on the cluttered table and went to check out the upstairs. Alex met him at the top of the steps with his comical half-purr, half-meow greeting. The dining room table was empty. Hmm. In the three and a half weeks she'd been coming, Ms. Houser had failed to leave a note only one other time. Art checked the kitchen. She'd been here all right. The clean coffee carafe, a soup bowl, and a cup and saucer were neatly stacked in the dish drainer.

He was surprised at the wave of disappointment that swept over him at the absence of that note. Maybe Dave was right after all. Maybe he seriously needed to get a life.

Alex pattered after him as he climbed the carpeted stairs to the second floor and opened the door to the narrow stairwell that led to the attic suite the weekend guests had requested. This had been his and Annie's room before the inn had become so successful. Later, they'd decided to finish the basement apartment and open the suite to guests. Art let his hand rest on the brass doorknob for a moment, steeling himself. It was still difficult to enter this space that held so many sweet, intimate memories.

He flipped the light switch and climbed the steps. The air grew chill as he reached the top. He walked over to the antique dresser on the far wall. Fine dust coated the smooth oak surface, and the beveled mirror that hung over the dresser was dim with grime. He ducked under the low-hanging eaves and stepped into the modern bathroom adjoining the room. A bulb was out on the Hollywood strip lighting that surrounded the mirror. The window that looked out over milo fields to the north of the house was open an inch, and the sill was littered with dead flies. A tiny spider scurried down the drain of the large whirlpool tub. He made a mental note to bring up some cleaning supplies and bug spray after supper.

As he stepped back into the room and pulled the bathroom door shut behind him, his gaze fell on an oval frame, convex glass protecting the photograph inside. As much as he wanted to turn away, he was drawn to the picture like steel to a magnet.

The sepia-toned image looked as authentic as the antique frame—just as Annie had intended. But the stoic couple standing side by side in the photograph was Art and Annie Tyler, circa 2001. It had been taken on their Colorado honeymoon at one of those Old West novelty portrait places in Durango. Annie had picked out their costumes, including the handlebar mustache Art sported in the portrait.

Art ran his fingers over the glass, gently wiping the dust from the image. A lump came to his throat as he gazed through the glass into Annie's eyes. Though her expression was stern and posed—as the long exposure time of the old tintype cameras necessitated—Annie's eyes held a distinct twinkle.

He remembered the day as if it were yesterday. When he'd stepped from the dressing room wearing the Western duds and the dark mustache that matched his hair, Annie had dissolved in hysterical giggles. The photographer had a hard time capturing the serious pose Annie desired. But

Annie had proudly framed the resulting print and penned the accompanying label, *Mr. and Mrs. Arthur Tyler,* in her flowing calligraphy.

Art shook his head to clear away the poignant memory. "Come on, Alex. We've got work to do."

Tail high, the cat followed him downstairs.

~

Maddie stared at the note, not quite sure how she should respond. Arthur Tyler had offered to proofread her manuscript. It would be wonderful to have an English professor read for her and especially helpful to get a male perspective on her story—even if that perspective did come from a generation or two before most of her readers were born. But how could she ask him for yet another favor? He'd already offered her so much. Still, she was desperate.

Before she could change her mind, she picked up her pen and accepted his offer as gracefully as she knew how.

Dear Arthur,

I sincerely hope you aren't making your offer to proofread my manuscript out of some altruistic, chivalrous sense of duty. Though we've never met, I fear that is just the kind of thing you would do. (Of course I use the word *fear* in a contrary sense. How I wish there were more men in my generation who possessed such a quality!)

I would love to take you up on your offer, under the following conditions:

1. You allow me to pay you a fair wage for your work.

2. You are brutally honest in your critique of my writing. (You would do me no favors by being kind!)

3. You feel free to drop the job at any time, for any reason, without explanation or guilt.

I will leave the first five chapters of my manuscript here, and if you are agreeable to these points, then have at it.

I know you must be weary of my gushing, but again, thank you so very much for all you've done to help me meet this deadline. You shall most definitely have a well-deserved mention in my acknowledgments page!

Have a lovely evening,
Madeleine Houser

That task out of the way, she plugged her computer in and set to work. She finished chapter twenty-seven but found herself at a loss as to what should come next.

Standing to stretch her cramped muscles, she walked from room to room on the main floor, barely noticing the now-familiar and dear features of the house as she mulled over her story. No great insights came.

She had learned not to panic when this happened—though it was hard not to when she was so close to her deadline.

She paced the hallway that ran the length of the house, her sneakers making an annoying squeak with each step. As she came to the staircase in the foyer, she remembered that she'd never explored the second floor since the day Ginny had waylaid her with the enticement of cheeseburgers. Her novel temporarily forgotten, Maddie trotted up the stairs.

Three doors off the main hallway at the top of the landing stood open, and Maddie walked first into a sitting room, part of a suite decorated in a Victorian motif, ruffled and elegant with a wonderful old porcelain claw-foot tub in the bathroom.

The room adjacent to the suite was more austere, with its Art Deco oak furniture and wall coverings. She meandered slowly through each room and back again, lingering over the trinkets thoughtfully arranged atop the antique dressers and armoires. The rooms were much as she had imagined, fitting the style of the old Victorian home, yet with modern comforts seamlessly woven in. Obviously a great deal of loving care and no small measure of creative talent had gone into the decorating of these rooms.

Maddie actually grew excited, thinking of a whole new part of the house she could dust and polish. She would earn her keep yet.

As she went back into the hallway to go downstairs, another door—this one closed—caught her eye. She tried the painted brass knob and was surprised when it swung outward, revealing a narrow, carpeted stairway. Feeling like a trespasser, she climbed the steps, relieved to discover that the room at the top was another cozy guest suite. Stooping to peer out the dormered window at the head of the stairway, she gave a little gasp. The window overlooked a patchwork of Kansas fields, and a row of ancient cottonwood trees stood against the backdrop of sky the color of sapphires.

The majesty of New York City paled by comparison. Maddie knelt there for a long time, surprised again by how deeply this open sky and prairie landscape spoke to her spirit.

Finally she stood and explored the suite, delighted to find a low bookcase filled with her favorite authors. Her eyes widened as she spotted hardcover copies of her first four novels lined up on the bottom shelf. Ginny mentioned that Annabeth Tyler had been a fan. These must have been Mrs. Tyler's copies. The book jackets were in pristine condition, as though the books had never been read. But some people removed the jacket before they read a book.

She crossed the room and peeked into the large, modern bathroom, complete with whirlpool tub. Mr. Tyler must be expecting guests for the weekend, for the room sparkled. Every chrome fixture shone, and every wood surface glowed with a warm patina. The room still smelled of lemon oil and Pine-Sol. Maddie had begun to wonder if the inn ever had guests anymore, but here was her answer.

As she exited the bathroom, her gaze was drawn to an old portrait on the wall in front of her. A well-dressed young couple struck a staid pose, staring straight ahead. Maddie had seen similar photographs while researching her historical novels. It always fascinated her to see such ordinary, often oddly familiar faces staring back from the past, and this portrait was no exception. The convex glass encasing the photograph had the wavy quality typical of old glass, making it a bit difficult to see the portrait clearly. Still, the faces intrigued her—the glint of mischief so apparent in the woman's eyes. And the man reminded her of someone she knew. Or perhaps he was someone famous, someone she'd come across in her research once upon a time.

Her fascination grew when she read the label at the bottom of the frame: *Mr. and Mrs. Arthur Tyler*. Judging by their formal clothing, this might have been their wedding portrait. What a handsome young man Arthur Tyler had been.

She could almost picture what he might look like now—the black curls and mustache grown white, the smooth planes of his face tanned like leather, crinkled with laugh lines. She could hardly wait to meet the man in person to see if her conjectures were accurate. If so, she could certainly understand Ginny's infatuation.

She cast about the room, hoping to discover a more recent portrait of the Tylers, but the only other frame in the suite held a faded, silvered mirror. Maddie studied her reflection for a moment, sweeping her hair up off her neck and twisting it into a wispy chignon like the one Annabeth Tyler wore in the portrait. Glancing back at the portrait on the wall and the handsome figure the young Arthur Tyler cut, a strange ache of longing came over her.

All the heroes in her novels were men of centuries long past. Men of honor and integrity. Gentle men whose strength didn't depend on vulgarity and macho blustering. The only peers she'd met who had those qualities were spoken for. She let her hair fall limply to her shoulders and sighed.

But as she descended the stairs, an idea flickered. She'd been looking for a face for Jonathan Barlowe, the protagonist in her novel who would sweep her hapless heroine off her feet and into his heart. She had certainly found him. A smile pulled at the corners of her mouth. She wondered how Mr. Tyler would feel if she told him his portrait had provided a model for one of her characters. No. She didn't want to creep the man out. It must be her little secret for now. But she knew she would come up to this room each day to gaze into the eyes of her new hero before going back, inspired, to her computer. Ah, how she envied Anne Caraway.

Seven

Art thanked the postal clerk, slipped the new book of stamps into his shirt pocket, and started through the post office door, stuffing his wallet into his back pocket as he walked. He glanced up in time to hold the door for an attractive young woman who was, like him, preoccupied, stuffing her gloves and keys into her purse. They almost collided, politely skirted around each other, then, in tandem, did a double take.

It was the woman from the white Mazda—the one he'd seen last week crying over some bad news the mail had brought.

Recognition sparked in her green eyes, and she flashed a little smile. "Oh, hi there." Her cheeks flushed a lovely shade of peach.

He didn't want to embarrass her, but took a risk, keeping his tone lighthearted. "You look considerably happier than the last time I saw you here."

The blush on her cheeks deepened. "Everything worked out fine." She looked up at him with a sheepish grin and started to say something, but stopped when Mabel Bachman, the elderly wife of Clayburn's mayor, shuffled toward them, weighed down with a bulky stack of packages.

Art hurried to hold the door open for the elderly woman. Green Eyes gave a little wave and hurried on toward her car. By the time Art helped Mrs. Bachman with the door to the inner office, the Mazda was crawling down the street, headed north.

He felt strangely disappointed. He'd meant to introduce himself to the attractive stranger. Art didn't think she was married. No wedding ring. He'd noticed while she was stuffing her gloves into her bag. Somehow he couldn't picture a married woman driving that sporty Mazda—especially not with a passenger seat that looked like a filing cabinet and library rolled into one. Not that he planned to pursue this green-eyed beauty. She must be new to Clayburn. He'd never seen her before, and he knew just about everyone in town—by face, if not by name. He thought about asking around to see if any of his golf buddies knew who she was, but he could just hear the ribbing he'd get. As it was, his friends were constantly trying to set him up with somebody's cousin or stepsister or the former college roommate of a buddy's wife. No thank you. He did not want to go there.

Art drove home, fed Alex, and fixed a bologna sandwich, which he took upstairs to eat while he read Madeleine Houser's missive of the day. A sheaf of manuscript pages lay neatly on the dining room table. Good. She must be agreeable to him proofreading her manuscript. He went into the kitchen for a drink, bending to peer out the kitchen windows as he ran fresh tap water over ice. Outside, the overgrown lawn rippled in the breeze. He made a mental note to remember to come home early enough on Friday to get it mowed before weekend guests arrived.

Back in the dining room, he read the note, smiling at the author's list of rules and her promise to list him in her acknowledgments for the book. He ran a hand through his hair. If the book turned out to be drivel, he might have to devise a graceful way to extricate himself from that dubious honor. He would never hear the end of it from his colleagues at the university if his name appeared on the acknowledgments page of a schmaltzy romance novel.

Brushing breadcrumbs from his hands, he pushed his sandwich plate away and drew the manuscript close. He pulled a pen from his shirt pocket. Alex jumped into his lap and turned a three-sixty to brush his tail across Art's nose before finally settling in.

"Hey, buddy, what do you think? Am I going to like this lady's writing?" He stroked the cat's thick fur, and Alex revved his feline motor in response.

Running one hand absently down the length of the cat's back, Arthur Tyler began to read.

Friday morning, Maddie went out to the garage, loaded down with her computer bag and the reference books she would need. Her mind on a new scene for Anne Caraway's story, she turned her keys in the ignition. Nothing.

Oh, great! She tried again with the same results. Sighing, she got out of the car and went around to open the hood. She knew as much about car engines as she did about computers—zip. There didn't seem to be any smoke, nor were any liquids dripping or spewing, so she slammed the hood down and ran inside to call a mechanic.

An hour later, with her Mazda at Bud's Automotive and driving a monstrous old Buick compliments of Bud, Maddie headed west on Main.

She was already behind schedule, but she hadn't had the energy to see Mom the night before, so she stopped by the Clayburn Market and picked up a bouquet of rather sad-looking daisies and carnations and drove to the nursing home.

Mom was having another bad day, fidgeting and sputtering nonsensical syllables in a tired voice. She didn't seem to realize Maddie was there. Maddie stayed just long enough to transfer the flowers to an unbreakable vase and to visit briefly with the nurse. She felt guilty about not spending more time with Mom, but what difference did it make when her mother didn't know her from the nurse's aide who came to deliver her breakfast tray?

She drove to the inn, feeling discouraged and depressed. But as soon as the old Victorian house came into sight, her spirits lifted. She tried not to think about how close the workmen were to finishing the remodeling on Jed and Kate's house. When the last tile was in place, she would have no excuse to come out here anymore.

Shaking off the thought, she let herself in, set up her computer, and immediately climbed the two flights of stairs to visit her new hero. The man behind the oval glass was as handsome as she remembered—as handsome as he'd been in her dreams.

Again, she was struck by how familiar he seemed. That often happened with her characters. She would have a vague picture of a character in mind, only to open up a catalog or magazine and see the perfect face staring back at her. She always clipped pictures of her characters for inspiration. But Anne Caraway's hero had been a long time making himself known. Maddie memorized the masculine contours of the young Arthur Tyler's face. The square jaw, the steel gaze of his pale eyes. Though she couldn't tell from the sepia-toned photograph, she imagined his eyes to be a mesmerizing shade of blue-gray. Oh, to have been born a few decades earlier!

She studied Annabeth Tyler's image—the playful glimmer in her eyes, the love on her face so tangible and compelling. Inspired, Maddie hurried downstairs to capture that passion on the computer screen.

She typed steadily, breaking for a quick cup of coffee and a bagel she'd bought that morning at Clayburn's newly opened Main Street Deli. The story flowed, and finally Maddie could visualize the perfect ending. She made her fingers fly across the keyboard, eager to finish her tale so she could reread it and add in the subtle nuances of detail and characterization that imbued her stories with her own unique style.

Shortly after three o'clock, the sound of a motor revving outside startled her. Oh, that's right . . . This was the day that high school kid mowed the lawn. Her concentration broken, she pushed back her chair and stood to stretch and knead the kinks from her spine.

She walked through the hallway into the front parlor and pushed the heavy curtains aside. Though he had his back to her, Maddie could see that the person pushing the mower wasn't the spike-haired teen who usually came. This guy had shiny black hair that curled slightly at the nape of his tanned neck. And he was older—late thirties, Maddie guessed. Tall and slender, but even beneath the long-sleeved T-shirt he wore, she could see taut muscles flex as he maneuvered the push mower across autumn-brittle grass.

As the man reached the edge of the driveway and turned the mower toward the house, she took in a sharp breath and let the curtain fall back over the window. She knew that man. It was the guy from the post office. The one who'd caught her crying over Peggy's returned manuscript.

Cautiously, she pulled the curtain aside and peered out again. She watched him for a while. But when she went back to the dining room and sat down at her computer, she'd lost her focus. She kept thinking about the handsome man from the post office. The same man mowing the lawn. She tried not to acknowledge the disappointment she felt at discovering he apparently was employed doing odd jobs. Not only was it small-minded and judgmental of her, but she was jumping to conclusions.

"Besides," she said under her breath, "you're not in the market for a man, Houser. Remember?" An odd nagging nudged the back of her mind—something she couldn't quite put her finger on.

Finally she heard the lawn mower's engine cut off and a few minutes later the sound of tires crunching on the gravel drive. She looked at the clock over the stairwell. It was time to leave anyway.

She'd toyed with the idea of staying until Mr. Tyler came home some night. She could finally meet the man and perhaps put in a good word for Ginny. But tonight wasn't the time for that. Seeing the stranger from the post office here at the inn had left her feeling oddly disconcerted. She just wanted to go home and hibernate.

Art delivered the lawn mower to Mike and Milt's Sharpening Service and drove back to the inn. When he pulled into the drive, he saw that Madeleine Houser's old Buick was gone. The inn looked neat and tidy, sitting on the freshly cut lawn, and Art admired his handiwork with satisfaction. If the weather cooperated, he could pick up the mower next week and park it in the garage, sharpened and ready to go for a new season. But if this Indian summer persisted, he'd probably have to cut the grass at least once more before it went dormant.

He'd rather enjoyed the task of mowing. The physical exertion, the sun on his face, and an October breeze cooling his skin gave him a feeling of gratification and . . . was it hope?

The verse from Genesis 8 that Pastor Rennick had read last Sunday floated through his mind: "While the earth remains, seedtime and harvest, and cold and heat, summer and winter, and day and night shall not cease." Of course the verse referred to God's promise to Noah that He would never again destroy the earth by a great flood.

Still, as Art looked north across the highway to the ripening milo fields and the trees in their autumn glory, he felt the hope of God's promise bloom in his heart. Tragic things happened. Yet in the midst of them, if one were watchful, he could see God's beauty manifested just as it was in the gold and russet of the dying leaves. Life went on, and God had given him strength and courage to keep living. The assurance of tomorrow, of a new harvest in the field, of springtime after a long winter.

Even after Annie.

Art got his weekend guests checked in and settled in their rooms, and after dinner, with Alex comfortably ensconced in his lap, Art settled into his recliner with Madeleine Houser's manuscript on his knee, a red pen at the ready. The pen mostly remained capped, however, for Art was captivated by the story. He had read two chapters the afternoon before and was immediately impressed—and sheepishly contrite over his premature judgment of Ms. Houser's writing. Now well into the third chapter, he was amazed at the way the author made him believe the book had actually been written in 1871. And yet she'd found the balance of speaking to the sensibilities of the contemporary reader as well. It was a rare thing.

The woman had obviously done her research. The historical details were sharply accurate. Her portrayal of the

Chicago fire was chilling. He could almost hear the flames from the great conflagration crackling and snapping around him. And her characterizations were multilayered, with intricately woven relationships that kept him turning pages. He especially liked the hero. Not usually one for love stories, he found himself intrigued by Jonathan Barlowe and could easily identify with this flawed man.

He stopped reading only long enough to scribble a note to Madeleine Houser.

> I am enthralled by your story, Ms. Houser. I had no idea what I've been missing all these years. I will finish these five meager chapters you've left me long before bedtime, and then I face the prospect of an entire weekend not knowing the fate of Anne Caraway, precocious little Charlie, and, of course, the quintessential hero, Jonathan Barlowe. (Please do not tell me you are one of those cruel writers who kill off beloved characters for no good reason.)

Art drew a happy face beside that last sentence, lest she take offense—or lest she *was* one of those cruel writers. He signed his brief note, picked up the manuscript, and was soon transported again to Chicago, 1871.

Eight

By the following Monday morning, Maddie had her Mazda back—complete with a new battery and spark plugs, plus a bill for almost two hundred dollars. But the car ran like a top. She packed up her computer and books along with a couple of granola bars to take to her mother before going out to the inn. The tile crew had finally arrived, and she had to skirt around the beefy father-son team and their assorted toolboxes to reach the back door. She'd almost made her escape when the telephone rang.

"Could I speak to Madeleine Houser, please?"

"Yes, this is Madeleine."

"Arthur Tyler . . . from Annabeth's Inn? Is this Madeleine *Houser,* the author?" The low, gravelly voice was just as Maddie had imagined Arthur Tyler would sound.

"Oh, yes, Mr. Tyler. Hello! So nice to talk to you."

The muffled sound of hoarse coughing, then, "I apologize. I seem to be coming down with something. I was wondering . . . were you planning on working at the inn today?"

"Well, yes . . . I was. But I certainly wouldn't have to. I could make other plans . . ." She tried to sound cheery despite her chagrin at the prospect.

"No. No. Please come ahead. I just wanted to let you know that I'm staying home in bed. Didn't want you to be alarmed if you heard noises coming from the apartment below. I—"

"Oh, I don't want to disturb you. Maybe it would be best if—"

"No. Please. I'm not trying to discourage you from coming at all. Judging by the way I feel right now, I'll probably sleep all day. I'll have no reason to leave my apartment, and it won't bother me one bit to have someone there. I'm used to having guests overhead. I just wanted to warn you that someone would be downstairs, that's all . . . in case you hear me rattling around down there."

The younger half of the tile-laying crew pounded a rubber mallet on the floorboards and sang off-key with his iPod. Maddie held her breath. She would get exactly nothing written if she stayed home and tried to work in this zoo. "If you're sure?" she said into the phone.

"Quite sure. Please, make yourself at home." Mr. Tyler cleared his throat again and gave a gruff chuckle. "I might warn you, though, I'm calling dibs on the famous foot-warming cat today."

Maddie laughed into the receiver. "I understand completely. It sounds like you need Alex's services worse than I do."

She put the phone back in its cradle and stared at it, unseeing. Because of the photograph in the attic bedroom, Maddie had a distinct image of Arthur Tyler—even if it was a half century old. She felt she knew him through the delightful notes he left for her, but it was strange to now have a voice to put to those notes. He had almost become like one of her characters—an intangible, yet beloved presence in her life. But hearing his throaty voice had made him seem all too real, and suddenly she felt very odd about going out to the inn, knowing he would be downstairs in his apartment.

The clatter of a slamming toolbox lid brought her to her senses. Mr. Tyler was expecting her, and she didn't want to call him back and risk disturbing him. Climbing over the flooring materials that littered the kitchen, she grabbed her things and made her escape.

On a whim, she stopped by the Main Street Deli and picked up two take-out tubs of chicken noodle soup. She'd heat up one for lunch and leave the other in the refrigerator for Mr. Tyler. That ought to be good for what ailed him, and it was another small way she could show her appreciation.

Arthur Tyler set his cell phone carefully on his bedside table, flipped off the lamp, and sat in bed, staring at the opposite wall. *Odd.* If he didn't know better, he'd have thought the woman he'd just spoken to was someone younger. Much younger.

But with his sinuses so clogged, his hearing was probably distorted. He shook his head and reached for a tissue, then blew his nose so loudly that Alex leapt from his nest at the foot of the bed and hissed.

"It's okay, buddy. Go back to sleep." Art stroked the gray-and-white fur that now stood comically on end.

The cat turned two full circles, plopped back on the bed, and resumed purring. Art tucked his feet into the warm spot the cat provided, slid beneath the fluffy down comforter, and drifted into a Nyquil-induced haze.

He awakened some time later to the sound of footsteps—decidedly feminine ones—overhead. Alex jumped off the bed and trotted down the hallway to investigate. Art glanced at the clock on the bedside table. 8:45. That would be Madeleine Houser. His head throbbed. Stifling a cough, he shrank under the covers.

He heard Alex pad softly up the stairs, then the youthful voice from the telephone cooing and clucking at Alex. There went his foot warmer. *Traitor.*

Curious, he crept out of bed and went to the foot of the stairs. He heard the refrigerator open and close, then the sound of water running and the coffeemaker beginning its cycle. With his stuffy nose he couldn't smell the brew, but he sure wouldn't have minded a cup. It would feel great on his scratchy throat.

He was tempted to throw a sweatshirt over his T-shirt and sweatpants and go up to introduce himself. But he dare not expose her to this nasty bug. At her age, a virus like this could easily turn into pneumonia.

Instead, he went to his kitchenette and boiled a mug of water in the microwave. He scooped in two spoonfuls of stale instant coffee and stirred. Wholly unsatisfying, but it would have to do. Someday he'd break down and buy a coffeemaker for the apartment.

He heard Ms. Houser talking upstairs again, presumably to his faithless feline. Carrying the steaming mug, he walked over to the partition between the stairway and his living area, careful to stay out of sight in case the woman should be at the top of the stairs. He didn't want to give her a heart attack.

"Come on, kitty," he heard her say. "Go on. Get back down there. You need to stay with your master today. Go on, Alex. I don't have anything for you."

How sweet. She was trying to coax Alex back downstairs. He liked this lady. And her voice—something about it struck a chord with him. It had a musical quality with the faintest hint of the East Coast in her accent. He was having trouble making that voice match the picture of the author he'd formed in his mind.

Feeling light-headed and groggy, Art went to his room and crawled back under the covers. He drifted off to sleep, thinking how nice it was to have someone upstairs puttering around in the kitchen and making use of his poor, neglected home.

Maddie had a hard time concentrating, knowing Arthur Tyler was practically right beneath her. Several times she heard his deep, wracking cough and was tempted to heat up the chicken soup she'd brought and take it down to him. But she didn't want to embarrass the man by catching him in his bathrobe—or worse.

She ignored Alex and focused on editing the chapter she'd written the day before. Finally the cat sauntered back downstairs.

At noon, she heated up a container of the soup. Careful as she was to tread lightly, the floors in the old house creaked with every step. It was a wonder Mr. Tyler didn't storm up the stairs and ask her to leave.

At two o'clock, having accomplished painfully little, she packed up her laptop and books. Before leaving, she composed a brief note.

Dear Mr. Tyler,

I'm so sorry you're ill. I hope I didn't disturb you too much today. It was probably a bad idea for me to come here with you home sick. I'm afraid every creak and squeak in the house must have sounded like a herd of camels to you. I do apologize and hope you're feeling better by the time you read this. I've left you some of the new deli's wonderful chicken noodle soup. As you may know, studies show that chicken soup actually has medicinal value for cold sufferers. I hope you enjoy it. Even if it doesn't cure what ails you, it *is* delicious.

Perhaps it would be best if I don't come back to the inn until you let me know you are well and able to return to work.

Praying for your speedy recovery,
Madeleine Houser

P.S. I apologize for "stealing" Alex away from you for a while this morning. I hope you don't think I enticed him with kitty treats or anything. I promise you, he came of his own accord.

She drew a smiley face after her postscript and signed the note.

Driving home, she fought discouragement at losing a whole day of writing. She simply must learn to discipline herself to work under adverse conditions.

When she pulled into her drive a few minutes later, Ginny Ross was next door sweeping the first of autumn's offerings off her front porch. Maddie parked in the garage and went around to the front of the house to talk with her neighbor.

"Well, hello there, Miss Madeleine." Ginny wielded her broom to scoot a giant red maple leaf onto the grass.

Maddie eyed the broom, then looked up into the branches of oaks and maples that had yet to shed their autumn coats. "That's kind of a losing battle, don't you think?"

"Oh, I know it is, but it's good exercise. Besides, I enjoy being out of doors on a day like this."

"Glorious weather," Maddie agreed.

Ginny leaned the broom against the porch railing. "So, how many words did you write today?"

Maddie sighed. "Not very many, I'm afraid. Mr. Tyler was home sick and I couldn't concentrate."

"Arthur was at home?" A strange expression crossed Ginny's face. "Did you meet him?"

"No. He was in bed sick. The poor man has a terrible cough."

Ginny clicked her tongue. "Oh, my. I don't suppose that was very conducive to a quiet day of writing."

"It's not that so much . . . It just felt strange to be in his house with him right downstairs."

Ginny didn't respond but picked up the broom and started sweeping again.

"Have you made plans for dinner yet, Ginny? Let me take you out to eat at the new deli."

"Oh, you don't need to do that, honey."

"I know I don't need to, but I'd like to."

"Well, I have been wanting to try out the deli . . ."

"It's settled then. Six o'clock?"

"Sounds great. Just toot your horn when you're ready. I'll meet you in the driveway." Ginny resumed sweeping, and Maddie imagined there was a livelier lilt to her friend's step.

"Well, I hate to admit it, but this chicken noodle soup is almost as good as mine." Ginny dipped into her bowl for another spoonful of the rich broth. She sat across from Maddie in a cozy booth at the Main Street Deli.

Maddie smiled and buttered a slice of wheat toast. "Well, yours must be wonderful then." An idea leapt into her brain, and she gave it voice, trying to sound matter-of-fact. "Ginny, you should make some of your homemade soup for Mr. Tyler. That ought to cure what ails him." It was the perfect opening Maddie had been seeking to get the two together. Ginny didn't need to know that she'd already taken Art some of the deli's soup.

Ginny nodded, eyes glistening. "Maybe I'll just do that. You could take it to him when you go tomorrow."

Maddie's head came up and she scrambled for a way to get her plan back on track. "Well . . . actually, as long as he's not feeling well, I'll probably work from home. I don't want to disturb him. But *you* could go and—"

"Nonsense!" Ginny said. "If you come bearing food, he certainly can't complain. Besides, I'd say it's high time you two met."

Feeling caught in a trap she'd set herself, Maddie didn't argue.

~

Ginny phoned early Tuesday morning to say she'd been asked to help with a funeral dinner at church, and that Arthur Tyler's chicken soup would have to wait a day. Grateful for the reprieve, Maddie spent the morning at home doing laundry and tidying up the house as best she could with the flooring guys in the kitchen.

The housework done, she called her editor in New York to discuss some questions that had come up as she wrote. Janice was talkative and enthusiastic, and Maddie hung up feeling encouraged. It *was* rather nice to take a day off from writing. Her story still perked quietly in the background, and she had a feeling that when she got back to her computer the words would flow.

She spent the afternoon sitting with her mother in the nursing home's large sunroom. Maddie had brought her mother's Bible and read quietly to her from the worn volume. She didn't know if Mom understood or even heard the words anymore, but Maddie had discovered the Scriptures often seemed to calm her mother's restlessness. And her own, as well.

She read aloud from 1 Corinthians 13. "'But when the perfect comes, the partial will be done away. When I was a child, I used to speak as a child, think as a child, reason as a child; when I became a man, I did away with childish things. For now we see in a mirror dimly, but then face to face; now I know in part, but then I shall know fully just as I also have been fully known.'"

Was this how it was for Mom? Seeing the world as if through a dim mirror? Yet the passage wasn't written only for people with dementia. Maddie's own vision was dark compared to what it would be when she saw Jesus face-to-face. Mom's mind had been ravaged by a horrible disease, yet her spirit waited for release, waited to soar to her Savior. It was an amazing thought.

She closed the Bible and patted her mother's cold hand. "I love you, Mom."

They sat together in silence for a long while, and Maddie tried to enjoy simply being in her mother's presence.

Shortly before five, a white-uniformed nurse's aide appeared in the wide doorway. "Mrs. Houser? Are you ready to go to the dining room?"

Mom fingered the crocheted hem of her sweater, not looking up. Maddie put a hand gently on her arm. "Mom, it's time for dinner. Shall we go to the dining room?" Her mother looked into her eyes but no recognition lit her gaze. Maddie dismissed the nurse's aide with a little wave. "I'll walk down with her."

Taking the frail hands in hers, she stood and gently pulled her mother up beside her. Maddie attempted to match the shuffling gait Alzheimer's had bestowed, and together they started down the long corridor.

Nine

Before the workmen arrived the next morning, Maddie heard Ginny's cheery greeting sail through the back door. The savory aroma of chicken broth wafted through the house, and Maddie followed the scent into the kitchen.

"Well, good morning." Ginny set the pot of soup on a dish towel on the kitchen table and looked around the room, taking in the newly laid tile and the granite countertops. "This is coming along nicely."

"I'm beginning to believe there might be light at the end of the tunnel." Maddie ran her hand over the smooth surface of the counter. "The guy who's doing the counters can't finish up until next week, but he thought he'd be done in a couple of days. The only thing left then is some touch-up paint."

"And then you won't need to go to the inn anymore," Ginny said. "I suppose it'll be a relief not to have to lug your things back and forth every day."

"Yes, I suppose it will." She was surprised at how gloomy the thought made her feel. Maybe after she got the new kitchen cleaned up and all her dishes put away, she'd feel differently. But when would she ever find the time?

"I'd better let you get going." Ginny gave the soup pot a proprietary pat. "Tell Arthur all he needs to do is put this on the stove until it's warm. I don't want him boiling all the flavor away. Or maybe you could heat it up for him, Maddie? Help yourself to a bowl." Ginny turned when she got to the back door, a wily glint in her eyes. "There's plenty there for both of you. You could have lunch together."

"Oh, well . . . thank you. I'm sure Mr. Tyler will appreciate it." She tried to hide her dismay. If Ginny kept this up, Maddie would soon be spoon-feeding the old gentleman.

Her neighbor flapped her hands like a mother hen directing chicks. "Go on now. Don't let me keep you."

When Maddie turned onto Hampton Road a few minutes later, soup in tow, she wondered what in the world she'd gotten herself into.

Art heard a car on the driveway and sat up in bed, disoriented. He'd tossed and turned all night long—burning up one minute and shivering the next. He reached for a tissue on the nightstand and blew his nose. This bug had laid him low, but it seemed his fever had finally broken.

The gravel crunched, and the car came to a stop. Madeleine Houser must have decided to come after all. He swung his legs over the side of the bed and went to the kitchenette to heat some water for coffee. He wished he'd gotten up in time to brew a pot of real coffee upstairs before she arrived.

He went to the view-out window overlooking the drive. Expecting to see Ms. Houser's old Buick in the drive, he was surprised to see a white Mazda.

His heart lurched. Had he scheduled guests for today and forgotten about it? He tried to think where he'd seen that car before. Someone was moving around inside the vehicle, but he couldn't tell who or how many.

Pulling on a pair of blue jeans, he flew up the stairs to the main floor and went to the desk in the parlor where he kept the appointment calendar. His head pounded as he flipped through the bookings, trying to remember what day it was. Wednesday. But no guests were scheduled until the weekend.

The sound of a key turning in the front door mere feet from where he stood shot adrenaline through his veins. That would be Madeleine Houser. Strange, he hadn't heard *her* car drive in.

Glancing up at the antique mirror over the parlor desk, he caught sight of his reflection. *Good grief.* Two days' worth of black stubble sprouted from his jawline, his hair spiked out in forty different directions, and his nose would give Rudolph a run for his money. He'd frighten the poor woman to death!

He clapped the appointment book shut and raced back through the house, practically diving down the stairs to his apartment. Out of breath with his heart thumping in his ears, Art draped himself over a bar stool in the kitchenette. Above him, the front door closed, and quiet footsteps echoed from the entry.

A repeat of Monday morning's litany of sounds began—a computer being turned on, water running into a carafe. What on earth . . . ? Had she sent the visitor in the Mazda away?

Soon the coffeemaker was chugging and hissing. His sinuses were considerably less stuffy today, and the delicious aroma tickled his nose.

The footsteps retreated through the house and back out the front door. Maybe she was going to talk to the driver of the Mazda. Curious, Art returned to the window and watched. No sign of Ms. Houser's Buick—or Ms. Houser—but the white Mazda was still parked in the driveway. The driver—a woman—had gotten out and was bent over, taking something from the backseat.

A brisk breeze kicked up, and she struggled to hold the car door open with one knee while she tugged on something in the car. Finally she stood and turned to face the house, cradling a large cooking dish of some sort. The wind whipped her hair in her face, and she flipped her head back, trying unsuccessfully to shake the thick mane out of her eyes. She turned slightly and gave the car door a shove with one hip—one very shapely hip, he couldn't help but notice.

Where had Ms. Houser disappeared to? The woman turned and started up the front walk. In that instant, something clicked in his brain. The white Mazda. Of course! It was the woman from the post office—the lovely Miss Green Eyes.

Coming up his walk.

His next breath came in a tight wheeze. What in the world was she doing here? And why was she bringing food?

He wasn't about to answer the door. Not in his condition.

But where *was* Madeleine Houser? He was sure he'd heard her go out just moments ago. Maybe she would tell Green Eyes he was indisposed.

He looked out on the drive again. The Buick was nowhere to be seen. But why would Ms. Houser set up her computer, make coffee, and then leave? It made no sense. Unless she'd forgotten something and run home for it. That must be it.

Art listened for the doorbell. Instead, he heard the front door open and the floorboards above him creak. He leaned against the wall that concealed the stairway. He heard the refrigerator open and close, the sound of coffee being poured, and soon the steady click of a computer keyboard. What was going on?

Alex slipped past him and scurried up the steps.

"Well, hello there, Alex," a familiar voice cooed. "Are you being a bad boy again? You're going to get me in trouble, you know. Now you go on. Get back down there and keep Mr. Tyler's feet warm."

Art closed his eyes and lifted his chin toward the ceiling. *Tyler, you idiot! How could you be so dumb?*

On impulse, he hurried to the bedroom and threw open Annie's side of the closet. Annabeth's sister and nieces had helped him pack up Annie's clothes and shoes more than a year ago, but two shelves in the back of the closet still held part of her beloved collection of books. Art knelt in front of the shelves and ran his fingers along the titles, looking frantically for one particular volume.

There it was. *Hope's Song*, by Madeleine Houser.

Art slipped the book from the shelf, knowing what he would find even before he opened the cover. He turned the book over, opened to the back flap of the dust jacket, and stared at the photograph.

A familiar pair of mesmerizing green eyes stared back at him.

The beautiful young woman at the post office—the one who'd made his heart beat a little faster—was Madeleine Houser. Green Eyes was the author of the compelling novel in which he'd immersed himself for the past few nights. This lovely creature—the one who'd penned the delightful notes Art had so looked forward to each evening—was Ginny's friend. Ginny's *young* friend. And she'd spent nearly every day of the past month in this very house—*his* house!

How could his perceptions have been so ridiculously off base? What happened to the gray-haired old lady? The one who walked with a cane and drove an old monster of a Buick?

Why hadn't Ginny *told* him? Yet . . . what had there been to tell? Ginny couldn't know he was infatuated with the lovely stranger at the post office. He looked at Madeleine Houser's publicity photo on the book jacket again. If he had only taken Ginny's advice, he would have read one of Ms. Houser's books and put two and two together long ago.

Art fell back against the bed and sat with his head in his hands, laughing softly to himself as each intricate facet of this great deception—one he'd apparently manufactured in his own mind—came to light.

Twenty minutes later, he felt a brush of soft fur against his bare arm. "Alex, you rascal. You knew all along, didn't you?" He chuckled and scratched the cat under the chin, then hauled himself off the floor and went down the hall to the bathroom.

It was time to shower and shave and properly introduce himself to the lovely, talented—and ever so young—Madeleine Houser.

~

Maddie heard the sound of running water downstairs. Mr. Tyler must be up and around. Maybe he would come upstairs and she could offer to warm some of Ginny's soup for him. That ought to make her neighbor happy.

She felt rather excited and just a bit nervous at the prospect of finally meeting her mysterious host—and the hero of her novel. But of course she wouldn't mention that. A flush of heat crept up her neck at the thought.

She saved her latest chapter to the computer and went into the kitchen to put Ginny's soup on to heat. If Mr. Tyler didn't come up, maybe she'd get up the courage to take a bowl down to him. Compliments of Ginny, of course.

She found a package of soup crackers in a basket on top of the refrigerator and fixed a tray with a cloth napkin and a glass of ice water. On a whim, she went out to the front porch and plucked one of the faded roses from the bush near the front porch. She placed it in a tiny bud vase she found in a cupboard. Surveying her handiwork with satisfaction, she stirred the soup once more and listened for sounds of life downstairs.

The water had stopped running, but all was quiet below. Maybe he'd gone back to bed. She certainly didn't want to wake him. Not sure what to do, she turned the heat down under the soup and went back to try to write another scene in her novel.

A few unproductive minutes later, Alex's meow caused her to look up from her computer. Footsteps sounded on the stairway not ten feet from where she sat. Ah, he *was* awake. She was finally going to meet the elusive Arthur Tyler. Sitting straighter in her chair, she slipped off her glasses, moistened her lips, and tucked her hair behind her ears.

But the head that appeared over the railing did not belong to Arthur Tyler. It was . . . the lawn guy. The man from the post office. Maddie took in a sharp breath, mildly alarmed that he had just walked into the house without knocking.

"Oh! Hello," she said, trying to appear calm. She pushed back her chair and stood, glad for the massive oak table between them. "Are you here to mow the lawn?" She motioned toward the front of the house.

"The lawn?" The man stared at her as though she were speaking Swahili.

"Um . . . Mr. Tyler is home sick today," she explained. "He's downstairs. I–I can get him if you like."

The man's bemused gaze made her extremely uncomfortable.

"Madeleine?"

Maddie gulped. *How did he know her name?* And today wasn't the day the lawn guy usually came. Her heart beat erratically and she struggled for a breath.

The man came up the last two stairs to the landing, and Maddie took a step back, bumping into the chair behind her.

He put a hand to his chest. "Ms. Houser, *I'm* Arthur Tyler."

"Wh–what?" What kind of nut case *was* this guy?

"I'm sorry if I frightened you." He shook his head. "And I

am home sick today. I–I don't think I'm contagious anymore. I just thought it was time I introduced myself." He waited, looking at her with something like amusement in his eyes.

"You're Arthur Tyler? But I thought . . ."

"Yes, I'm Art Tyler. You thought I was someone else?"

Maddie reached behind her, felt for the brocade seat of the straight-back chair, and crumpled onto it. "I'm sorry. I'm . . . a little confused right now. I thought . . ." The truth began to unfold in her mind, and she giggled. "Well, I thought you were . . ."

He waited, dark brows knit together.

She started again. "For some reason, I assumed you were Ginny's friend. Well, I know you *are* her friend, but I thought you were Ginny's age. I thought you were *old.*" She knew she was rambling, but her brain was having trouble wrapping itself around the now obvious truth.

Arthur Tyler threw back his head and laughed. "You thought *I* was old?" he said, when he finally caught a breath. "I thought the same thing!"

"You thought you were old?" Maybe he *was* a nut case after all.

He laughed again. "No, no. I thought *you* were old. Ginny said she had this writer friend and I just jumped to conclu—"

"Apparently we both jumped to some conclusions." Her mind whirled, trying desperately to sort out this whole outrageous scenario.

"Yes," Arthur said, a hint of suspicion creeping into his voice, "and I don't recall our friend Ginny doing anything to correct those misperceptions."

Maddie thought for a minute, remembering the mischievous gleam in Ginny's eye earlier that morning. "You're right. I'm sure I said something that would have let her know I thought—wait a minute! And to think I was trying to—" She stopped, feeling herself blush.

"What?"

Maddie giggled again. "I was trying to set you and Ginny up. I thought she had a crush on you. But all this time—"

Arthur Tyler took a step toward her and a light of recognition came to his eyes—eyes that, up close, were exactly the shade of blue-gray Maddie had imagined.

"Ginny Ross was trying to set *us* up? Is that it?"

Maddie smiled and nodded slowly, remembering her neighbor's insistence that Maddie deliver the chicken soup in person. "I have a feeling that's exactly what she was up to."

Arthur pulled a chair out from the dining room table, turned it around, and straddled it, resting his arms on the high back. "Well, isn't this one for the books? No pun intended." He grinned, looking for all the world like Jonathan Barlowe.

They sat looking at one another, shaking their heads. Finally Arthur unfolded his lean body from the chair, rose, and stretched out a hand. "Madeleine Houser, I'm Arthur Tyler. I'm very pleased to finally meet you. The *real* you."

Maddie took his hand, smiling broadly. "And I'm pleased to meet you, too, kind sir. After all our correspondence, I—I wish I could say, 'I feel like I know you,' but I'm so confused right now, I'm afraid that wouldn't be altogether true."

"No," he laughed. "Not for me, either." He dipped his head. "But I'd certainly like to remedy that."

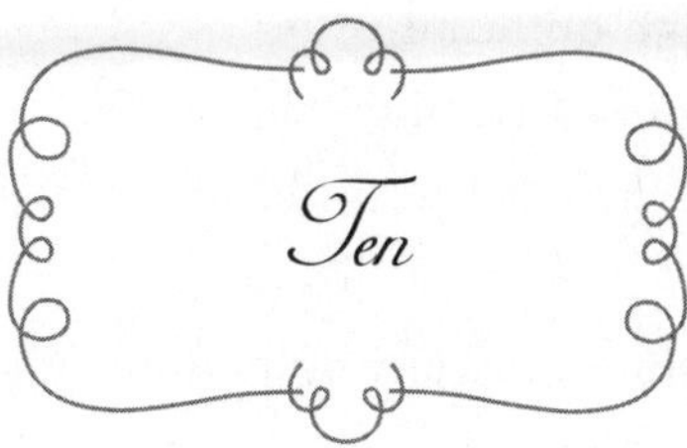

Ten

The kitchen smelled of chicken broth and coffee and the slightest hint of some delicate, feminine cologne. After being without his olfactory senses for several days, Art inhaled each scent with fresh appreciation.

He smiled at the woman sitting across from him and spooned another bite of the fragrant soup into his mouth. "Mmm . . . this is wonderful," he said over a mouthful of noodles. "I think I feel better already. I can see why they say this stuff has medicinal value," he added with a wink.

"Well, I'd say this goes down a bit easier than any medicine." Madeleine Houser dabbed at the corner of her mouth with a paper napkin.

For a few minutes the two ate together in silence—a remarkably comfortable silence, given the fact they'd met only twenty minutes ago.

Yet watching her, Art felt he knew the soul of the beautiful woman sitting at his table. His heart swelled at the amazing discoveries they'd made. To think they'd each had such skewed perceptions of the other. Every time he thought of the comedy of errors that had brought them to this moment, he wanted to laugh out loud.

Madeleine looked up and caught him watching her, but the quirk of her shapely lips told him she was having similar thoughts.

"So all this time you've imagined me as a doddering old man?"

"Not exactly doddering." She tilted her head. "I was thinking more along the lines of distinguished and . . . dapper."

Art was charmed by the blush of crimson that climbed her throat.

"I wish I could give parallel adjectives for the picture I had of Ms. Madeleine Houser, elderly author. But the truth is, I thought you were just plain *old.*"

"Hey!" She shot him a look that was exactly what he'd aimed for.

He cocked his head to one side and held up a finger. "Ah, but let's talk about my opinion of the mysterious woman at the post office."

"Let's not," she protested. But her smile clearly said the opposite.

"I desperately wanted to get to know her." He hesitated. "Do I dare ask what you were so upset about that day—in the car?"

Madeleine put her spoon down and thought for a minute, then giggled like a schoolgirl.

"What?"

She put an elbow on the table and rested her chin on one hand. "I was upset because my proofreader had just returned my manuscript with a note saying she was quitting."

"Oh . . ." One more piece of the puzzle plunked into place. "Well, hey, didn't you tell me that one day you'd probably be able to laugh about it?"

She laughed again, a sound Art was quickly growing to love.

When her amusement subsided, a wistful note crept into her voice. "I really didn't expect that day to come quite so soon."

"I'm so glad it did."

She rewarded him with another smile. "Me too."

"Your book is wonderful, Madeleine—may I call you Madeleine?" It felt right, but he wanted to be certain.

"My friends call me Maddie."

He nodded. "Then Maddie it is. And I mean it. Your book is excellent."

"Thank you, Arthur—"

"Please, my friends call me Art."

"Art, then." She bobbed her chin. "I was nervous . . . about having you read it."

"What? You, nervous about some old geezer's opinion?"

"I'd grown to like that old geezer quite a bit. And to respect his opinion." A mischievous glimmer came to her eyes. "Frankly, I'm not sure how much I'd value the critique of a young whippersnapper like you."

If he'd believed in love at first sight, he would have dropped to one knee and proposed on the spot. But he managed to restrain himself and simply enjoy her clever wit.

Maddie. Yes, the name fit Green Eyes perfectly.

She jumped up and went to the kitchen, came back with a pitcher of water, and refilled his glass.

"Thank you. You don't have to wait on me, you know."

"I don't mind. You're not feeling well. Besides, I can never begin to repay you for allowing me to take over your house like this."

"Speaking of which . . ." He balled up his napkin and pushed back his chair, "I need to let you get back to work." He gathered up their bowls and spoons and carried them into the kitchen. Poking his head back into the dining room, he added, "Pretend I'm not here. I'll take care of these dishes. You get back to that story. I'm ready for more chapters."

He went back to the kitchen and ran the sink full of hot water. While he washed dishes, he listened to the rhythmic *tap tap tap* of her keyboard. He was wiping off the counters when he heard her giggling again.

He poked his head into the dining room. "Did our story take a humorous turn?"

She looked up and studied him for a moment. "I may as well tell you. You're my hero."

"Wow . . . Just because I did the dishes?"

"No. The photograph upstairs." She pointed toward the ceiling.

He waited, dish towel in hand.

"Would you care to clue me in? Or would you rather write me a note?" He grinned.

She gave him a crooked smile and dipped her head. "I saw the photograph upstairs of you and your wife. The old-fashioned one. I thought it was you when you were young—before I knew you weren't old, I mean—" She shook her head. "This is very complicated."

He waited, rather enjoying her discomfort.

"I needed a face for my hero and . . . well, I borrowed yours. I hope you don't mind."

Art curbed a grin. "No wonder I liked Jonathan Barlowe so well."

Maddie laughed again and turned a luscious shade of pink. But he was flattered at the implication.

"Ginny said your wife—Annabeth—died." It was almost a whisper.

His breath caught at the sound of Annie's name, but the sympathy in Maddie's expression touched a place deep within. "Yes." He looked at the floor. "Cancer. It'll be three years next April."

"I'm so sorry. She was very beautiful."

He nodded, unable to speak. Suddenly desperate to change the subject, he moved toward the stairway. "I'm keeping you from your work . . ."

"Oh, no." She scooted her chair back from the table. "I'm not going to kick you out of your own dining room. I'll go now. I can come back after you've returned to work."

"Please. Don't go, Maddie. I needed to get busy anyway. I have papers to grade downstairs."

"Well . . . if you're sure . . ."

"Positive. It was very nice to finally meet you." He smiled and stretched out a hand again. "Madeleine."

She took it, and the pink in her cheeks blossomed. "You too . . . Arthur."

Downstairs he retrieved a stack of freshman essays from

his briefcase and took them to the bar in the kitchen. But thoughts of Annie—and of the woman upstairs—wouldn't let him concentrate.

More than once, the music of feminine laughter floated down the stairway. He didn't know if Green Eyes was writing a funny scene, or if she was, like him, remembering some little incident, some little providential twist of timing that had led to their meeting today.

All he knew was that this house had been too long without a woman's laughter.

Eleven

The next morning when Maddie emerged from the steamy bathroom, hair still damp from her shower, the answering machine blinked at her. She listened to the message while she did her makeup.

"Hello, Maddie. It's Art. Just wanted to let you know Ginny's soup worked its magic and I'm going back to work today, so the house is all yours. Please make yourself at home. I–I've left you a note . . . in the usual place. Well . . . that's all. Bye now."

A twinge of guilt accompanied the thrill that went up her spine at the sound of Art's voice. But she detected a note of hesitancy, too, and wondered what it meant. She'd dreamed of Arthur Tyler—Art—both waking and sleeping, since she'd left the inn yesterday. She had fallen and fallen hard.

But how could that be? She didn't even know the man. Was she just in love with the idea of being in love?

She stared in the mirror as she ran a brush through her

hair. "You don't know what love is, Houser." But oh, how she wanted to learn.

Sitting across from Art over chicken noodle soup yesterday, talking, laughing together, it seemed as though they were dear, old friends. She smiled at her reflection. *Old.* And she did know something of Art's dreams and desires. In a way, they'd been courting since the second day she went to the inn and found his thoughtful note in reply to hers. They just hadn't realized it.

Maddie wondered what he was feeling this morning. Had he sensed the connection as strongly as she? Even though his wife had been gone for several years, it was obvious from his reaction yesterday that he was still reeling from the loss. She'd need to tread lightly.

With a swarm of butterflies in her stomach, she drove out to the inn, feeling a new kind of anticipation over the note that awaited. She let herself in and hurried to the dining room. Without bothering to set up her computer, she picked up the sheet of paper on the table.

As she read, her heart dipped and soared and dipped again like a kite in a fickle Kansas wind.

Dear Maddie,

Not Ms. Houser, not Madeleine, but dear Maddie. I'm still trying to sort out all the crazy misunderstandings that kept us from meeting until yesterday. But somehow I know it was for the best. I think perhaps if we'd met that first day you came to write at the inn, we never would have grown to know and respect one another as we have. (At least I hope you share those feelings.)

I suppose you need to know that I've put up some walls where women—especially beautiful, talented, available women—are concerned. My marriage was an extremely happy one, but it had a tragic ending. And since you and I have been honest with each other from the start, I'll confess to a tremendous fear that I will never be able to love that way again. I don't want you to expect what I'm not sure I can give.

Perhaps I am seriously premature in sharing these things with you—and now in making a request—but what I said yesterday was true: I would like to get to know you better. Could we have dinner again soon? A real—dare I say it—date? If I've misread your interest, please be honest with me, and please forgive me. But if not, are you free this Saturday night? The college symphony is performing, and I have two tickets. (And someone told me about a new restaurant not far from campus. We could eat before the concert.)

I admit I'm a little nervous about this next step in our friendship. Frankly I adored the elderly, charming, *safe* Madeleine Houser. I'm a little sad to think she's gone from my life. But I have a feeling her younger counterpart will win me over just as quickly. In fact, I'm not so sure she hasn't already.

I'll hope to find your response when I get home tonight, but if you need to think it over for a few days, I will understand.

Your friend,
Art

Maddie read the note again, caressing the smooth paper beneath her palm. How was she supposed to finish her novel, make her deadline, *breathe,* when his letter contained such undisguised hesitancy—such fragile promise?

She read it a third time and found herself more confused than ever. What did the man want? First it seemed as if he were making romantic overtures, but then he held out a warning that no one could fill Annie's place in his heart. Yet in his very next breath he was asking her for a date. Did the man have a clue what he wanted? Did he care that he was stringing her along like some kind of puppet?

She picked up her pen and turned over Art's note, ready to write her reply on the back. But she didn't want to part with this paper. She needed to take it home and read it again, attempt to decipher the true message his words held.

Digging in her computer bag, she found a legal pad. She sat for several minutes, pen poised, mind reeling, before she knew what she wanted to say.

Dear Art,

Rest assured, I am every bit as frightened and uncertain as you are. Having said that, my calendar is free for Saturday, and I can't think of a more pleasant way to spend it than at dinner and the symphony with a friend.

Shall we keep it at that, with no other expectations or potential? Just friends? I could use a friend right now.

Maddie

She laid the pen and pad on the table. She understood what Art meant about being sad to see the imagined, elderly friend go. She felt the same about "old Mr. Tyler." With him, she'd never had to measure her words so carefully.

Never had to worry that she would be judged the way men her age judged women.

Had they ruined a wonderful friendship by the simple act of being introduced? Did the mere fact that they were the same age, and therefore eligible for romance, doom their friendship? This surely broke her track record for destroying a relationship. Friends to strangers almost before she met the guy.

She opened her laptop, pulled up her manuscript, and forced herself to start typing. But what she really wanted was to put her head in her hands and weep.

~

On Thursday evening Art sat in Ginny Ross's cozy living room, sipping tea from a fragile china cup. They'd discussed global news and local politics, and now they'd worked their way down to the weather.

Beside him on the slipcovered sofa, Ginny set her own teacup on the doily-strewn coffee table. "Well, enough small talk. What did you really come for, Arthur?"

Art smiled. Ginny had never been one to mince words. Okay, he would lay it all out for her and see if she had a cure for his jumbled emotions. "I think I'm in love with your neighbor."

Ginny hooked a thumb to the north and feigned shock. "Elma Wheaton? I don't know, Art. She's awfully old for you, don't you think?"

"Very funny, Ginny. You know exactly who I mean." He sobered. "I think I'm in love with Madeleine Houser."

Ginny's expression was unreadable. "So why are you telling *me*? Seems Madeleine ought to be the first to hear this startling announcement."

"She already has . . . well, sort of."

"Arthur, how do you 'sort of' tell a woman you love her? Seems to me either you do or you don't."

"Ginny—"

Her eyes softened, and she reached over to pat his knee. "It's Annie, isn't it?"

"I know it's not right to hold on, Ginny. I know it, but I don't know what to do about it."

"Art, Annie's not coming back. Ever. I know you understand that," she said gently. "And I know Annie wanted you to go on with your life."

He swallowed hard. "I'm just . . . so afraid that no one will ever be able to compare to her. We had such a good thing, Ginny. Right up until the end—a *perfect* thing and—"

"No, it *wasn't* perfect, Art." Ginny wagged her head. "My memory sometimes tends to gloss over the bad times Grover and I had too. But that wouldn't be right. It wouldn't be honest. Oh, it was *mostly* good, just as it was for you and Annie. But don't forget the struggles, Art. Don't romanticize things. That's not fair—not to Annie, and certainly not to Madeleine."

Art thought about Ginny's words. Yes, he and Annie had sometimes fought. But they'd never let the sun go down on their anger. They'd never hurt each other beyond forgiveness. It was nothing he could take credit for. It was all Annie. Her spirit had been ever gentle and loving, even after she'd become so ill.

"What if . . . what if I marry someone else and it's not as good as it was with Annie? I've known what marriage can be. I can't risk ruining the memories I have with Annie."

Ginny leaned in and took both his hands in hers. Her frail, veined hands were dwarfed by his own, but there was surprising strength in her grasp.

"Arthur Tyler . . ." She gave his hands a little shake that made him look her in the eye. "I know you well enough to know that you, of all people, are not going to do anything to sully the institution of marriage. Unless you're putting your faith in yourself. But I know you better than that. You've always been one to trust God for your life. Why are you withholding this one thing now?"

"I–I guess I didn't realize I was."

"Well, you are."

He didn't reply. Didn't need to.

~

Art looped one end of his necktie over the other and tied the knot unconsciously. The man staring back at him from the mirror certainly didn't *look* riddled with guilt. He wished they could trade places.

It was wrong to feel this way. He knew that. Annie had been gone a long time. And Ginny was right: Annie had given her blessing for him to find love again. At the time, he'd resented it, still refusing to believe God would ever take his Annie from him. For a long time after she died, her blessing was meaningless, since he'd had no desire to even look at another woman.

But now there was a living, breathing woman who had stolen into his life under cover of acute misunderstanding, and he'd fallen in love almost without realizing it. Okay, maybe it was a stretch to call it love. He didn't really know Maddie. Yet he felt he did. The notes they'd shared had opened windows into each of their hearts. Reading her manuscript had opened a door. And now having met her, having discovered that they shared much more than he'd ever imagined, he could not deny she made his heart pump to a rhythm he'd long forgotten.

Wednesday he'd sat across the table from a beautiful woman, and for the first time since Annabeth McGee, he'd experienced that enthralling pull on his heartstrings. It had energized him like nothing had in a very long time.

Three days later, that tug on his heart had become a tug-of-war. And right now, guilt was pulling far more weight on the rope of his emotions. Luckily, Maddie didn't appear to be as smitten as he was. In truth, his heart had sunk when he read her rather cool note. She seemed determined to remain friends and nothing more. But perhaps that was a good thing.

Then there was the matter of their date. No, he mentally corrected himself. If she only wanted to be friends, he had to quit thinking of tonight as a date. Maddie was probably dressing for the evening this very minute. He wondered how she would look all dressed up.

Stop it, Tyler. She's a friend. That's all. An image of her smooth, pale hair and those tantalizing green eyes popped into his mind. He could almost hear the melody of her laughter. His thoughts were hardly appropriate toward a woman who was only a friend. But he couldn't help it.

He was going to drive himself insane thinking this way. With a sharp tug, he finished his tie, patted his pockets to be sure the symphony tickets were there, and headed out to the pickup.

Twelve

Maddie paced the living room, making occasional forays into the bathroom to check her lipstick, add one last spritz of hair spray, and adjust the collar of her white silk blouse.

It wasn't often she got to dress up, and it had been rather fun to go all out this evening. She just hoped she hadn't overdone it. She didn't want Art to get the wrong idea.

The front doorbell chimed. Maddie's breath caught in her throat. She slipped on a cashmere sweater, rubbed damp palms on her long velvet skirt, and went to answer the door.

Art stood on the porch, handsome in a dark suit with a tie the same shade of blue as his eyes. "Maddie. You . . . look lovely."

Maddie felt certain, looking into the deep pools of those eyes, that it wasn't the appreciation of a mere friend she saw there. "You clean up pretty nice too," she teased, determined to keep things light.

Art led the way down the front walk. November had come in on a crisp breeze, and she shivered and pulled her sweater tighter. Art went around to open the door for her. It was a bit of a climb to get into his pickup, but she managed to do so without looking like a total klutz. He carefully tucked the hem of her skirt out of harm's way before closing the door.

They were silent while Art navigated the tree-lined streets to the edge of town. He merged easily into the flow of traffic on the interstate and set the cruise control. "This symphony is probably going to seem pretty Podunk to you—compared to the concerts you hear in New York, I mean."

She waved off his warning. "It's been so long since I've been to a real concert, I doubt I'd know one from a kindergarten kazoo band."

He laughed. "That's good, because that may be exactly what this group sounds like to your ears."

"Art, I do love classical music, but I'm no critic."

"Well, we'll see after tonight." He flashed a droll grin.

For the rest of the drive into Wichita, they talked animatedly about music and movies and books they'd enjoyed. In the space of an hour, she successfully eliminated her earlier image of Art as a distinguished, elderly professor and replaced it with the witty, handsome, flesh-and-blood man seated behind the wheel of this Chevy 4x4—an exchange she made gladly.

Art asked about her writing career and gave a glowing critique of her work-in-progress. "I'm not finished yet," he said, "but what I've read so far is beautifully done. I will truly feel guilty if you pay me to proofread this, Maddie."

"Well, if you won't let me pay you, then you'd better quit

reading right now, because I'm already so indebted to you for the use of the inn, I'll never get out of hock."

"Hey," he said lightly, "can we come to some sort of understanding about this? We both feel we're cheating the other, so let's just call it even and not bring it up again."

She nodded. "I could go with that plan."

They ate at a new Italian place on the east side of town. Dinner brought more pleasant conversation. Again, Maddie had the sense she'd known this man forever.

Later, in spite of Art's caveat, Maddie thoroughly enjoyed the concert. The small symphony was quite accomplished, and several of Maddie's favorite concertos were on the program. She was sorry when it was over. On the way out the door, he purchased one of the group's CDs, and they listened to it on the drive home.

"You know," she said, as strains of Mendelssohn threaded around them, "when I saw this pickup truck, I was just sure we'd be listening to country music all the way."

Art smiled. "I like to keep people guessing."

Boy, did he have that *right.*

"Actually, I do listen to country," he said. "I like the stories those ballads tell. But there's something timeless about the classics."

"Did your wife . . . did Annie like classical music?" Maddie ventured, wanting to be sure he knew the topic wasn't off limits for her.

There was an overlong silence.

Maddie remembered Art's quick exit the last time the topic of Annabeth came up, and for a minute she was afraid she'd stepped on sacred ground.

"Yes, she did like music," Art said finally. "Annie played the piano beautifully and always had Mozart or Vivaldi going on the stereo." He rested one wrist on the steering wheel. "Do you play? Piano?"

She cringed and shook her head. "Only for my own enjoyment. I play by ear—by heart, my mom calls it."

"I'm sure you play beautifully."

"Oh, I would never inflict my pathetic attempts on an audience. But it's cheap therapy. I'm out of practice, though. My sister's piano is desperately out of tune, and I left my piano in storage in New York."

"Are you going back?" he asked abruptly. "To New York, I mean? Is Clayburn only temporary?"

She wondered how much rode on her answer. "I honestly don't know. My mom is only sixty-eight. She could live for many years. I want to be here for her."

"How is she doing?"

Maddie was moved by the genuine concern in his voice. "That's a hard question to answer. I don't think she's known me for quite a while now."

"That must be really difficult for you. I admire you . . . for wanting to be there for her."

She shook her head. "I'm not doing anything heroic. But I am glad it's worked out for me to be here. And I do like Clayburn. More than I thought I would." She didn't tell him that *he* was a lot of the reason why. "If it weren't for the house being so torn up, I couldn't complain."

"Oh, but if it weren't for the house being torn up, you wouldn't be sitting here beside me right now. I tend to think that was a gift."

His words confused her as much as his note had. This had to stop. She drew herself up in the seat. "Art, I—I'm too old to play games, so I want to get this out in the open."

"Okay . . ." His tone was understandably cautious.

She took a deep breath. "Your note the other day confused the life out of me."

He seemed surprised. "What do you mean?"

"In one breath you're asking me for a date, and in the next you're warning me you've put up this wall because of Annie. Then you change gears again and say I've already won you over—whatever that means." Against her will, her voice went up an octave. "And now you're saying our friendship is a gift. At least I think that's what you meant. The thing is, I don't have a clue where I stand with you. I don't know if you're determined we can never be more than friends or if you truly meant this night to be . . . a date." She felt a little foolish—and more than a little vulnerable after laying everything out so blatantly.

Art raked a hand through his hair, then put both hands back on the steering wheel and stared straight ahead for a long minute. She was afraid she'd ticked him off.

When he finally spoke, his voice was so quiet she could scarcely hear it over the truck's engine. "Maddie . . . I'm sorry."

He reached across the seat and took her hand in his. A tiny tremor went up her spine.

His Adam's apple bobbed in his throat. "If I've confused you, it's only because I'm confused myself. I—I do want to get to know you. No . . ." He turned to meet her gaze briefly before training his eyes back on the road. "As long as we're being totally honest here, the truth is, I feel as though I *do* know you. And I–I like what I see, Maddie. I like it a lot. I don't just mean what I see with my eyes, although that's altogether pleasant too."

For a moment, his eyes sought hers again, and he gave her hand a squeeze. Maddie felt the pleasure of his words warm her cheeks.

"What I really mean is . . . well—" His grin turned impish. "I had a bit of a crush on you when I thought you were eighty years old. But you were *safe* then. You weren't going to mess up the comfortable little world of grief I've lived in . . . gotten comfortable in, as dumb as that might sound." He waited, as though wanting a response.

But she didn't know what to say.

"I know this sounds totally unreasonable, Maddie, but now that I've met you, I feel like I'm almost . . . I don't know . . . in love with you–which would be wonderful if that feeling weren't eating me alive with guilt."

What? She stared at him. Now he was in *love* with her? The man was crazy—and driving her there on a fast train. She finally found her voice. "You feel guilty because of Annie?"

He nodded, but even in the darkness of the truck's cab, he couldn't hide the emotion that tinted his expression.

"Art . . ." She pulled her hand out of his warm grasp. "I've had my heart broken enough times that I don't go seeking out the experience. There's no way I can compete with . . . with a memory. And if you're looking for someone to ease your guilt, I'm sorry, but I don't think I'm your gal."

"I'm sorry," he said. "I want to be able to open my heart

again. I truly do. And I've never said that to any woman before. But . . . I can't seem to find the way."

She stared at her lap. "Thank you for being honest with me. I think."

"I'm trying, Maddie, that's all I can promise."

"I know . . . I know you are. But I don't know if my heart can take the chance that you'll fail."

They drove the rest of the way home in silence. When they got to her house, Art came around and opened her door. She rummaged frantically in her purse, looking for her keys, not wanting to create an awkward moment at the door.

She finally found them in a corner of her bag. She jangled them in front of her.

"Let me walk you to the door." Art smiled, and she felt her heart respond.

"It's okay. You don't have to."

"Maddie—" He scuffed the toe of his shoe in the gravel. "I don't want to sound like a broken record, but I'm sorry. I've ruined what has been a delightful evening till now."

"It's okay, Art. You can't help what you feel." She made her voice bright. "I enjoyed the concert very much. And thank you for dinner. It was delicious."

She turned and started up the walk. She was aware of his pickup idling in the drive until he saw she was safely in the house. She locked the front door behind her, flipped off the lights, and parted the curtain. She watched him back out of her driveway, and followed the taillights of his truck until they disappeared from sight. Letting the drapes fall, she put a hand over her heart in a futile effort to assuage the ache there.

Art had said he wanted to open his heart again.

Well, she'd done just that, and look where it had gotten her.

She crossed the room to Kate's old upright piano and ran her fingers idly over the dusty keys. Their sour, metallic clang pierced the stillness. A dissonant note hung in the air, and Maddie closed her eyes. She was playing at love the way she played the piano—by heart.

Thirteen

Back at the inn, Art got ready for bed, but sleep eluded him. Finally he crawled from beneath the covers and paced his apartment into the wee hours of the morning, thinking, praying, agonizing. The pain he'd seen in Maddie's eyes tonight broke his heart. He'd done that to her.

He wanted so desperately to put the past behind him, to offer Maddie his love with no reservations. But what kind of man would he be if he could let Annie go so easily?

On a whim, he went to the closet and pulled their wedding album from the top shelf. He sank to the floor at the foot of the bed and put the album in his lap. He'd nearly worn the pages out those first weeks after she died. But months had passed since he'd last looked at the photographs and mementos tucked inside. As he leafed through the pages, he remembered why. The vivid images made him remember every curve of her face, every nuance of her smile. In one shot, the camera had captured Annie's luminous expression as she walked down the aisle toward him. She'd been oblivious—they both had—to the horror that would ravage their lives a short decade later.

Art turned the last page and slowly eased the cover closed. As he put the album aside on the floor, another book caught his eye.

The hardcover copy of Maddie's novel, the one that had revealed her identity to him. *Hope's Song.* He slid it from the shelf again, flipped open the back cover, and stared at her image. Judging by the book's copyright date, the photograph must have been at least four or five years old. Maddie's hair was shorter and curlier. But her smile was the same . . . and the sparkle of her eyes.

He riffled the pages absently, deep in thought. Something caught his eye. Yellow highlighting and notes scribbled in Annie's handwriting. How often had he scolded her for dog-earing and marking in their books? It had been a source of frustration for him. But her friends loved to borrow her books. It was like getting a free study guide, they always said.

He thought about what Ginny had said that afternoon and remembered a heated argument he'd had with Annie over what he viewed as her careless disrespect of books. He'd called her irresponsible and wasteful. And brought her to tears.

Ginny was right. It hadn't all been a bed of roses. They'd had their ugly moments.

He flipped through the pages and read a few of Annie's cryptic marginal notes. "Echoes the theme of Pastor Rennick's sermon," one read. "Share with study group!" said another.

It was a gift to have this peek into Annie's heart. But his

own heart stuttered when he saw his name in the margin. "Read this section to Art."

Had she done so? Annie was always reading him snippets, but he didn't remember her ever reading from Maddie's books. Of course, he hadn't known Maddie then. He read the highlighted paragraphs and scratched his head. What had Annie intended him to glean from the words? Turning to the cover flap, he read the synopsis of the book, trying to put the passage she'd marked into context.

The novel was set during the Civil War. His gut twisted when he read that the heroine was dying of consumption. No wonder Annie identified with the storyline. He read the paragraphs again.

> *Maizie came in and flung open the window, muttering something about fresh air. A minute later, the servant sashayed out of the room with the wash basin sloshing, leaving the scent of lavender in its wake. Sarah watched from the bed, her thin fingers worrying the rough hem of the coverlet. Maizie had not so much as glanced her way. Sarah blanched. Had she become invisible in her confinement?*
>
> *Her gaze traveled to the window, and in an instant, she felt transported beyond the splintered sash. Her sick room faded to nothing, and she was somehow dancing among the willows that bent in the April breeze. She could almost feel the cool grasses between her bare toes, relish the warmth of the sun on her arms. For one moment, she remembered what it had been like to be healthy and whole. It was a gift. And even as her spirit danced, she thanked the Giver.*

Had Annie experienced something similar during her illness? Or was there some deeper meaning he wasn't quite getting? He would show the passage to Maddie. Maybe she would understand what Annie might have wanted him to learn from it.

Paging through the last half of the book, he came to a notation on the last page. It was printed in bold letters and underlined twice: "I LOVE this author!"

Stunned, he lifted his eyes to the ceiling—and beyond. *Amazing.* Annie had met Maddie through her words—had connected with her heart, her soul, her faith in God—and had come to love her. Perhaps *this* was the message he most needed to hear right now. The sign he'd been looking for.

He turned to the author's photograph again and brought it slowly to his lips. He was finally ready to let go. And he could hardly wait to tell Maddie.

Fourteen

The granite countertops were elegant, and Maddie's good china gleamed behind glass-fronted cabinets. She walked across the pristine tiled floor and stood in the doorway surveying the results of weeks of chaos and labor. It was finally finished. And it was beautiful.

Maddie sighed. Her days would finally belong to her again. No more letting in a crew of noisy workmen every morning or tripping over sawhorses at night. No more microwaved suppers. No more hauling her entire office back and forth each day. The house was livable, and she could set up her office and finish her book in peace.

So why did she feel so melancholy?

Stupid question. She knew why.

It had been almost a week since her disastrous date with Arthur Tyler. Except for the friendly, noncommittal notes on the dining room table, she had not seen him or spoken to him. And today would be her last day at the inn. She would sit at the smooth oak table and listen to the familiar, soothing creaks of the old house. She would write her chapters and coax Alex to warm her feet. She would jot down one last note of thanks to Arthur Tyler. And then she'd come home.

Home. The very word filled her with longing. As beautiful as it was, Kate's fancy house with its new kitchen and spacious rooms had never quite felt like home to her. Even the New York loft Maddie loved couldn't hold a candle to the one place that had worked its way into her heart. In the space of a few weeks, Annabeth's Inn had become home to Maddie.

It wasn't the bricks and boards or the cottonwoods and rosebushes—or even the lovable cat—that made it feel like home. It was Art. And knowing that, she wasn't sure she could ever really feel at home again anywhere else.

Sighing again, she went to gather her things. She loaded the car and backed out of the driveway. Today, the short drive to the inn felt like a walk to the gallows. She turned onto Hampton Road and a few minutes later turned the key in Art's front door. She walked through the hall to the dining room. As always, his note was waiting—a short one today. Had he remembered this was her last day?

She set up her computer and started coffee, putting off the moment when she would read Art's final note. When she finally picked it up, his salutation startled her.

Dearest Maddie,

Today is supposed to be your final day at the inn. I know you have a book to finish and I know your deadline is tight, but could I bring lunch at noon and steal a few minutes of your time? There's something I'd like to talk to you about. (If you can't spare the time, I understand. Just leave a message on my cell phone.)

Happy writing,
Art

She turned the note over, hoping to find a postscript that would offer a clue. But the page was blank. How did he expect her to concentrate, knowing he'd be walking through the door in a few hours?

She went into the bathroom off the main-floor bedroom and inspected her reflection. Why hadn't she bothered to fix her hair this morning instead of gathering it into a sloppy ponytail? And chosen something besides yoga pants and sweatshirt—although she did like the way the teal color brought out the green flecks in her eyes.

What difference did it make what she wore, how she looked? It didn't matter. None of it mattered.

She barely managed to write a thousand words before the clock struck twelve. Right on schedule, she heard the key in the door to the apartment below. She moistened her lips, quickly saved her file, and put her computer in sleep mode.

Footsteps sounded on the stairway, and Maddie went to meet him. Art balanced two round plastic containers in his hands and was attempting to secure two large paper cups with his chin while the cat wove a figure eight between his feet.

She hurried down the steps. "Here, let me take some of this. Alex, shoo! Mmm . . . smells good. What are we having?"

"Chicken noodle soup." Art grinned and winked at her. "I'm told it's good for what ails you."

Why did he always have to flirt with her? If he didn't have

room in his heart for another woman, why did he turn on the charm when he was with her?

She took the soup into the kitchen and transferred it to thick pottery bowls. Enticing aromas filled the room. "Is this from the deli?" she called out to the dining room, where she heard him scooting chairs around. The drinks bore the deli's label, but their takeout usually came in Styrofoam containers.

He came and stood in the doorway between the two rooms and watched while she fixed a tray with crackers and spoons. "The drinks are from the deli. Actually Ginny made the soup."

"Really?" That was interesting. Ginny'd been over the night before to borrow the newspaper. She hadn't mentioned anything about soup.

Maddie swept past Art, carrying the tray to the table. Art put folded napkins at each place and removed lids from their drinks. He came and held her chair for her.

"Thank you, sir."

He took the chair to her left and spread a napkin on his lap. "Shall we bless the food?"

Maddie nodded and bowed her head.

Art surprised her by reaching for her hand. His grasp was warm and firm—and unsettling.

"Father God, we thank You for this day and for this food. Please bless our time together, and especially bless the dear hands that prepared this food. In Jesus' name, amen."

He squeezed Maddie's hand before he let it go.

They ate in silence for a few minutes, then Art wiped his

mouth and pushed back from the table. "I want to talk to you about something."

She swallowed a mouthful of soup and put down her spoon. "So you said, in your note."

Art bent his head and rubbed circles in the smooth finish of the table with his fingertips. "I owe you an apology. You . . . well, you took me by surprise that day I first realized who you were. Before I'd had time to think about the consequences, I'd already asked you for a date. That wasn't fair to you."

Maddie's defenses went up. Here it came—the big breakup scene that was all too familiar. Never fear, though. She had her lines memorized.

Meanwhile, Art dutifully delivered his own lines. "The truth is, I was a very confused man. I wasn't looking for another relationship because . . . well, I guess I'd known true love, and I didn't believe I could ever find that with anyone else."

From the edge of her consciousness, Maddie became aware that Art was speaking in the past tense. She started to pay attention.

"For a while, grief crippled me," he said. "But I've been talking to some very wise counselors recently, and I do believe they've brought me to my senses."

"C—counselors?" She waited.

With one easy motion, he straddled his chair and moved it closer to hers. He enveloped her right hand in both of his. "Maddie, I don't want to rush you, but I don't want to let you get away, either. When you told me your house was finished and that you wouldn't be coming out here to write anymore, it . . ." He shook his head and swallowed hard. "It scared me. I know it sounds crazy because it's not like we were ever here together. But I liked coming home to find your notes. Highlight of my days, and I'll miss them like crazy. I liked walking up the stairs and catching the faintest whiff of your perfume. And that day I was home sick . . . Oh, Maddie, you can't imagine how wonderful it was to hear your laughter up here. I don't want to lose that."

Though her backside was firmly planted on the brocade pad of the chair, Maddie felt some part of her rise up and begin to soar.

Alex sauntered to the table, tail held high, and situated himself between them. The cat looked from Maddie to Art and back again, then pushed his weight hard against Maddie's leg, begging to be petted.

"Go away, Alex." Art gave the cat a gentle shove with the side of his foot. "Come on, buddy. You're cramping my style."

Alex plopped down on top of Maddie's feet. Art ignored him and scooted his chair another inch closer. "What I'm trying to say is, I know now it's very possible I may find love again. And I'm ready to embrace the possibility."

She sat, speechless. One hot tear escaped and rolled down her cheek.

Art let go of her hand. He reached up to thread his fingers through her hair and smudged the tear away with his thumb. "Oh, Maddie, I'm so sorry if I hurt you. Could we begin again?"

She nodded, her heart as full as her throat.

Art stroked her hair away from her temple and looked into her eyes. "I desperately want to kiss you right now. Would that be okay?"

In an instant, she was in his arms, and then he was kissing her forehead, her temples, his lips brushing away the tears of joy that streaked her cheeks. Finally, gently, he matched his lips to hers.

When he drew away, they were both breathless.

"Wow . . ." Maddie drew out the word.

"Yeah, wow," he echoed, kissing her again. He brushed a strand of hair from her face, then cupped her cheek in the palm of his hand. "I have so much I want to tell you. God has done some pretty incredible things in my life these past few days."

"Really?"

He nodded. "You may be the writer, but I have some stories of my own to tell."

She reached up and put her hand over his, savoring the warmth of his skin. "I can't wait to hear your stories, Arthur Tyler."

That familiar spark flared in his smoky eyes. "What if I told you that you were the heroine in some of them?"

She flashed him a grin. "I'd say turnabout is fair play."

Their mingled laughter rang through the house.

Fifteen

Art tamped the snow shovel on the driveway and stepped back to admire his work. The walk was clear, but the porch railings wore pristine shawls of snow that sparkled in the late January sun. Maddie had allowed him to shovel the walk only for the sake of the guests, who'd be arriving within the hour.

But she'd been adamant about leaving the snow on the railings intact. If he remembered correctly, *picturesque* was the word she'd used. And he had to admit, the inn did look nice after the skies had deposited eight inches of the white stuff on its roof and eaves.

With her manuscript barely turned in on time, he'd expected her to be frantic about the wedding plans and logistics of their friends and family who were coming in for the event, but if Art had learned anything about Madeleine Houser—soon to be Maddie Tyler—it was that she didn't let many things rattle her. "God has it all under control," she'd told him before they kissed goodnight on the inn's front porch last night.

The last night they'd spend apart. *Ever*, if he had anything to say about it. He could hardly make it seem real that today was his wedding day. He'd been afraid thoughts of Annie—and a twinge of guilt—might dampen his joy. But he was surprised to discover that although Annie, and the wedding day he'd shared with her, were very much on his mind, he was flooded with peace in the midst of it all. *Thank You, Lord.*

Maddie's sister, Kate, had come earlier in the week and quickly assumed the bossy big sister role. His instructions were to stay out of their way and do whatever Maddie told him in preparation for the wedding. When Art told Pastor Rennick that, the man had nodded knowingly. "Sounds like everything is under control then."

Now the inn was ready inside and out, and he went to get the car. His final duty before donning a tux and assuming his position in front of the fireplace, was to pick up Maddie's mom from the nursing home. He and Maddie had taken her out for a drive in the country a couple of weeks ago, and he'd practiced, with Maddie's help, transferring Mildred Houser from the wheelchair to the car, folding the chair and stowing it in the trunk, then doing it all in reverse.

Half an hour later, with Mrs. Houser seated at the back beside Ginny near the aisle Maddie would walk down, he ran down to his apartment to get dressed. He hadn't seen Alex since breakfast, but no doubt the cat was hiding out from the strangers who'd been coming and going all week getting things ready for the wedding.

Knotting the silver tie Maddie picked out for him, he heard Jed and Kate and the girls upstairs greeting guests. Chairs scraped on the floor overhead and a pleasant murmur of mingled voices floated down to him. He adjusted his cuff links and checked his watch. Almost time. His nerves ratcheted up a notch. He gave his tie a final tug, slipped into his jacket, and headed upstairs.

Six rows of rented chairs had been arranged facing the fireplace, and from the back of the room he observed the small gathering of friends and family unnoticed. He was surprised how many had come out on a Saturday. Three fellow professors and their wives visited in hushed voices on the back row, and a knot of friends from church held down the fort on the other side of the aisle.

Dave Sanders, who'd agreed to stand up with him, caught his eye and came to clap him on the shoulder and shake his hand. "Hey, buddy . . . You ready for this?"

"I'm ready."

Pastor Rennick went to the front and Dave joined him while Art went to get Maddie's mom.

In the corner of the dining room, a string quartet from the college tuned their instruments. The exquisite dissonance seemed a perfect metaphor for this new beginning. The room quieted in anticipation.

Art bent to kiss Ginny's cheek, and the lump that moved into his throat surprised him.

"Break a leg," she said, with a comical pump of her fist.

Chuckling and feeling instantly more at ease, Art patted Mildred Houser's hand and wheeled her to the spot reserved on the aisle at the front row. He kissed her cheek as he had

Ginny's and took his place at the front of the room beside Dave.

Kate came from a side door and joined them on the other side of the fireplace as the opening strains of Purcell's "Trumpet Tune" swelled and overflowed the inn.

Ginny rose from her chair and went to stand at the bottom of the stairs. That was the cue for all to rise and face the staircase. The banister was festooned with ivy and baby's breath, and candles glowed from hurricanes tied to each baluster post. The inn had never looked better.

Annie would have been delighted. Art somehow knew that . . . knew it as surely as his love for Maddie Houser grew with every moment he spent with her. He turned toward the staircase.

This was it. And he'd never been more ready in his life.

~

Maddie stood at the top of the stairway looking down, her heart—and nerves—aflutter. *Please don't let me fall.*

As soon as that prayer left her heart, another took wing behind it. A simple prayer she welcomed and hoped would never leave her repertoire. "Thank You, God," she whispered. "For . . . everything."

The string quartet's echoed strains of Purcell's lovely air wafted up the stairs, giving the moment a surreal quality. Maddie took a deep breath and gripped her elegant bouquet of white roses in one hand. She caught her reflection in the ornate mirror on the landing and for once she was pleased with what she saw there. She'd planned to wear a cream-colored suit she'd owned for years, but Kate had found this simple tea-length gown on clearance in a Cincinnati boutique and frantically texted photos to Maddie mere days before she'd flown in for the wedding.

The dress was perfect. Absolutely perfect.

The fitted strapless gown had a bodice of appliqué lace and a matching sheer shrug. The satin skirt had just the right amount of flounce and showed off her satin and lace slippers. Kate had helped her with her hair, pulling up the sides, but leaving the back down the way Art liked it. Her sister had tried to talk her into a frothy veil, but Maddie hated it the instant Kate popped it on her head. They'd settled instead on a fragile wreath of baby's breath tucked at her crown.

Maddie descended the first step. Seeing Ginny waiting for her there, her heart swelled. How dear this woman was to her. She blinked back tears and prayed she wouldn't ruin her mascara.

The slanted ceiling prevented her from seeing more than Art's feet until she was halfway down, but when his eyes came into view, all she saw there was love.

She reached the bottom step and took Ginny's arm, but she only had eyes for this man—this amazing man. She couldn't help the smile that came. Nothing had ever felt so right, so true.

When she reached her mother's wheelchair, she knelt beside it and whispered, "I love you, Mom." Maddie kissed her cheek and stood quickly before the tears came again. Taking Ginny's hand, she squeezed it and stepped up to the altar, Ginny still beside her.

Pastor Rennick greeted the audience and said pleasant

words that Maddie barely heard. But when he asked, "Who gives this woman to be married to this man?" Ginny lifted her chin and answered strong and clear, "Her mother and I."

The guests sighed in unison, obviously moved by the moment. Maddie hugged Ginny and waited for her to find her seat beside Mom. Then she turned to her groom.

Art took her hand in his, squeezing her fingers, stroking her palm with his smooth thumb in a silent language meant only for them.

"You look so beautiful," he mouthed when they'd turned their backs to their guests.

Pastor Rennick let them have a moment, and then he spoke the timeless vows. "Arthur Tyler, do you take this woman . . . ?" And, "Madeleine Houser, do you take this man . . . ?"

Yes. Oh, yes . . . I do.

She repeated the promises, committing to memory the planes of her beloved's face, the glint in his eyes. "I promise to love and cherish you, in sickness and in health, for richer or for poorer, and forsaking all others as long as we both shall live."

They exchanged rings and the pastor smiled as he addressed them before the congregation. "Therefore, by the power vested in me, I now pronounce you husband and wife. You may kiss your—"

Meow.

Muffled gasps rose from the audience and Dave Sanders's children laughed out loud. In unison, Art and Maddie looked down to see Alex winding figure eights between their legs, tail fluffed and held high.

Maddie stifled a giggle.

Art winked at her and reached to scoop up the cat with one arm. He placed Alex ceremoniously in the surprised pastor's arms. Then he turned and took Maddie into his arms and kissed her long and sweet.

The guests rose, clapping and cheering, and the string quartet burst into a joyous rendition of Mendelssohn's "Wedding March."

Art slid his hand down her arm and grasped her hand again, entwining her fingers with his. Together, they turned to face their loved ones for the first time as husband and wife.

Maddie practically floated down the aisle beside him.

A new year, a new life, a new beginning.

1. Do you think it is possible to fall in love with someone you've never met except through letters? What are some of the dangers of courting only through letters or e-mail? Some of the advantages?
2. Art and Maddie have very different backgrounds. He is a small-town boy, she is a city girl. He likes classic literature, she's a romance writer. What kind of problems might those differences create after Art and Maddie are married?
3. If you are married, do you and your spouse have more in common, or more differences? How do commonalities and differences each add something positive to a marriage?
4. Ginny actively played matchmaker to Art and Maddie. Do you know anyone who fancies themselves to be a matchmaker? What are the pitfalls of playing matchmaker? Have you ever known it to work successfully? To be a disaster? Share your stories.

5. God had to heal places in both Art's and Maddie's hearts before they could be ready to love one another. Have you experienced something similar in a relationship?
6. If you are married, how did God prepare you to have the capacity to love your spouse? Do you think God sometimes asks spouses, even if they are long-married, to undergo change for the other's sake?

I would like to express my deep appreciation to the following people for the roles they played in bringing to life the original version of this novella, first published as *Playing by Heart.*

Tammy Alexander and Jill Eileen Smith, who went over the manuscript with a fine-toothed comb and the eagle eyes of gifted writers and editors. Thank you for contributing incredible ideas and insight and for feeding and encouraging my writer's heart. I think you'll love this expanded version of Art and Maddie's story, and especially watching Maddie walk down the aisle!

Debbie Allen, Lorie Battershill, Terry Stucky, and Max and Winifred Teeter for reading the manuscript in its early stages and offering encouragement and advice.

Dan and Jeanne Billings, owners of the former Emma Creek Inn, Hesston, Kansas, for providing the lovely writing retreat that inspired this story more than a decade ago.

A special thanks to the inn's original Alex, who inspired Art and Maddie's feline friend.

And as always, thank you to my precious family for always being there for me. I love you with all my heart.

Deborah Raney

September 2013

About the Author

Photo by Ken Raney

Deborah Raney's first novel, *A Vow to Cherish*, inspired the World Wide Pictures film of the same title and launched her writing career after twenty happy years as a stay-at-home mom. Deb now has more than two dozen published novels. She and her husband, Ken, live in Kansas and have five children and four small grandchildren, who all live much too far away.

A February Bride

BETSY ST. AMANT

To my Groom, now and forever—Jesus Christ. Your romance and heart for me transcends any other love. I am yours forever.

Prologue

Allie Andrews couldn't breathe, and it had nothing to do with the yards of tulle wrapped around her waist. Or the fact that the air conditioner in the crowded small-town, southern church was on the fritz again, resulting in the sporadic waving of wedding programs in front of flushed faces she'd seen when she peeked through the sanctuary window ten minutes earlier. No, her lack of breath had everything to do with the ticking clock. The literal one on the wall *and* the figurative one thumping an unsteady rhythm in her heart.

Married.

A bead of sweat trickled between her shoulder blades, sure to dampen the silky ivory fabric that cascaded down her back like a white-chocolate waterfall gone wrong. So wrong.

Married.

She twisted the stem of her rose bouquet and paced the faded orange carpet inside the bride's room, her thoughts churning along with her breakfast. She slipped one heel out of her three-inch pump, anxiety tying her stomach into a knot that would make a Boy Scout proud.

Married.

It wouldn't take much to toe off one shoe, then the other. Dig her painstakingly pedicured feet into the carpet for traction, grab the hem of this cursed dress, and just . . . bolt.

Better now than later, right?

Marcus. She couldn't do that to Marcus.

But wasn't marrying him doing him worse?

She strode to the window overlooking the gravel parking lot and stared at the onslaught of cars baking in the late September sun. It was a good turnout. Looked as if half of Beaux Creek had shown up. There were probably loads of gifts on the covered table in the reception hall by now—a forever-sentimental collection of floral-patterned china she'd rarely use, gift cards to home repair stores, and likely more than one toaster and blender. All gifts she'd have to return if she let her toes touch the carpet.

But would dividing them up in a divorce property settlement however many years down the road be any easier?

She started to turn away, then squinted at her reflection, seeing skin at her shoulder where there should be lace. Oh no . . . yes. She twisted for a better view. A tiny tear, right on the seam of the sleeve. Her heart stammered.

Not a sign. Just a rip. It happens.

Right?

She pushed away from the window, wringing her bouquet. Now what? She wished Hannah, her maid of honor and only attendant, was still with her, but she had taken the flower girl for one last trip to the bathroom. Besides, Hannah, while her best friend, was also Marcus's sister. The loyalty line would be blurred if she knew Allie's doubts, and Allie couldn't do that to either of them. She had to figure this one out alone.

Married.

She swallowed hard and pressed one hand against her stomach. Just prewedding jitters, right? That's all it was, surely. She loved Marcus.

Maybe too much.

The organ reached a crescendo, the opening strains building in strength and cuing her grandmother and her mom down the aisle. Soon it would be time for Hannah, followed by the flower girl, Marcus's little cousin. The little curly-haired blonde would toss more red roses onto that awful carpet that they'd attempted to hide with a lacy runner, and then it'd be Allie's turn, for better or for worse.

She hated roses.

What was she doing here? The flowers. The carpet. The dress. It was all wrong. None of it went together. It wasn't . . . her. No, it was her mom. Her grandmother. Her aunt.

Not exactly the role models on which to base a marriage. That poison was in her blood, and she couldn't escape it. Just as she hadn't been able to avoid this dress all the women in her family had worn in generations past, or been able to choose her own wedding venue or floral arrangements or even the topper on the cake, which, ironically, featured a groom dashing away from a wide-eyed bride clutching the back of his tuxedo collar.

Marcus didn't have a chance.

And it was all her fault.

The music faded into a key change and then struck up a slightly off-tune version of the wedding march. The unmistakable squeaking of bodies rising from time-warped pews filtered through the space leading from the bride's room to the main entrance of the country chapel, sounding suspiciously like the creaking of gallows.

And her poor groom didn't have a clue of the noose dangling above him in the form of a white-gold wedding band.

Allie toed off her shoes, hitched up her skirt, and dug her toes into the carpet.

One

If wedding dresses could talk, Allie Andrews was fairly certain hers would have a sailor's mouth.

Four months later—to the day, actually, after she'd shucked out of her wedding dress in the backseat of the meant-to-be honeymoon car and gunned it down the highway with nothing but a bottled Yoo-hoo and her favorite faded jeans for company—the dress hung on the inside of her closet door, the once small tear in the seam now gaping and taunting her. Every time she opened the closet, that rip reminded her how she'd severed one of the few relationships in her life actually worth keeping.

Which was precisely why she had to give it away in the first place.

Allie grabbed her favorite purple sweater, the one she often wore to work at her antiques store since the air conditioner in the quirky old building refused to shut off year round, and tugged it over her head. She could use all the cozy comfort she could get today at lunch with Hannah. She'd put it off long enough. After ditching her best friend's brother at the altar, she'd fully expected Hannah to hold a grudge. Hannah's unconditional love expressed through multiple phone calls and text messages had been almost worse than the cold shoulder—harder to face than a much deserved grudge—which was probably why she'd been avoiding this meeting.

Besides, Hannah looked so much like her brother.

Allie's arm brushed against the dress as she adjusted her sweater, and the frothy number swayed on its padded hanger. The swish of the fabric only seemed to whisper more condemnation.

With a groan, she shut the closet door harder than necessary. She should just get rid of the thing, but it wouldn't be worth the wrath of her mother, grandmother, and aunt. Yet even though they all threatened her within an inch of her life if she sold the dress or threw it away, not one of them would store it at her own house. *"It belongs to you now, and will until you wear it. Then you pass it down to your daughter."*

Right. A daughter? Not at this rate.

And zero hope of getting over what she did to Marcus. Even if it was for his own good.

A knock sounded on her apartment door, and Allie dashed to get it, checking her watch. She needed to leave in less than ten minutes if she didn't want to be late, and with a long-time friendship already riding on this lunch, she really shouldn't push it by appearing like she didn't care. She pulled the door open.

Hannah, looking at once like her best friend and a total stranger in a pink cashmere sweater and skinny jeans tucked into boots. She looked great—like she hadn't lost her best friend or spent the past several months comforting a broken-hearted brother at all.

Maybe Allie hadn't mattered all that much to begin with.

"I was just heading out to meet you." Allie cautiously opened the door wider to allow her friend inside, bracing herself for . . . something. And not just the chill of the January air that rushed to meet her despite the heated hallway. "Did I mess up the time?"

She took a step backward, and the heel of her boot caught on the striped rug under her feet. Maybe Hannah had changed her mind and decided to tell her off privately instead. Maybe she'd realized a polite lunch in public was way more considerate than Allie deserved.

"I couldn't wait another minute to tell you." Hannah shoved her left ring finger in Allie's face and let out an excited squeal. "I'm engaged!" She jumped up and down, her curly dark hair bouncing against her shoulders.

Engaged.

The word twisted in Allie's throat and refused to rise to her lips. "That's . . . that's . . ."

What was it? Surprising? Not really. Hannah and Zach had been dating for about six months, but she supposed not everyone had to be together for several years before tying the knot. A long courtship hadn't exactly worked out for her and Marcus . . .

"I know, right?" Hannah pushed past Allie and sank down onto the arm of the overstuffed turquoise chair, exactly as she'd done a million times over the years. As if it were that easy to pick up. Like the past few months hadn't changed everything.

Maybe they hadn't.

Hannah held up her hand again, this time keeping it steady enough for Allie to focus on the significant princess-cut carat adorning her finger. "Zach is perfect. Well, no, he's not. He's pretty much a slob, and we don't like any of the same movies." She snorted a laugh. "But we're perfect together."

Allie slowly sank to the edge of the couch near Hannah. "Right. I understand." Sort of. She'd never felt like anything between Marcus and herself had been perfect. He was perfect, to be sure. As much as any six-foot, dark-haired, chocolate-eyed, car-loving athletic guy could be. The problem had been Allie. She'd been the one to fall short, thanks to her family—and the curse that ran though her blood.

Once upon a time, when gazing into Marcus's eyes and feeling the heady weight of that diamond on her finger, she'd thought she could break the family scourge. Break the effect of the words her mom had whispered when Stepdad #2 had roared off on his Harley, and when Stepdad #4 had slammed the door on his way to the bus stop, and when unofficial Stepdad #5 had plucked his clothes from the front yard and shoved them into a trash bag before calling a taxi.

"Remember, Allie, this is what Andrews women do. We break hearts before we get ours broken."

She could still remember the firm set of her mother's lips, the expressionless twist of her eyebrows, the wall of steel in her eyes. It was the same look Grandma had when anyone mentioned her first or second husband, and the same look Aunt Shelly got when she announced she was meeting another man from her online dating profile.

If a leopard couldn't change its spots and a zebra couldn't change its stripes, who was Allie to change her blood?

Since Marcus was way too gentlemanly to break a promise or dodge a bullet, she'd been the one forced to remove him from the line of sight.

A point no one seemed to understand.

Hannah grinned. "Of course you get it. I knew you would, since you've been engaged . . ." Her voice trailed off, and she averted her gaze to the carpet. "I didn't mean to bring that up. Honest."

Her eyes radiated sincere regret, and Allie relaxed slightly. No firing squads. Just good ol' Hannah. "I was thinking George."

Hannah gave her a sharp glance, her brown eyes, as vivid as Marcus's, sparkling suspiciously beneath her furrowed brow. "What are you talking about?"

"Maybe Bob."

"I don't get it." Her voice hitched. "Are these guys you've dated since—"

"Calm down." Allie winked. "I'm just trying to name that elephant in the corner. He's been sitting there since you walked in, so I thought we ought to give him a collar and a home."

Hannah stared at her a minute longer before her lips quivered into a hesitant smile, then morphed into a full-out grin. "Funny. You had me there." She straightened her shoulders and arranged her features into a deadpan mask. "Clearly, though, he's a Steve."

"Steve it is."

That hadn't been so hard. Maybe her years of friendship

with Hannah demanded loyalty in spite of the sibling relationship.

Not that she would ever ask Hannah to choose—in fact, that was why she had refused all contact with her friend all these months. She didn't want to put her in an even more awkward position. And Marcus had enough to deal with without her creating family drama for him.

But the fact that Hannah was right here in her living room meant maybe they could find their way around this. After all, it wasn't like she'd have to see Marcus if she and Hannah remained friends. Maybe he wouldn't even have to know.

"Anyway, Steve wasn't why I came. You've made it clear you don't want to talk about that, and I'll respect your wishes." Hannah rose from the chair and began to pace the small living area, pausing every few feet to nervously rearrange a knickknack on the mantel or straighten the royal purple pillows on the couch Allie had recently recovered. "I came to ask a favor."

"Anything." The word leapt from Allie's grateful lips before she could self-edit. She really would do anything to get her relationship with Hannah back, to grasp something good and familiar during this dismal season in her life. Maybe she'd brought it on herself, but that didn't make everything any easier to cope with.

Because one fact remained—if she'd run down the aisle instead of to her car that day, she'd have been married for four months right now. She and Marcus would probably be getting ready to go to a celebration dinner, where he'd have sneaked a card under her dinner plate or arranged for the chef to make a heart with cherry tomatoes in her salad. That was Marcus. Considerate. Romantic. Always thinking.

No question, she had done him a favor. They might have made it a few months, but they wouldn't have made it a few years. No one in her family had ever made it past three—and good grief, they'd all given it multiple tries.

"I'm glad you said that." Hannah's voice, and the squeak of a glass vase against the coffee table as her friend absently redesigned the floral arrangement, jerked Allie away from her thoughts. She wondered if Hannah realized that the vase had taken the place of the giant framed engagement photo of her and Marcus snuggled under an oak tree. "Because my favor is sort of big."

Couldn't be as big as Steve.

"You know how I've always wanted a Valentine's Day wedding."

Hannah's eyes gleamed, and Allie could almost see cartoonish, pulsing pink hearts shooting out of her gaze.

"Well, that means we only have about six weeks. Actually, more like five."

"Five weeks. Wow, you're right. That *is* soon." Allie knew better than to assume there was a secret reason, though others surely would speculate. Marcus would hate those rumors about his sister. He'd always been so protective of the women in his life.

"Really soon. So there's no time to lose." Hannah took a deep breath and twisted her ring on her finger.

"Whatever it is, I'm in." *I owe you.* The words faded from her tongue but still burned an aftertaste. She did owe her friend. Whatever Hannah needed, it was Allie's turn to support *her*. After all, Hannah had reluctantly honored Allie's desperate request to give her time and space after the wedding-that-wasn't, time and space from all things Marcus-related. Hannah had met her several hours after Allie sped away from the church that day to pick up Marcus's car, and their brief conversation had been tear-filled and beyond awkward. But Allie needed the chance to process her decision, and in allowing her that time, Hannah had given her a gift that beat all the premium toasters and coffeemakers in the world. Allie'd had to return those to the store, so it was the least she could do to return this favor for Hannah and keep their friendship alive.

Besides, what could be so bad? If Hannah's obvious willingness to bury the hatchet was anything to go by, this opportunity—whatever it may be—could be the catalyst to proving her ability to remain loyal to at least one member of the Hall family. And having Hannah around again would ease that unbearable loneliness that had taken over these past few months. There was no reason they couldn't rekindle their friendship apart from her brother. No reason for her to have to be around him at all, really.

"I want you to be my maid of honor."

Except maybe that reason.

Marcus Hall wiped his grease-stained hands on an even dirtier shop rag, then tossed it onto the bench inside his garage before bending back over the car's fender. Rebuilding the engine in this '67 Corvette Stingray had proved to be a little more complicated than he'd anticipated—and he still had to check the clearance on the headers—but ever since his sister broke the news of her particular choice in bridesmaids, he'd appreciated the distraction.

She'd had to pick Allie? *His* Allie? The only woman who'd ever made sense to him. The only woman who could make an obsession with anything in the shade of turquoise seem cute. The only woman who had ever possessed the power to steer his heart straight over a cliff—and probably still did.

Guess he'd be finding out.

When Hannah broke the news yesterday, he threw his wrench against the wall and nearly broke it. The resounding *clang* had been all but drowned out by the warning alarms wailing in his head. Wasn't the fact that Valentine's Day was right around the corner bad enough? The day he'd planned to take Allie back to the scene of their first date, a day he thought he'd be spending as a happily married man. Now he'd be spending what should have been a special holiday at his little sister's wedding.

Standing across from his should-be wife as maid of honor.

He groaned. It was like a reality show setup gone bad. He'd always hated those things. Now he could practically star in one.

One thing was certain—Allie Andrews meant personal system malfunction. It'd been a solid four months since she'd pealed out of the church parking lot, and he still couldn't take a full breath when he heard her name. He should be livid over what she'd done, leaving him at the altar with no explanation—or at least, so everyone told him. Maybe anger would be easier to deal with than the ever-present pain, but the emotion just wouldn't stick. Rolled right off like Rain-X on a windshield.

The familiar click of heels on concrete alerted him to the fact he was no longer alone. Hannah. He folded his arms over his chest and leaned against the wall, tipping his chin to acknowledge her presence. Two visits in two days. Never a good sign.

"You busy?" She offered a timid smile, and he dropped his crossed arms, trying to make his own smile appear more genuine than it felt. This was his little sister's big moment in life. He wouldn't ruin it because of his own problems.

Even if Allie was a *big* problem.

"Just fighting this Chevy." To prove it, he picked up a ratchet he didn't need and pretended to resume his work. There would probably be a whole lot more "fighting" if Allie showed up to every prewedding shindig and unnecessary couples showers people held for engaged people.

Definitely a whole lot more pretending.

Funny how he hadn't minded all that frou-frou stuff when it'd been his and Allie's celebration.

"I just drove over to make sure you weren't mad at me." Hannah shuffled inside, twisting her new diamond ring around her finger. She had the same look on her face that she'd had as a kid when he busted her for playing with his model cars.

He straightened, mentally noting a need to check the timing on the engine. "Not mad." Not really. More like confused. Why resurrect her friendship with Allie now?

Some things just needed to stay dead.

Too bad his heart couldn't remember that fact.

Hannah shoved her dark hair behind her ears, the overhead garage light catching the shine in her giant diamond. He wondered briefly—and not for the first time—what Allie had done with hers. And what had happened to all those gifts that had been piled up in the church?

And why he'd never taken his and Allie's wedding bands back to the jeweler's instead of shoving them in his top dresser drawer.

"So did you hear any more about Texas?"

So obvious, his sister's change of subject. But he wasn't going to argue. Marcus shrugged. "It's pretty much up to me right now, if I want to go there as regional manager for the new store or just keep my franchise going here in Louisiana. Not sure I have the time right now." Well, he did, though business had clearly picked up. He just wasn't sure he wanted to leave. Moving over the border, even temporarily, seemed like some kind of significant Next Step. In the aftermath of losing Allie, it had seemed genius, a decent goal to work toward. Now that it was within reach, it just made him feel like he was slogging boots through mud. Sticky. Heavy.

He hated that decisions were so hard these days.

"You know, you sure are here a lot now. You used to do more of your work from home." Hannah glanced around the packed garage, full of his company's half-finished motors, three parked cars—one of which remained on a lift—and a grimy workbench covered in tools that his employees had apparently not put away.

Marcus's heart constricted, desperate to prevent his sister from saying the words he knew were coming next.

"Don't you think it's time to go back into your home gar—"

He intentionally nudged the factory headers across the floor with his boot, the squeal of metal against concrete worse than fingernails on a chalkboard.

Hannah either got the hint or lost interest. "Look, I know it's going to be weird for you. And Allie." She hesitated. "I just miss her, and well, it's my wedding and I can't imagine her not being there." She sighed. "Maybe that's selfish."

"It's not selfish." He gritted his teeth, looking back down at the engine to hide his expression. He was the one being selfish—this was his sister's wedding. She had to be more important than his leftover drama. "It's fine." Or it would be, at least, soon as it was all over.

He tried to redirect his attention. More Stingray, less Allie. Let's see, next he'd tighten down the bolts on the new intake manifold and then check the timing—

"I'm glad you're okay with it." Hannah's voice pitched, the stifled sound breaking the stillness of the garage. "I just can't help but hope—"

He brought his hand down on the radiator shroud with a solid thud, dropping the wrench he'd used on the bolts. "No, Hannah. Don't hope." There was no hope. Not with Allie. Not with him. That hope had driven away with her in the passenger seat of their getaway car—*his* car—when she'd sped from the church.

And not even tapped the brakes.

He felt a little bad as Hannah quietly slipped outside, their conversation clearly over—but not bad enough to go after her. Not right now. He turned back to the car, relieved to see that the timing was correct. Finally, something was falling into place. The owner would be thrilled at the improvement.

But he couldn't help but wonder if sometimes, new would be better than restored.

The catchphrase "Always a bridesmaid, never a bride" might not be technically true, but it sure felt like it at the moment. Allie flipped another page in the bridal invitation catalog.

Across the table, Hannah and her mom perused another thick gray booklet. Julie Hall had smiled at Allie when she'd met them there, as if it were perfectly normal for her son's ex-fiancée to be crashing their mother-daughter time of wedding planning. But Hannah had demanded that Allie be involved in all the details, and there was no time to waste.

So two days after Hannah had shown up on her front door with the big news, here they were, poring over samples of invitations. Allie had had a hard enough time picking out her own invites last year, yet Hannah asked her opinion like she was some sort of expert.

At least Hannah had a mother whose company she enjoyed. Picking out all of this stuff with Allie's mom, aunt, and grandmother had been torture. At one point Allie had picked up the display book from the table and gone clear across the room while the three of them argued without her. It was fifteen minutes before they'd noticed she was gone.

"What about these?" Hannah slid another stock-paper card from the pocket of the book and passed it across the table.

Allie tilted her head. Two linked hearts with flying doves. Exactly the kind of frilly stuff Marcus hated. She shook off the memory. His opinion didn't count this time. "It suits you. Does it fit Zach?"

Hannah opened her mouth, then shut it. "Well. No." She turned the page.

"What about this one?" Julie—no, Mrs. Hall, now—turned the book so she and Hannah could both see the simple elegance of the invitation. The corners of the trim thickened into squares, while the sides—any color you chose—cascaded like liquid ribbons to the bottom of the card.

A card almost exactly like Allie and Marcus's. Except their trim had been turquoise, while the example was red. Perfect for a Valentine's wedding. Had Mrs. Hall shown her that particular design on purpose? Or had she truly forgotten what they'd selected last year?

Her face, so gracefully aged, with precision-arched brows and warm-toned makeup, gave no sign of foul play. This was the same woman who had been so excited to discover Marcus was proposing that she planned a celebration party with *Welcome to the Family* written in chocolate icing on a cake and cried happy tears when presenting it. The same woman who'd shared her secret family recipes with Allie after their third date, and bought her a Bible with her new last name imprinted on the cover as a wedding gift. The same woman who accompanied Allie to the bridal boutique to play referee between Allie's aunt, mom, and grandmother, and bought her coffee afterward as a congratulations for surviving the day.

The woman radiated family, love, and faith. It wasn't in Julie Hall to be vengeful.

Then again, if Allie had ever given someone a reason to seek revenge, it'd be this woman, whose beloved youngest son Allie had left at the altar.

"It's . . . nice." She swallowed and looked back at her book, holding her breath for Hannah's opinion. If she loved it, Marcus would see it and remember. He might not have been all that active in choosing flowers or china patterns, but he'd remember the argument she'd had with her mother over the invitations as they'd flipped through those very books. The same argument that had led to a full-out fight, that had led to tears, which eventually led to Marcus blissfully comforting her in her driveway for twenty minutes.

Oh, he'd remember.

Allie peeked from under her lashes at Hannah as her friend studied the invitation. She wrinkled her pert nose and shook her head. "No offense, Mom, but definitely not. Too plain."

She breathed a sigh of relief. No offense taken.

Not a single bit.

The bell on the door handle of Allie's Antiques hadn't jingled in over an hour. Which wasn't exactly great for business, but was even worse for her sanity. Spending time with Hannah the other day had been like turning a key in the lock securing Allie's closetful of Marcus-memories. And they'd been pouring out ever since, paying no heed to the damage to her heart left in their wake.

She stared blankly at the tired chest of drawers across from where she perched on a stool behind the front counter, the distressed wooden surface serving as a movie screen for the past. One after the other, memories flashed before her:

The first time she'd seen Marcus, three years her senior, during a visit to Hannah's house. She'd been a sophomore in high school, he a freshman in college. He'd seemed so out of her league. It was all she could do to contain her hormonal immature blush after he'd snagged an apple out of the fridge, tossed it in the air before polishing it on his sleeve, and shot her a wink that took her about six weeks to recover from.

Then there was the first time Marcus had finally seemed to notice her. He'd come home from college, using his business degree to dive into a chain of auto shops across southern Louisiana, and opened a franchise that found immediate success. The mercury had risen into triple digits, taking her temper with it. Twenty-one years old and more than a little impatient, she'd driven up in her protesting old car, ready to junk the entire thing, when Marcus slid from underneath a Camaro he was rebuilding. Without hesitation he'd wiped his hands on a rag, popped the hood of her clunker, and spent the next hour pointing out the value in things she couldn't see.

Allie fell in love, both with her best friend's brother and his unique eye for restoration and worth, which had led to her finally settling on a career choice and opening an antiques shop that barely paid the bills but let her heart soar.

They became inseparable, marriage a foregone conclusion. She refurnished furniture on the side to make ends meet and knew once she married Marcus she wouldn't have to worry about bills. Not only was his shop successful, but he rebuilt engines as a well-paying hobby, usually for wealthy car enthusiasts willing, based on Marcus's stellar reputation, to drive for hours and drop their babies off in the middle of nowhere, aka Beaux Creek, Louisiana.

Now she had to worry about bills. But that was the least of her concerns—until the rent was due, anyway. No, the top of her list had nothing to do with her budget or monthly sales, and everything to do with how in the world she'd survive the evening—Hannah and Zach's engagement party at the Beaux Creek Boardwalk.

Bankruptcy might be preferable to seeing Marcus up close and personal for the first time since she'd jilted him.

The bell on the door chimed as Mrs. Hawkins, a faithful customer, walked in with a smile. Allie always enjoyed their visits, and today the distraction was especially needed.

"You didn't bring me anything today?" Allie faked indifference as the elderly woman laughed and held out her empty hands. Mrs. Hawkins loved to frequent estate sales and was notorious for bringing in junk pieces that were a challenge for Allie to restore.

"No treasures today." She shot Allie a feisty wink as she adjusted her purse strap. "But you never know when one might turn up."

The older woman went to peruse the back of the store, and Allie refused to let the memories hold her captive again. She turned her attention to the dresser she'd been staring at and whispered truth to herself instead. "Not a movie screen. Just a chest of drawers." She kept her voice down, though the elderly Mrs. Hawkins was accustomed to all of Allie's quirks. "Not scarred. Distressed."

She squinted. Well, maybe both. There was a fine line between "intentionally distressed" and plain old "beat up."

Maybe the dresser just needed a boost. Everything could be redeemed, right? Something to hide its flaws. Highlight its potential.

Just a little something.

Something like . . .

She smiled. Turquoise paint.

It was like waking up from a bad dream and finding yourself in a nightmare.

Heart in her throat, dreading and anticipating the inevitable all at once, Allie scanned the crowded dock for any sign of Marcus.

Why?

So she could talk to him?

Or so she could make certain to keep one hors d'oeuvres–toting waiter between them at all times?

She hadn't decided yet, but if they were going to be thrown into each other's presence during the never-ending course of prewedding—not to mention *actual* wedding—events, they needed to somehow face it, deal with it, and move forward. For Hannah's sake, of course.

Allie smoothed the front of her tan sweaterdress, glad she'd decided to wear tights with her chocolate-brown boots since the party was clearly an inside/outside event and the night air beyond chilly. The reception room of the Beaux Creek Boardwalk boasted a picturesque window overlooking the body of water that passed for a lake, except in the heat of summer, when it really did dry up to something more along the lines of a creek.

In January, however, the water served as a beautiful backdrop alongside the tiny twinkling lights tacked around the trunks of the nearby cypress and pines. Glowing tiki torches provided celebratory lighting around the patio tables, while the strains of a country ballad, courtesy of the hired DJ, drifted from inside the reception room, where two couples were already braving the makeshift dance floor.

But nothing could compete with the sight of Marcus standing by the outside soda bar. Dressed in tailored beige pants and an untucked navy-blue button-down, sleeves rolled to his forearms, collar opened at the neck, he was the very expression of attractive. Having an in-demand seamstress for a mother had always worked in his favor—he cleaned up well, regardless of how casual or formal the event.

Tonight was the perfect balance of both.

He braced one elbow on the tall wooden counter as he

sipped from a fizzing cup and scanned the room in typical Marcus-surveillance style.

Even from a distance she could see the evidence of at least two days sans razor coloring his jaw, a sure sign he was working on a new car that probably had him robbed of anything more than the bare minimum of sleep. His dark hair, normally cropped close for less maintenance, curled slightly long over his ears and collar in waves. New look? Or just too busy to take care of it?

It looked good, regardless.

He looked good, regardless.

And in about five seconds he'd see her.

Allie's stomach tightened, then roiled like a traitor. Her palms grew sweaty as her mouth dried. Yep. His gaze would sweep from left to right here any minute now, and she'd be right in the middle of his line of vision. In about three . . .

Now or never . . .

Two.

Fight or flight . . .

One.

Sink or swim . . .

Their gazes locked, and there was nowhere to hide.

Not that she felt particularly interested in getting away. No. Wait. What was she thinking? She opened her mouth, then closed it, then wished she'd worn a different dress. Any other dress, one that showed off the twelve pounds she'd recently shed, or one that showcased her eyes a little more or one that—

Oh no, he was coming toward her.

She fought the urge to wipe her palms on her dress and

schooled her features into a casual expression as she zipped her necklace charm around its chain. Not that there was anything remotely casual about seeing your ex face-to-face for the first time in four months. At a wedding party—a *family* wedding party—they should have been attending together, rather than staring awkwardly at each other from six feet away like they'd never met. Like they'd never slow-danced under a starlight sky, never shared their deepest secrets, never kissed like the other held their very last breath of oxygen.

Nope. Not awkward at all.

She steeled herself for his first words. A stiff and formal hello? A brief nod as he passed by without speaking? Or worse, an obligatory "You look good"?

And more importantly, *did* she?

She drew a deep breath and braced her heart as he opened his mouth.

"So I hear there's an elephant lurking around lately."

Didn't see that one coming. She raised her eyebrows, unable to commit to a full-sentence response.

He shoved his hands into his pants pockets and shrugged, a borderline shy move reminiscent of his early college days when she knew him only as her best friend's brother. Yet despite the hint of shyness, confidence filled his demeanor, sort of like his muscles filled the space under his dress shirt.

But that line of thinking wasn't productive.

"Hannah says his name is Steve."

Ah. *That* elephant. Allie licked her dry lips. "Right. Steve." Aka *you*. "Yeah, he's been around." They *were* going to have to talk about it, weren't they? Her face heated. What could she say? *Sorry for running out on you four months ago? Sorry for embarrassing you in front of everyone in the entire town?*

Sorry for spilling Yoo-hoo on the floor mats when I stole your car?

"Can I bring you a soda?"

Always the gentleman, even when he had every right to throw said soda in her face. She almost wished he would. Then she could get mad in return, and her heart would be safe.

And more importantly, so would his.

Her gut clenched, and she found herself nodding, going through the motions, because really, what choice was there? The only reason she was here right now, facing Marcus's potential wrath, was for Hannah. All for Hannah. Her heart could hang in there a little bit longer. If it hadn't completely shattered by now.

"Sure, that'd be nice. Thanks."

He started toward the bar, then stopped and turned. "Diet?"

Something flickered in his eyes, and she wondered if he was remembering all the times he'd tried to convince her to give up her one vice—diet soft drinks—and failed miserably. Or the times she tried to convince him to convert to scrambled eggs instead of preferring over-easy. Or the times he teased her for painting everything within reach of a paintbrush turquoise. All were laughable attempts—because they were all the things that made the other person who they were, part of those unique differences between two people who loved to debate and eventually be completely satisfied with exactly the way the other was.

She forced a smile she didn't feel. "Diet is great."

Some things never changed.

And maybe some things never should.

~

Marcus felt a little like a stalker as he watched Allie from his position half hidden behind the DJ table. The long-haired guy was busy packing up his equipment, but so far, the podium-style speakers still on their mounts allowed him a moment to watch as she unzipped her boots and flexed her toes against the hardwood floor. Her feet had to be killing her if the heels on those boots were any indication.

The party was long over, and around them the reception hall's cleanup crew were stacking chairs and rolling tables away to be stored. However, Allie's aching feet had to be nothing compared to the torture it'd been just being around her this evening. Watching that slightly crooked smile of hers that always made him want to smile back. Watching her pretend like she wasn't watching him as he'd spun his young cousin around the dance floor and let her stand on his shoes. Watching her nibble the top off a cupcake over the course of about twenty minutes.

From her spot at the table, Allie reached up and pushed her fingers against her temples, a sure sign she had a headache. Because of him? His stomach knotted with regret and a twisted kind of hope.

No, not hope. Hadn't he railed against that very thing with his sister the other day?

Allie wasn't stressed over him—she'd been the one to leave, after all. If her headache did have anything to do with him, it was probably because she was counting the minutes until she could escape the awkwardness of his presence. They'd attempted small talk over their sodas earlier in the evening, before his family dragged him away for brother-of-the-bride duties—small talk that was more like epic failure.

Probably a good thing they'd been interrupted, though. With the way he'd felt looking into her eyes again at that close distance, he'd have made a fool of himself for sure. Like by blurting out how her gaze still had the power to burn a near tangible hole in his heart, or how he still knew all of her idiosyncrasies and preferences, far beyond that of Diet Coke. They were permanently seared in his brain.

Sort of like turquoise paint that wouldn't wash off.

"Can you give me a hand?" The DJ motioned to the speaker mount, and Marcus snapped out of his miserable reverie.

"Sure thing, man." He helped the guy dismantle the speaker to pack on his rolling cart, then turned for one more glimpse of Allie.

Gone.

He really didn't know why his heart sank like that. Disappearing was sort of her specialty.

Still, he'd hoped she'd have bothered to tell him good-bye before she left the boardwalk. If they didn't pretend that everything wasn't awkward, then it would never stop being awkward. Fake it until you meant it, or something like that.

Games had never worked between him and Allie, though, which oddly enough had been one reason he'd been so certain they would make it to their golden anniversary one day. They never did the hard-to-get thing or the "push you away so you'll come close" thing. They always told the truth, even if it stung a bit.

Yet he still didn't know the real reason why she had run away.

He shot one more glance at her empty chair, then jerked at a tap on his shoulder. "You hiding out over here?"

Allie.

He turned slowly, ignoring the "busted" smirk the DJ shot his direction as he edged away, rolling cables around his arm.

"Just helping with the takedown." He casually shoved his hands into his pockets, hoping the joy he felt didn't show on his face.

Allie hitched her purse strap higher on her shoulder and held up her car keys. "Your truck is blocking me in."

It was almost midnight, yet Allie had the feeling there would be no glass slipper tonight.

Marcus had quickly moved his truck, which his dad had apparently pulled around to load up the party decorations, not realizing he had blocked Allie's car by a telephone pole. But her royal carriage had already gone back into pumpkin mode, complete with a flat tire. She stared at her listless vehicle.

She hated being a damsel in distress. But that tire wasn't going to fix itself, and while she knew how to do it, she'd never changed one alone in the cold and in the dark. Her mother had always made sure she'd known how to change tires and check the oil in her vehicles. But unless she wanted to sacrifice her sweaterdress and tights on the altar of frozen January ground, she needed help this time.

And help was slowly driving across the nearly deserted parking lot away from her.

"Hey! Wait!" Ditching pride—was there any left at this point?—she ran after Marcus's truck, waving her arms.

Brake lights flashed, and he rolled down his window as she breathlessly approached the driver's side. "You need something?"

He almost looked as if he hoped she might. But that was ridiculous. She'd broken his heart, so why would he want anything to do with her? It was the manners speaking again, as they had earlier when he got her a Diet Coke. His mama raised him well, that was all. She'd be ignorant to try to read more into it than that.

Guilt pricked her back like a thousand tiny needles. He shouldn't be the one doing this—wasn't fair on so many levels.

She gestured behind her in the general vicinity of her car. "Flat tire."

His expression morphed into neutral, the glimmer she'd mistakenly defined as hope fading, and began edging the truck away from her. "I'll handle it."

Of course he would. He handled everything. That was Marcus, always ready, always prepared, always willing.

It was one of the things that had attracted her to him—his confidence and ability to take charge in a situation made her feel safe and protected. It was the perfect balance—she *could* take care of herself, but with Marcus, she never had to.

To think she'd thrown that away for a lifetime of Triple A and tow trucks.

Had she made a mistake?

No. That line of thinking was pointless and painful.

She'd saved him. Saved them both from misery. No

custody battles over who got the toaster, no worries of greedy lawyers pushing for alimony. She wouldn't be her mother after all.

But if she tried to win him back now, she'd be an Andrews all the way. Putting herself first. Getting what she wanted and discarding the rest. Ignoring the trail of broken hearts in her wake.

Only to end up bitter and alone.

If she was going to end up a spinster anyway, at least it'd be for nobler reasons. She'd break the curse once and for all.

Even if it meant sacrificing her own heart.

She stepped back and waited for Marcus to park, then led the way to her car, pointing needlessly to the offending tire. He didn't say a word, just popped the trunk and dug out the jack and the small bag of tools she kept on hand. He set it all on the ground before hefting out the full-size spare.

"Anything I can do to help?" She crossed her arms over her dress, partially to block the late night January wind and partially to hide her heart.

Marcus shrugged. "Unless you're really good at removing lug nuts, no."

Then no it is.

He began applying the jack to the flat, then stopped, stood, and unbuttoned his dress shirt. "Just in case." He tossed it to her.

Allie caught it automatically, and resisted the urge to lift it to her face just in time. Those days had long since passed. A whiff of his familiar spicy cologne—that tangy citrus blend always made her mouth water—would only serve as a brutal twist of the knife.

How had she even gotten herself into this mess?

Oh yeah. By agreeing to be Hannah's maid of honor.

She calmly draped it over her arm and kept her voice brisk. "No problem."

Just as she began to assume he was as irritated as she feared, he shot her a quick wink over his shoulder. "A song and dance might help, though. See you take another turn in those boots."

Warmth crept up her face and heated her neck, while butterflies invaded her stomach. Had he really been as aware of her as she'd been of him all night? Every time she'd glanced his way, he'd been involved in conversation with someone else.

Maybe not as involved as she'd assumed.

But assuming never helped anything.

Even more important than the question of whether he was flirting, however, was the unavoidable question of why the thought of it made her feel equal parts elated and numb . . .

Not to mention what the view of his muscles flexing beneath his thin white T-shirt was doing to her heart rate.

Allie forced her eyes away from his form as he finished up her tire. Talk about shameful. One lousy wink and her knees turned to Jell-O. How, after all these months, was just being within a few feet of him capable of making her feel so alive?

Alive. That feeling was probably the worst.

Marcus was over her. Moving on was the only way he'd ever find the lifelong happiness he deserved.

Well, she took that back. Clearly, feeling alive wasn't the worst. Visions of Marcus with someone else irked way worse.

She dug her fingernails into the shirt she held, lips chattering in the wind, feeling two parts frustrated and one part nostalgic—the dangerous mixture bubbling in her throat like poison. "I would never sing karaoke with you before, and trust me, nothing's changed."

Marcus hopped up, grabbed the wrench, and knelt back by the tire. "I don't know about that, Allie. I'm starting to think maybe it has."

Well, if that wasn't the most cryptic thing he'd ever said.

Marcus's words from the night of the engagement party a week ago replayed in Allie's mind as she walked up the flagstone path through the Halls' perfectly manicured lawn. Every blade of grass saluted at the same height, while bushes and trees trimmed in high-dollar symmetrical design dotted the yard. Glossy wooden double doors graced the front of their home, complete with embellished wrought iron hinges that complemented the deep red of the brick.

Every element of Marcus's family resembled a Norman Rockwell painting. Annoyingly perfect but too charming to despise. Rather than be jealous, it just made one ache for the same.

His declaration still rang in her memory with the same clarity in which he'd spoken the words—then promptly refused to elaborate.

He thought things had changed? In what way? And from her side or his?

Did he mean it in a positive way or a negative?

Had he forgiven her?

So many unanswered questions.

Not that it mattered. Because when it came to who they were to one another, nothing had changed at all. The vast differences between Marcus's and her heritage remained as insurmountable as ever.

Thankfully, tonight was a bridal shower, which meant Zach, his groomsmen, and the rest of the guys wouldn't be around. Allie could cram in all the finger food she wanted without worrying about her nerves, visit freely with the other bridesmaids, and write down gift items as Hannah opened lingerie and dish towels and bath soaps. Though she could have done without the theme.

She glanced down at her sweater, which still made her want to cringe and giggle at the same time. Hannah had insisted this particular shower be "Über-Valentine's" themed—everything from tacky clothes to gaudy accessories to over-the-top decorations.

Allie had dressed the part, for sure—plastic heart clips in her hair and an oversized, late-eighties-era sweater with pink hearts and lightning bolts she'd found at a thrift shop. She quickly checked to make sure she'd remembered her camera—Hannah would definitely want a record of this night—then knocked.

Muffled voices echoed from the other side. Hannah opened the door and burst out laughing. "Oh, that is priceless." She spun in a quick circle, showing off her own tacky sweater, leggings, and red and pink bangle bracelets. "How do I look?"

"Über-Valentine's, for sure." Allie pointed to the headband Hannah wore with heart antennae attached. "I don't even want to know where you found those."

"Actually, Marcus bought them from the dollar store. Grab one." She motioned Allie inside and pointed to a basket full of headgear on the glass-topped entry table.

Allie tried to ignore the way her stomach flipped at the mere mention of him as she followed Hannah through the house.

Talk about memory lane. The last time she'd been there was for the impromptu engagement party in her honor. The floral arrangement on the wall sconce hadn't changed, nor had the striped carpeted aisle runner stretching the length of the polished wooden hallway. The low table by the foot of the stairs still held the same framed photo montage of the Hall kids growing up, and Allie realized with a start that her and Marcus's engagement photo hadn't been removed. Rather, it'd been pushed to the back of the table, halfway hidden behind a more recent picture of Hannah.

Odd.

She followed Hannah past the guest bathroom to the bigger of the two living rooms, where a trail of laughter drifted from the gaudily dressed guests sitting on the wraparound sofa.

Coed guests.

Allie grabbed Hannah's arm, tugging her halfway back out of the room. She nearly bumped into a giant heart balloon display, and sidestepped around it. "Hannah. I thought this was a girls-only party." Panic swelled in her stomach as she took in her ensemble once more and felt the sway of the heart antennae on her head. She looked like a complete idiot. "You said Über-Valentine's, and—"

"Don't worry, the guys are totally wearing tacky sweaters too." Hannah bounced on her toes as she pointed at Zach, lounging in the leather recliner and looking like a "which of these does not belong?" game in his psychedelic sweater and khaki pants. "Doesn't he look adorable?"

Maybe, but the guy sitting at the end of the couch wearing jeans with the knees ripped out definitely did.

Marcus. Looking sharp as always, even with a big, glittery heart sticker stuck on the pocket of his long-sleeved black tee.

While she resembled some sort of lovesick alien.

Allie sucked in her breath.

~

Allie looked like some sort of cute lovesick alien. Too bad the lovesick part was clearly not the truth. At least not toward him, anyway.

Marcus couldn't bear to think of her with anyone else. Made him want to rip that glittery sticker his sister had slapped on his chest right off of his shirt and tear it to shreds.

Nothing symbolic there or anything.

He took a deep breath and swirled his too-sweet red punch around in his plastic cup. So what if the woman of his dreams-turned-nightmare would be sitting across from him for the next umpteen hours. It was just a party, he could handle it. It was just Allie.

Right. That was like saying the Sears Tower was sort of

tall. Just as surely as he knew better than to nab a cupcake at the party before his mom gave official permission, he knew not to underestimate Allie's hold on him.

He watched her in the corner with Hannah, whispering furtively before reluctantly taking a seat in a straight-back chair across the room. She couldn't get farther away from him if she tried.

And after the lame flirting he'd attempted during her tire change the other night, he couldn't really blame her. He'd probably given the exact opposite impression he'd been trying to, though on second thought, he wasn't sure what that even was. The impression that he still cared? That he wanted to be friends?

That he wanted her back?

Loaded questions, and zero answers to be found.

Maybe he should go to Texas for a while.

He half listened as his sister and his mom explained the rules to some silly shower game involving heart-shaped game pieces and score sheets, and kept one eye on Allie as she scribbled on her sheet of paper. Man, he wished he could know what was going on under those bobbing antennae.

Which were ridiculous, but it seemed to make Hannah happy to have everyone in goofy mode. Zach, too, apparently, by the way he grinned as Hannah perched on his knee and tried to cheat off his paper. Maybe silly themes and corny games were the way to go—his wedding showers with Allie hadn't been nearly this fun or held nearly the same amount of laughter and whispers. Even his parents were getting in on the fun tonight. He looked up to see his mom turned to use his dad's back as a writing board.

He swallowed and looked away, absently shading in the numbers on his score sheet with a pencil. He'd never admitted this to anyone except Hannah, but he'd always dreamed of having what their parents had. Love that lasted. Love that, like the Bible instructed, never failed. Believed. Endured. His parents' lives hadn't been perfect, but they were blessed in many ways. They'd made it so far and were still going strong. He'd envisioned himself and Allie the same way.

Until she stopped their golden anniversary path dead in its tracks before it could even get started.

He eyed his parents as they collected the scorecards, then his sister as she squeezed Zach out of the chair and onto the floor, taking over the recliner. Maybe if his and Allie's prewedding season had been more lighthearted, Allie wouldn't have bolted.

If that had even been the problem. She refused to tell him what it'd been, and four months later, he figured asking wasn't going to reveal anything new. She clearly had reasons for not explaining herself, except maybe for the one scenario that he almost couldn't bear to imagine—that she just plain didn't love him and had realized it in time.

He glanced up at Allie's smiling face as his parents awarded the door prize to the winner, wanting to smile himself at the way her antennae bobbed so freely on her head. And where in the world had she found that sweater? He wouldn't use that thing to buff a car. Yet even in that ridiculous pattern, she shone. That was Allie.

There wasn't a cruel bone in her body, and dumping him at the altar because she just didn't want to get married anymore wasn't Allie. No one changed that completely, that fast. No, there had to be a better explanation for what she had done.

The question was, would she ever trust him enough to tell him the truth?

"All right, everyone, we're pairing up into teams of four for the next game." Mom clapped her hands to gather the room's attention. "I'll number everyone. Ones, gather by the recliner. Twos, you're over by the far end of the couch . . ."

Marcus accepted his number and ambled over to his meeting spot.

Near Allie's straight-back chair.

"Hi." She offered a grin as wobbly as her headgear, and he wished for the tenth time he hadn't allowed Hannah to put that sticker on his shirt. Though he really shouldn't be concerned how silly he looked, considering the entire room looked like a Valentine's Day crime scene.

"Hey." He drank her in before remembering to acknowledge the other two people in their group—a red-haired girl he'd seen with Hannah but whose name he couldn't remember, and one of Zach's groomsmen, Tyler.

"Here you go. You have ten minutes." His mom suddenly shoved a giant roll of toilet paper into his hands. "Pick a bride, and make a wedding dress out of the TP."

"Make a *what*?" He sounded like the expression on Tyler's face looked. The girls, however, appeared as if they received such instructions every day. "Did she just say wedding dress?"

Not a trigger for a bad stroll down memory lane there or anything.

"You should definitely be the bride," Allie adamantly

instructed Redhead, who bobbed her head in agreement. Though who wouldn't be afraid to argue with the no-nonsense tone in Allie's voice? Was that sweat forming on her brow? Marcus shook his head. Clearly, the very thought of being in a wedding dress, even of the TP variety, sent her into a mild panic.

Allie talked about the dress her mom wore in her wedding, back when they were planning their own. Something about her entire family wearing it and passing it down through the generations. Wasn't that a good thing, though?

Sure beat constructing one out of toilet paper.

But she'd said the dress was cursed. At the time he hadn't thought much of it. He'd been more focused on finishing up Allie's wedding present—restoring her 1973 Mustang Mach 1. The same car she'd dragged by the hair into his garage that summer—the day he finally realized he didn't want his sister's best friend to be her friend anymore.

He wanted her all to himself.

But what if something about that "curse" had actually meant more to Allie than she'd let on? What if her joking around about the tainted outcomes of the other marriages in her family hadn't been a joke after all?

Judging by the look in her eyes at the moment, her current thoughts weren't very pleasant.

The dress mattered. He could sense it. Maybe Hannah could find out . . .

No, he couldn't let her get in the middle. She and Allie were just finding their footing again. He wouldn't risk their friendship to satisfy his own curiosity.

What would it matter anyway? Knowing wouldn't change the past. Knowing might even make things worse.

"What do I do with this?" The groomsman in their group looked terrified as he glanced back and forth from the thick white roll in his hands to Redhead, who stood stock-still with her arms stretched out as if waiting to be wrapped.

Marcus's mom strolled the perimeter of the room, grinning and tapping her watch. "Seven minutes."

Well, Marcus might not be a dress designer or even a talented seamstress like his mom, but he was an athlete, and that meant one thing—he knew a little something about competition.

"Give me that." He snatched the toilet paper and began to unroll it several feet at a time. "Here." He tore some off and handed it to Allie. "You're in charge of the sleeves."

She hesitated, then lifted her chin slightly and began to fashion long sleeves for their mutual bride, tucking and folding the edges to make the paper lay flat.

And leaving him to wish he'd been able to see Allie in her own wedding dress that day before she'd left.

I can't believe you didn't tell me it was a coed shower." Allie tied another pink bow around a white mesh favor bag, snipped the ends with scissors, and set it down on her kitchen table. One down, two hundred to go.

She really wasn't in the mood for precision work, especially since she'd just gotten off the phone with her aunt and heard yet another lecture about the dress in her closet and the fact that she wasn't getting any younger and it was "time for her first marriage." She yanked the ribbon a little tighter than necessary.

Hannah filled another bag with pink foil-covered chocolates. "I didn't realize you were assuming otherwise. Just because your and Marcus's wedding showers weren't done that way doesn't mean—"

"I know, I know. It's my own fault." Allie set the next bag down and ripped open a piece of chocolate instead. "It was just a little embarrassing."

"Why?" Hannah frowned.

Allie popped the candy into her mouth and mumbled around it. "Maybe because I looked like some kind of Valentine-obsessed Martian the whole night?" Her blood pressure shot up just remembering how awkward it had been seeing Marcus's gaze flit across her sweater and headpiece. Not exactly the impression she'd hoped to leave—though why she was still worried about it, she had no idea.

"You looked cute. I know Marcus thought so." Hannah's eyes widened, and she suddenly focused a little too hard on the ribbon in her hand.

Allie nudged her leg under the table. "What do you mean?" Oh, she hated the hope in her voice, hated that tell-tale lilt. Had he said something to Hannah about her?

Hannah set the bag aside and reached for another. "He's my brother, Allie. I can tell by the way he looked at you all night."

That wasn't necessarily a serious indication. More like a fascination with how ridiculous one could look at a theme party.

"If you don't believe me, bring me your camera." Hannah stood up, palm stretched out like she expected Allie to pull the thing from her back pocket. "I'll show you."

"It's in my room. But I don't see how that's going to prove anything." Allie led the way down the hall and handed her the small camera.

Hannah perched on the edge of the bed and clicked her way through the most recent pictures. "See? Right there. No, wait, not there. Mom's hair got in the way." She clicked another one. "There!" She turned the camera around with a triumphant grin.

Allie took it from her and slowly sank to the bed as she drank in the image. It was a candid group shot Hannah had sneaked of the dress-making competition. In it, Allie knelt in front of their makeshift bride, adjusting the hem of the toilet-paper gown, while Tyler stood back with arms crossed and a nervous furrow in his brow. Marcus hovered next to Allie, holding out a fresh roll of paper, his eyes focused on Allie's face as she looked up at the bride. But the expression on his face as he gazed down at her radiated light.

"Now are you going to argue?" Hannah hopped off the bed and began pawing through Allie's closet. The wedding dress on the back of the door swung slightly from its hook. "And can I borrow your red cardigan?"

"Yes." Allie turned off the camera and stared at the tiny blank screen, trying to figure out why her heart rate couldn't slow down and if Hannah might actually be right.

And if it changed anything if she was.

"Yes to the arguing? Or the sweater?" Hannah's hand hovered near the cardigan.

"Both." Allie stood and tossed her camera on the bed, decision made. "Marcus was probably just excited about winning. You know how he gets about competition."

"Allie. It was toilet paper. No one beams over toilet paper." Hannah pulled the cardigan off the hanger and draped it over her arm. She bumped into the dress on her way out of the closet and looked it up and down, nibbling her lower lip. A rush of emotion flickered through her eyes. "Oh wow. What happened here?" She ran her fingers over the rip in the shoulder. "Are you going to fix that tear?"

The Tear. As in, capital *T*. Hadn't that been what sent

yet another dart of doubt spiraling into place in the bridal room last September? Still, looking at it there—if she had to look at the dress at all—sort of kept her grounded. Like she'd done the right thing. Like that tear could only symbolize their future if she'd marched down the aisle as expected.

Allie drew a shuddered breath. "It ripped on our wedding day."

Hannah slowly drew her hand back. "Wow." She glanced at Allie, then at the dress, as if she couldn't look away. "Let me take it to my mom. She can fix it."

She reached for the hanger, and Allie barreled into her arm. "No. Wait."

Hannah froze, eyebrows lifted in surprise. "Why not? Isn't your family crazy about this dress? I bet your mom freaked out over the tear."

Actually, Mom didn't know. Allie had made sure she and Aunt Shelly and Grandma hadn't seen it in the aftermath of the nonwedding. And after they insisted she keep the thing anyway, it hadn't been hard to hold back the secret. It wasn't like they ever came into her closet.

Because if they knew, they'd march straight to the nearest tailor and sew it up tighter than that noose she'd almost slipped around Marcus's neck.

It needed to stay torn.

"I can't. I mean, she can't." No, especially not Julie—Mrs. Hall. How could she ask her to sew up the dress that had betrayed her son?

"Can't what?" Hannah folded her arms around the cardigan, hip cocked slightly to the side. "Allie, you're losing it."

"Your mom, I meant. Your mom can't fix my dress."

Allie reached inside the closet and began to pull Hannah out. "Don't you see how awkward that would be?"

Hannah made a half-snort, half-hissing sound through her lips as she shook free of Allie's grip. "Not at all. She'd be happy to. Being a seamstress is her career, you know." She reached up and pulled the dress free of the door.

Allie grabbed for the gown, letting go of the ripped sleeve just in time to prevent further tearing. She gripped the skirt instead. "Hannah. It'd be rude, like throwing it in her face. Your mom was devastated after I left."

Hannah rolled in her lip, averting her eyes. "We all were, Allie."

Silence hung in the room, thick and heavy like the fabric between them. "I'm sorry."

"Are you ever going to tell me what happened?"

Allie loosened her grip slightly. "I didn't want to hurt him."

"So you left him at the altar." Hannah's tone filled in any blanks her words left.

"I did what I had to do. Trust me, he's better off." Better off than the men who had gotten tangled up with her mom and her aunt over the years, and been carnage in their wake.

"Better off than marrying the love of his life?" Hannah tugged the dress closer to her. "Listen, I don't know the whole story, and you don't have to tell me. I'm your friend no matter what. But let me do this. Let my mom fix this tear. I think it'll provide closure, actually."

Closure for who? Mrs. Hall or Allie? If the former, Hannah had a decent point. If the latter, well, fat chance.

Regardless, she had to let go of the dress.

Allie stepped back and reluctantly let the material slip through her fingers.

Hannah pulled the gown closer to her and draped it carefully over her arm on top of the cardigan. "It'll be in good hands. I promise."

That might be the problem.

~

His little sister might drive him crazy, but unfortunately, she was right. Sometimes. Like about the garage.

Marcus tossed the handheld remote between his hands, wondering if he could actually go through with pushing the button. Allie's Mustang, the one he'd bought back for her and restored for her wedding present, still sat inside.

It'd taken four months to realize that ignoring something didn't make it vanish, especially something that weighed roughly four thousand pounds, but the time had come.

He had to deal with the past.

He quickly pushed the small red button, and the door to the detached garage began to creak open. Shadows and sunlight mingled, illuminating the timid dance of dust particles.

The Mustang waited under a thin black car cover, exactly the way he'd left it. He'd planned for a groomsman to drive it to the church after the ceremony so it would stay a surprise to Allie until the very last minute.

It never even had a chance.

Marcus tossed the garage opener onto the dilapidated bench inside, then gripped one edge of the cover. His dad had come and covered the car a week after the wedding, at

Marcus's request. Dad had asked about it just once since, and after Marcus's emotional response, he'd wisely never mentioned it again.

Hesitantly, Marcus began to pull. More dust flew as he maneuvered around the car, peeling back the cloth bit by bit until the entire car was revealed.

It still looked amazing. Some of his best work. He'd replaced the wheels, completely redone the interior, enhanced the suspension, installed a sound system, and added a custom paint job, turning the entire car from a faded green to a shiny black.

Allie had always been one of his biggest champions in the garage. Ever since their first conversation years ago about the beauty and power in restoration, she'd been hooked, always eager to see what he'd transformed next with a few tools and a lot of elbow grease.

But he couldn't transform everything.

Over the past several days she'd crept back into his thoughts, despite his heavily guarded walls that proved to be no thicker than the car cover. After helping to create that ridiculous wedding dress at the party, he'd wondered if maybe he could learn to be around Allie and still breathe. Look at her without a knot in his stomach. Even enjoy being around her again, as a friend.

He missed her.

But watching her laugh with those crazy antennas on her head, seeing her break into a sudden smile without being able to find out why, watching her shine without being able to embrace that light . . . torture. Like being handed the keys to a brand-new 'Vette and then being told he could just sit in it in the showroom. He wanted it all with her, wanted to keep the vows he'd memorized and still felt running through his heart every time he caught her eye.

It was all or nothing, and Allie had chosen nothing.

The car had to go.

He couldn't keep stale reminders of the past in his garage forever. Couldn't keep stale memories of Allie in his heart forever, either.

Marcus studied the Mustang, ignoring the ache in his chest, and tried to evaluate how much he could sell it for. He wasn't after profit, but maybe he could break even.

He absently rubbed at a dust smudge on the side-view mirror. After the wedding festivities were over, he'd leave. Take that job opportunity in east Texas and head out. There was no reason to stay. But there might be plenty of reasons to go.

He knocked lightly on the hood of the Mustang, the slight sound echoing through the garage. First he had to rid himself of the car. Then he had to let go.

Completely.

~

Maybe she didn't have to completely let go of Marcus after all.

Allie ran her favorite blue feather duster over the tableful of ancient vases in her store, careful not to knock over the antique birdcage set up on the end. The more she thought about that picture Hannah had shown her, the more she wondered if she and Marcus could find a new normal. Maybe not the future they'd imagined, but a friendship, at the least. A way to be around each other, perhaps even enjoy each other's company, for the sake of her connection with Hannah.

And okay, a little bit for her own sake as well. Because if she and Marcus could figure out how to redefine their former relationship into a current friendship, everyone won. She could stop being the bad guy for ditching him, he would finally see that he was better off without her as a wife, his family would feel like her own again, and she and Hannah could stay friends—everything would be as it should.

Or close to it. If she couldn't have it all with Marcus, *something* would be better than *nothing*.

Because right now, having gotten a taste of his presence again, having seen his interactions with family and his smile up close and the way his eyes crinkled in the corners when he laughed . . . it'd be worse torture letting him go again.

She moved away from the table of vases and began to dust an old china cabinet and the collection of porcelain bunnies perched on the bottom shelf. He didn't hate her, at least. The picture revealed that much, even if it was blurry on everything else. And if he didn't hate her, then there was a chance for her plan to work. They'd find a way to be friends, stay in each other's lives.

She missed him.

But it was going to take a gesture. Something to show him that while he might not understand why she did what she did—and he couldn't, because if she ever told him, he'd surely try to talk her out of it—it wasn't because she didn't care about him.

The chime of the bell and a whiff of floral perfume announced Mrs. Hawkins's presence before the top of her gray bun appeared over the dresser. Allie peered around the piece of dusty furniture and grinned. "Did you bring me a treasure today?"

Her elderly friend smiled back. "It's a good one too. Seemed perfect for you."

Allie came out from behind the dresser. Mrs. Hawkins's great-nephews, teenagers who had served as her musclemen many times over the years, stood in jeans and slightly rumpled T-shirts beside a long, almost dilapidated piece of wood with back shelves that might have been a workbench at one point. Allie squinted as she set down her duster and moved closer.

Mrs. Hawkins stood back, her hands in the pockets of her elastic-waist plaid skirt, and rocked slightly on her therapeutic shoes. She knew not to interrupt an evaluation, and so did her boys.

Allie ran her hands lightly over the piece. The backing had partially torn away from the bench seat and needed some screws. The wood itself was scuffed and faded, needed sanding at the least, definitely a stain.

She rocked the piece slightly with her hand a few times. The legs still seemed sturdy, which meant at one point it'd been quality craftsmanship. She could fix it up, probably turn a profit without too much effort. Though she was starting to run out of places on the floor to display these bigger pieces.

Unless . . .

She looked harder. It was exactly the style bench Marcus used to compliment, and had always needed in his home garage. She had no idea if he'd ever gotten one, but maybe . . . maybe this was the answer to her dilemma. If she restored the bench and gave it to him as a gift, he'd know they were on good terms and had a future as friends. That she hadn't iced him out, that she still cared about him—probably more than she should.

But the bench wouldn't say *all* that.

"I'll take it." Allie held out her hand to Mrs. Hawkins, and they shook before Allie excitedly turned back to her treasure.

She'd make sure it said just enough.

Five

Allie was everywhere.

It was like as soon as Marcus decided he couldn't handle being around her and he should pull back, there she was. They'd managed to go for four months in the same small town without running into each other—he avoided her shop, she avoided his garage and his family's house, he started attending a different church.

Now she was suddenly at the bank when he stopped to make a business deposit, at the post office when he went with Hannah to buy stamps for Zach's tool shower invitation mail-out, at the grocery store when he pushed the cart for his mom to buy a ridiculous amount of beef jerky to use as centerpieces for the shower.

He was almost starting to hate tools.

Then one afternoon there she was sitting in his mom's kitchen assisting Hannah with thank-you notes, surrounded by fresh-baked cookies and smiling at him sweeter than the chocolate chips themselves.

It didn't help that February had also invaded Beaux Creek, ushering in a plethora of cut-out hearts and lace in store windows and dangling off end-cap displays like nothing he'd ever seen. It almost put Hannah's party decorations to shame. The entire town had been bitten by the Valentine bug. The reminders of what could have been—*should* have been—were enough to drive a man insane.

He got in his truck after leaving the grocery store, the radio set to his favorite country station, and flinched at the lyrics to a popular song referencing how mid-February shouldn't be so scary. He couldn't agree more—as he quickly changed the dial. To hard rock. Since he hated the genre, at least Allie couldn't linger *there*.

If he hadn't seen Allie so much in town the past few weeks, he'd have been surprised to see her strolling into his garage at work that morning, looking cute in a turquoise sweater and jeans tucked into boots—too cute, in fact, to be parading around in front of his grease-stained, male-minded employees.

"Outside." His voice was harsher than he meant it to be as he took her arm in his gloved hands and steered her back out the way she had come, careful to stay close behind her to shield her from view. He loved his team of workers but didn't love the way they were eyeballing and elbowing.

Especially now that they knew Allie was single.

She protested and tried to look at him as he propelled her back toward her car in the nearly empty lot.

They finally stopped near her driver's side, and he pulled off his work gloves and shoved them into the pockets of his coveralls. He'd been working on engines today in the bay, so he'd traded the jeans and company polo in for the working gear. Not that he cared how Allie thought he looked.

Though his biceps were definitely more defined in the polo.

"What's wrong?" She shaded her eyes against the setting sun as she peered up at him.

"Nothing's wrong."

"Then what was all that about?" She shifted, attempting to gain her footing in her boots on the gravel ground. He automatically reached to steady her, and the electricity from his touch against her shoulder sparked his hand—and it only had a little to do with winter static. He dropped his grip and stepped back a bit. That was all he needed—a chemistry fire at his garage.

"It was nothing." He shifted his weight slightly to help block the glare of sunshine for her. "Just . . . nothing." Yeah, he wasn't going to explain his desire to protect her still. Not even.

He cleared his throat. "What's up with you?" In other words, *Why are you here?*—but he couldn't be that rude. Not while looking down into those green eyes, almost the same color as her sweater. He suddenly appreciated her turquoise obsession in a new way.

"I wanted your opinion on a gift for Zach." The chilly February wind lifted her hair as she played with the flower petal charm on her necklace, zipping it around the chain. A nervous habit she'd always had.

"Didn't he make a registry?" He and Allie had certainly made enough when they were going through the process last year.

"Well, yeah, but with tools I still don't know the right thing to get, and I want it to be nice." Allie let go of her necklace and grinned. "I know what tools to use to restore furniture, but not to repair a toilet or any other random household issue."

Marcus loved his soon-to-be brother-in-law, but Zach wouldn't have a clue either. The poor guy would have to call a plumber regardless of how many tools sat in his barn.

"Just get something in your price range. If it's on his list, it's something he'll appreciate."

How many showers were these guys going to have, anyway? He didn't remember having that many with Allie; then again, he'd been distracted during that entire season. He'd been more invested in the marriage coming afterward than in registering for silverware and oven mitts.

He'd trade all his tools for Allie in a heartbeat. That is, he *would* have—he needed to remember to keep that sentiment in the past tense.

"Maybe you could come with me." Her tone pitched slightly higher. With nerves? Hope? "Or we could go in together and get something really nice, if you haven't bought anything yet."

He hadn't, but that wasn't the point.

He crossed his arms, using the excuse of a motorcycle roaring down the side street to turn slightly away from her as he tried to steel himself against her request. *She* left him. *She* bailed.

And now she was asking him to be her hero with a toolbox?

No. He couldn't do it.

He understood playing nice for the sake of his sister's wedding, but if he kept giving in to Allie's requests for help, he'd be back to square one on the misery scale. The flat tire he couldn't avoid, not without being a jerk. He'd have helped anyone in that situation.

But this he could avoid.

He couldn't let her do that to his heart again.

"I'm really busy here at the garage." He gestured behind him to the car business that ran like a well-oiled machine itself.

Allie followed his gaze, confusion and doubt highlighting her eyes. "Lunch break?"

"I'm on a special project." He kept his jaw tight, gaze averted. If he looked her in the eyes now, he'd cave. Take her to the hardware store in a dang limousine and probably buy flowers along the way.

Not happening.

She pulled open her car door, and the key chime dinged. "I see."

He risked a glance and regretted it. Hurt had replaced the confusion in her eyes, and he struggled to stand his ground. She didn't really see at all, but she needed to.

Because after this whole shindig was over, he was going to find out how fast his car could go from zero to sixty across the Texas border.

Maybe she shouldn't have gone.

Allie strolled the main aisle of the hardware store, staring at hammers and screwdrivers and various pouches of nails as if they might hold the answer to Marcus's sudden attitude change. What had shifted? It was probably a little gutsy of her to show up at his work, especially considering that the last time she'd done so, she'd been bringing him lunch the week before their wedding.

But still. She'd been sure after the coed party and that picture of him looking at her that way that he'd be on board with the attempt at friendship. Didn't he feel the same way she did, wanting to make things civil? Why else would he be so lighthearted during the faux-wedding-dress game, enough for it to have been captured on camera? Why else would he have been so sweet about changing her tire and so friendly every time he ran into her in town these past few weeks? She'd thought they were on the same page, but now he was acting really distant. Almost rude.

They had to figure this out.

Allie glanced again at the registry list she'd printed out, absently scanning through the price column until she found a number she could handle. She was going to finish the workbench for Marcus regardless. He deserved it. She'd already sanded and stained the piece, and secured the back to the bench. Now she was just waiting to give it a second coat of stain, and it'd be ready to give to him. Maybe after that he'd see how she felt, understand what she meant.

Or maybe she'd misread the entire thing. And was now going to have to try to sell a restored workbench.

She picked up an electric drill, then put it down again. The bench still didn't feel quite finished. It needed a message, a signature or a quote or a picture engraved. Something that meant something to Marcus specifically and would remind him of her—in a positive way.

So what positively said, *I still love you, even though I left you at the altar, and trust me, you're better off avoiding my curse, but I do care about you regardless*?

She groaned and flipped to the next page of the printout. Maybe this was a bad idea. One of many, the first being the antennae headband. Or no, the first being agreeing to wear her mother's stupid dress in the first place. She didn't believe in curses, not really—not in the New Orleans voodoo sense or anything. But she believed what the Bible said about generational sins, and she knew that her baggage weighed heavily on her shoulders. She didn't want to transfer that to Marcus, not when he'd come from such perfection. How could he carry that and not resent her later? Not regret the entire marriage? It was too much, even for someone as good as gold like Marcus.

He deserved better than what she and her family had to offer. Better than a cursed future and a cursed dress and a wife destined to repeat history.

The figures on the page before her blurred as her eyelids welled with tears, and she blinked rapidly to clear them, swiping one finger under her eye and taking a deep breath.

"Hey, no crying on the registry." A familiar voice broke through the noise in her head, and Marcus's hands tugged the stapled papers from her grasp.

Allie sniffed and wiped her eyes again before forcing a smile, taking in his jeans and company polo shirt, and the way the fit hugged his muscles. Great, now not only was she a lovesick Martian, she was an emotional one with raccoon eyes from smeared mascara.

But he'd come.

And that just made her want to cry all over again.

She drew a ragged breath, trying to push back the emotion. It was just a hardware store. None of that changed the way he'd acted at his garage. "What are you—"

"Doing here?" Marcus tapped the page she'd just been looking at, and his gaze said a whole lot more than his words. Her breath caught in her throat at the apology in his eyes. "Shopping for a tool shower. You?"

"Same, ironically." She snorted back a laugh. He'd always been able to diffuse a tense situation.

Too bad he hadn't been in the bridal room with her last September.

"Then why don't we go in together on the drill?" His eyes softened. "Sound good?"

Yes. Too good. This team thing was going to mess with her head. But she managed a nod and a real smile, and he tugged the drill box off the shelf, tucking it under one arm as he handed her back the list.

She followed him to the checkout line, hovering near his elbow and trying to drink in his citrus cologne without his noticing. As long as this new "same team" effort only messed with her head, and not his.

He'd hurt enough already, but her pain quota would, rightly so, never be full.

Six

Marcus sat on the couch and eyed the blue-striped gift box that held a card touting his and Allie's names. Together.

As it should have been, except nothing was as it should have been. He sat on one end of the sofa in Zach's mother's living room, while Allie sat in an armchair too many feet to his left. She should have been perched on his knee so he could run his fingers through the ends of her hair while she laughed at the small talk and awkward ice-breaker games everyone played when blending families tried to get to know each other. She should have been offering him the last bite of that artichoke-and-cheese quiche thing she'd eaten half of and hadn't finished, should have been using him as her cup holder while she touched up her lipstick. All those couple things he'd taken for granted when they were together.

Now, watching her swing one jean-clad crossed leg absently

in that chair, her high-heeled shoe dangling from her toes, sitting much too far away, he just wanted to ask if he could hold something for her. Hand her her purse. Refill her soda.

If any of his employees ever talked like that, he'd smack them. Yet here he was, moony over the woman he should be closer to despising than loving.

He knew he shouldn't have gone in on that gift with her. But when he'd shown up at the store on an errand for work, half hoping she'd already be gone and half hoping he'd run into her, he'd caved. Melted, like that tear that he saw dripping down her cheek as she stared hopelessly at the registry list.

She hadn't been crying over the list. He knew Allie well enough to know that much. She'd been upset over something else, and he couldn't shake the thought it might have been over the way he'd acted at the garage. She might have ditched him at the altar, but for whatever reason, she was now trying to be nice. Not flirty, but sweet. Sincere. Genuine.

Just *Allie*.

Which was almost worse.

Flirty he could fend off. He could guard against that, could see through it and know it was a game or an angle he didn't want anything to do with.

But when she was just herself, her old self, the Allie he could recognize a mile away, well . . . his wall crumbled faster than those darn cookies she'd made the other day with Hannah. And he started doing ridiculous things without his wall, like offering to pay for half of electric drills and picking out gift wrap at the hardware store counter.

"Time for a game!" Zach's mom suddenly stood up from

the fireplace hearth, the same manic gleam in her eye that his own mother had displayed before announcing the toilet-paper dress competition.

Marcus stood as well and made a beeline for the kitchen with his trash. He'd be sure to take his time throwing it all away so he'd miss whatever crazy concoction they'd come up with next. And if anyone said anything about a Valentine, well, he might have to find a hammer from the gift basket on the table and put himself out of his misery. At least the wedding was in a few days, and all of this madness would finally end.

He dumped his plate and cup in the trash, then turned and nearly collided with Allie.

"Sorry." They both spoke at the same time.

"My fault." He took the plate from her hand, noting the still unfinished quiche, and tossed everything into the garbage.

"What, you're not in a hurry to play the game?" Her eyes twinkled as she pulled her cell from her pocket and laid it on the counter. "Sounds like they're having fun." Behind her, loud laughter rang from the swinging doors that led to the living room, where, judging by the instructions he'd heard on his way out, the guests were playing some kind of purse scavenger hunt.

He leaned back against the kitchen counter, scooting her cell to the side to brace his hands on the tile. "Don't have a purse. I'm safe."

"The men are the ones having to find the items in their dates' purses."

Ah. Well, that wasn't awkward. Especially since, by the

looks of the room earlier, he and Allie were the only ones older than sixteen who had come without an official significant other.

Some days the knife just kept twisting.

Allie shifted closer, leaning one hip against the counter beside him. The low light above the kitchen sink shone against her hair, pulled halfway up with a clip the way he'd always loved. She wore the same dark dress she'd worn a few weeks ago at the engagement party, the night they'd first seen each other again. She wore it well.

Talk about knives.

"I'm sorry if I shouldn't have come by your garage." Her voice was barely above a whisper, but the hum of the refrigerator and the rush of the heater in the vents above them would have kept the conversation private, even if the noise from the party room didn't.

They were alone. Too alone.

His arm drew nearer to hers on the counter, as if pulled by a magnet, and he shifted toward her to answer. "It wasn't a problem." Well, a little bit of one. But that wasn't her fault. She didn't know what he'd resolved.

Same resolve that was currently slipping away like oil through a filter.

"Felt like a problem." Now she was whispering and edging closer to him too.

His heart thundered against his button-down, and somehow his fingers grazed hers on the countertop. Like moths to a flame. "I'm sorry if I was rude. You're not ever a problem, Allie." He was the problem, clearly, if she'd left him for no reason.

A reason she might have currently forgotten, as now her eyes were dipping from his own to his lips.

No. He couldn't. He pulled in a tight breath and she mirrored the action, her gaze still darting back and forth, a dozen questions mingling inside. The same questions that his heart shouted, had shouted for months now, demanding answers.

Demanding action.

He cupped her face in his palm and kissed her.

~

Allie returned Marcus's kiss, her lips mingling with his in a dance they'd performed countless times, yet somehow it felt brand-new. She rose slightly on tiptoe and pressed in closer, his hand warm against her face. His free arm came around her waist and fit snugly as ever.

A knot of hope and dread tangled in her stomach. Hope that they had a chance, dread that they didn't. Hope that she'd been wrong about Marcus's feelings toward her, dread that now she'd ruined any chance of friendship they could have had after all.

Yet even with the tug-of-war in her heart, she couldn't bear to pull away.

Marcus's hand against her face slid into her hair, and her fingers found the collar of his shirt as he deepened the kiss. A rush of old and not-so-old memories poured over her, triggering a tidal wave of regret. But it was quickly drowned out by reality.

And the sound of the kitchen door squeaking open.

Allie pulled away at the same time that Marcus slammed back against the counter, his hands thumping against the sides. The sound startled Allie, but her surprise was nothing compared to the shocked expression on Hannah's face.

"Sorry. I didn't mean to interrupt." The grin that spread across her cheeks made her seem a whole lot less than sorry. "I just noticed you guys had disappeared, and we're about to start opening gifts."

"Of course. We're coming." Allie coughed, reaching up to wipe her lips, then catching herself just in time. "I mean, I'm coming." She didn't know what Marcus was doing. Or what she was doing, for that matter.

She really just wanted to do it again.

"Be right there." Marcus shot his sister a pointed look, and her smug-kitty grin only deepened before she slipped back into the party. Allie's heart stuttered. She'd so be hearing about this later.

The door swung shut behind her, once again engulfing them in the solitude of the kitchen. She turned to Marcus, wishing she could read inside his head before having to speak.

"Allie, I—"

"Marcus, we—"

They both stopped, and tried again.

"We can't—"

"I really—"

"Wait." Allie held up both hands. "We can't what? Your turn."

He hesitated, bracing both arms against the tiled countertop. "We can't . . . this. That." He gestured between them. "That was . . . well, it was. And it can't be."

Sort of how she felt, except . . . no, it was the opposite. Oh, she knew better, her head agreed tenfold, but her heart . . . it had somehow missed the logic memo and was still wrapped up in the warmth of Marcus's arms.

She started to fan her face, then caught herself. "I agree." How could she not? In the face of rejection. Rejection she deserved, sure, but he'd just kissed her and then told her he couldn't do it again. She swallowed, hoping her expression didn't betray her thundering nerves. "It's not a good idea."

"Right. A bad idea." Marcus's eyes searched hers, as if seeking a different response, but that wasn't fair. What was she supposed to do, beg him to change his mind? He hadn't begged her after she left the church or in the days to follow. He was the one making the call this time. Not her.

But the rush of familiarity between them and the built-up emotion of the past few weeks loosened her tongue and her resolve. "But maybe . . ."

No, he was right. It *was* a bad idea. She'd been trying to find a way for them to be friends, and somehow they'd ended up making out in Zach's kitchen. Clearly their physical connection was alive and well—no surprise there—but the curse was still the curse.

"Maybe what?" His breath hitched visibly in his chest, and she fought the urge to press her hand against his heart. She'd loved doing that when they were together, feeling the beat of it beneath her palm, listening to his whispered promises about whom it beat for.

"Maybe . . ." No, she couldn't think straight. Nothing had changed.

But maybe it had. Maybe she'd been wrong about it all.

What if she and Marcus really could create their own life and leave all her curses behind? Leave the dress behind, her family behind, and start over on their own, as they'd always wanted.

What if—what *if*—it was possible?

Her cell lit up in a silent ring on the countertop. Her mother's number.

"You take it." Marcus squeezed her hand before he eased away, the unspoken understanding that they weren't finished yet lingering in his wake. "I'll see you in there."

Yes. Yes he would.

Allie scooped up her cell. Impeccable timing on her mother's part, as always.

"Hi, Mom." She turned away from the kitchen light and pinched the bridge of her nose, fighting the headache that always seemed to spring up right along with her mom's voice. "What's up? I'm at Hannah and Zach's party." *Kissing my ex-fiancé.* Her face heated, and she cast a glance over her shoulder to make sure Marcus had left.

Gone.

Not that she really blamed him. She didn't want to be around her mother, even via cell phone, either.

"Another party we weren't invited to?" Her mother's voice barreled through the reception, and Allie yanked the phone an inch away from her ear. "That's what, three now?" Confusion filled her voice more than shock, which wasn't at all surprising. For all her mother's coldhearted calculations, she never was big on getting a hint.

"Mom, just because you know Hannah as my friend doesn't mean you're invited to every event they have."

She'd explained this once before, a week ago, actually,

when her grandmother had started griping about all the things she'd done for Hannah over the course of their friendship. Eventually Allie figured she'd stop being shocked over her family's naïveté. Did they really have no idea how people perceived them? How obnoxious they were at social events? How offensive they were by throwing around their opinions, and how obvious they were about scouting for a new man at every public outing?

"Well, being invited to one of them might have been nice." Her mom sniffed, and Allie fought the urge to roll her eyes.

"What do you need, Mom? I'm supposed to be writing down the gifts Hannah and Zach open." She assumed so, anyway, since she'd done it at the previous showers, but even so she just wanted to get off the phone. Wanted to figure out what she'd tell Marcus. Wanted to process his kiss.

Or had she kissed *him* first?

Now she couldn't even remember.

"I just wanted to ask you about the dress." Her mom's tone turned borderline cajoling, a surefire sign Allie wouldn't like what was coming next.

She braced one arm against her stomach. "What about it?" She couldn't turn off the warning in her voice, not that her mother would heed it.

"I need to borrow it for a while."

Oh no. "What do you mean?"

There was an expectant pause. "I'm getting married."

Of course. Allie's stomach clenched. "Congratulations." The word came out more monotone than she meant. Or maybe not monotone enough. "So you want to use the dress again."

"Well, it's not like you need it right now."

That one sank in deep. Allie briefly closed her eyes. "They're opening the gifts now. I've got to go."

"Just get the dress to me in two weeks or sooner. I'll make sure you get an invitation, dear."

Yes, because she definitely couldn't miss this one.

Allie mumbled good-bye and clicked the power button on her phone, squeezing the small contraption until her hand ached as much as her heart. They'd never learn. Not any of them. They were living, generational proof that some curses couldn't be broken. That some destinies were meant to happen, and all you could control was who you took down with you.

She straightened with a sigh and marched determinedly toward the living room, her previously soaring heart now as heavy as that workbench she'd spent days restoring.

She refused to take Marcus down with her.

Seven

He'd kissed her.

And he'd do it again, given the chance.

Marcus couldn't contain his whistle as he climbed out of his truck in the dimly lit church parking lot, ignoring the uncomfortable pinch of his dress shoes, not even minding that tomorrow evening during the actual wedding he'd be stuck in a full suit for hours on end as an usher. None of that mattered.

He'd kissed Allie.

And she'd kissed him back.

The purple twilight around him only heightened the expectant pulse in the chilly February air. Tonight would be good, maybe life-changing good. He could feel it.

"Hey, Marcus! Wait up!"

He slowed to a stop outside the sanctuary doors, turning as Zach jogged toward him in a pair of dress pants and a button-down—not his usual look. He shoved his glasses further up on his nose, out of breath as Hannah hurried up behind him.

Zach slowed to a stop. "I just heard from one of my groomsmen, my buddy from college. He isn't going to be able to make it to the wedding."

Marcus frowned, though the news didn't do much to dampen his elation. "I'm sorry to hear that."

Hannah pointed at him from behind Zach with a grin. "In other words, brother, *you* just got promoted."

"Me? What?" He looked from Hannah to Zach and back again, his elation slowly leaking out. Uh oh. This wasn't what he'd meant by expectant pulse. "Which guy is it, exactly?" But he already knew. The only one coming from out of town was—

"The best man." The words rolled matter-of-factly off Hannah's tongue, and Marcus did a classic double take.

"The best *what*?" If that were true, he'd be walking down the aisle with Allie—the maid of honor.

Which should have been matron of honor by now.

His stomach pitched a little, sort of like the time he'd been in a rear-end collision. He could see it coming, could feel the panic squeezing his chest, but the brakes just weren't working quickly enough.

Hannah clapped his shoulder and squeezed. "Best *man*, silly. You'll be great—you've had practice."

"Thanks for the reminder, little sis." He shot her a warning glare, and she brushed him off with a flippant wave of her hand.

"You'll be fine." She grabbed his arm and tugged him toward the sanctuary doors. He paused, shrugging out of her grip as reality sucker-punched him in the gut.

This was the first time he'd entered this church since that fateful day last September. Now he'd be standing there in a wedding not his own—with Allie ironically on his arm.

They'd never been able to finish the conversation they'd left hanging at the tool shower a few days ago. When Allie finished her phone call, she'd gone straight to the notebook Hannah had set aside for her and begun scribbling down names and gifts as the presents were methodically opened. After the party, she'd stayed to help with the cleanup. There was no reason for him to stay without looking suspicious, since his offer to help around the house was quickly dismissed by Zach's mother.

Thanks to Hannah and their mom, who always had one more errand for him to run, the next forty-eight hours had been a blur of work and wedding prep. He'd been hoping for a repeat of that kiss, despite their mutual agreement that it couldn't happen. But more than that, he just hoped Allie didn't think he was avoiding her.

Though come to think of it, he hadn't run into her again out and about, and she hadn't texted him. Or called.

Speaking of . . . her car pulled into the lot behind them, and Allie got out, the hem of her long dress fluttering against her legs. She looked beautiful, but when did she not?

"I'll meet you inside." He nudged his sister along, determined to tell Allie the news about the change in the wedding lineup himself. She deserved to be warned, because he had a feeling walking back into that same church might be even weirder for her than for him.

He started toward her, and she offered a half smile that didn't meet her eyes as she shoved her keys into her purse. "Hi."

Something was definitely wrong. She probably thought he'd been avoiding discussing that kiss. He ran his hand over his jaw, eager to use the right words to put her mind at ease. "Allie, I didn't—"

The spinning of gravel drowned out his apology. A blue four-door sedan pulled into the spot near Allie, and her face drained of color as the driver's door popped open.

"No." The word escaped and lingered on her lips, morphing into a half groan. He turned just as the backseat doors flew open. Several pairs of legs in panty hose slid out of the car, and he winced at the panic crossing Allie's face.

Her family.

Then a look of horror replaced the panic as a tall, thin man slid out of the passenger side.

~

Allie marched slowly beside Marcus down the carpeted aisle to the front of the church, her shaking hand tucked inside his elbow. Hearing about his upgrade to best man hadn't exactly done much to calm the nerves that had been shot at the sight of her family cruising into the parking lot like invited guests—including her mother's new fiancé. How dare they?

Nor did it help the quiver in her legs as the reality of entering the church she'd once sprinted out of hit her full force.

Couldn't Hannah have chosen a different venue?

Not to mention that this church aisle was clearly about three football fields long. Her palm grew slick against Marcus's sleeve, and she briefly clenched her hand into a fist. They'd been walking this aisle forever, and each step just intensified how awkward the entire ordeal was. The former bride and groom, strolling casually toward the altar as maid of honor and substitute best man. Who would have thought?

God definitely had a sense of humor.

Her shoe caught in the thick carpet and she pitched forward, straightening as Marcus's strong hand gripped her tighter.

Marcus deposited her on the top step with a brief squeeze of her arm, and she listened as the wedding coordinator stopped to instruct the sound man in the balcony when to press play for the unity candle song.

But all she could really hear was the not-so-whispered conversation going on between her mom, her aunt Shelly, and her grandmother, who all perched on the first pew of the bride's section like it was already tomorrow evening and time for the wedding—which they also weren't invited to.

Allie shifted the pretend bouquet Hannah had made them out of rolled-up newspapers, wishing she could hide her face behind it, and shot a glance at Marcus. If he hadn't changed his mind about her already since their kiss, he surely would now. Who crashed a rehearsal? Her family's true colors were bleeding all over the place.

His gaze appeared riveted to her family, all three women sitting there with legs crossed, feet bouncing, ashy blond or gray hair piled on top of their heads, smug smiles highlighting their intent—they were going to hit up the rehearsal dinner. If free food was involved, her aunt was all over it. And they were just tacky enough to do it, not caring about decorum or embarrassing Allie in the least.

"Allie! Don't forget my dress." Her mom pointed at her as if they were the only ones in the room, not concerned that she was interrupting a ceremony taking place. "Two weeks, remember?" She patted the arm of the man at her side, who smiled and waved as if he had no idea he'd just joined the circus.

Mrs. Hall shot a concerned look between the two of them as the pastor began instructing Hannah and Zach on where they'd stand during the ceremony. She focused on Allie once again and mouthed, "Are you okay?"

Okay was pretty relative at the moment. Maybe even rhetorical. Allie forced a nod, her face burning, as mortification, razor sharp, swelled inside her. First the confusing back-and-forth with Marcus and his roller-coaster reactions, then her inner debate over the workbench. Then the phone call and wedding announcement from her mom, the kiss with Marcus that was completely left hanging in midair, and now her family crashing her best friend's rehearsal—inside the same church where she and Marcus had nearly wed.

She eyed him across the steps from her, and he caught her eye and winked.

Her stomach flipped. He still thought she meant what she'd started to say before her mom's phone call interrupted them in the kitchen. He had his hopes up again, just as she'd feared. Dreaded. Wished for.

She squeezed her newspaper bouquet with clammy fingers. She'd *wanted* Marcus to hope. Wanted to plant that seed of expectation and possibility in his heart after the kiss. Why? Why would she do that when she knew deep down it couldn't happen?

That nothing had changed, and never would.

Because clearly, she was just like her mom. And her aunt. Taking advantage of men, using them for her own purposes, her own pleasure, her own means of beefing up her self-esteem. It would only be a matter of time before she tossed them—tossed Marcus—aside in the same way they did, moving on to the next victim when the last didn't fully satisfy.

She looked back at Marcus, who seemed transfixed on the ceremony before him, and her heart cracked.

Some things couldn't be restored.

Not Marcus. Not her engagement or her family.

Definitely not her heart.

She couldn't breathe.

Allie pressed her hand against her stomach as the church closed in on her, until all she could hear was the snort of laughter from Husband #27 coming from the front row near her mom and the stage-whispered criticisms from her aunt and grandmother over every carefully handcrafted decoration in the church. This was her life. She didn't belong with Marcus and Mrs. Hall. With Hannah and Zach and the purity and love shining in their eyes.

She was part of the circus too. Bound to it by chains of blood and DNA and whispers of memories that never fully left her alone. She was crazy to think she had a chance of escape.

Marcus caught her eye, and the suffocating feeling intensified. Losing him again after their glimpse of reconciliation would be a hundred times worse than the first time. He'd never understand, and this time he'd hate her. How could she have been so selfish, giving him hope with that kiss?

His brow furrowed in concern as her face heated, and she swayed on the stairs. The ceiling dipped and panic gripped her in a vise. She had to get out of there or risk fainting in front of everyone.

Marcus took a step toward her, but the pastor's microphone squealed a protest. He tapped it with a grin. "And then at this point in the ceremony I'll say, 'Zach, you may kiss your bride.'"

The wedding party raised their arms and cheered as Zach blew a kiss to Hannah. Allie's mom planted a smack on her soon-to-be husband's cheek. Mr. Hall dipped Mrs. Hall into a backward kiss.

And Allie hitched up her dress and bolted down the aisle.

Eight

Funny how history had a way of repeating itself.

Once again Marcus stood in front of Beaux Creek's only pawn shop, his and Allie's wedding rings clenched in his hand—except this time he was determined to actually go inside.

Because this time he'd actually *seen* Allie run away from him in full Technicolor instead of only imagining it. This time was different.

This time he was done.

The morning sun screamed a contradiction to his mood as he pushed open the door, the dusty scent of unmoved merchandise and cheap cologne slapping him in the face. He nodded a curt greeting to the owner behind the counter. Bert nodded back as he paged through a fishing magazine. "Have a look around," he said in a monotone. "Let me know if I can help."

Marcus thanked him, though help from anyone at this

point seemed impossible. He hesitated at the counter, taking in the selection of jewelry beneath the smudged glass. Could he really add his and Allie's rings to that random collection of gold, white gold, and sterling silver?

Yes. Because he couldn't get the image of Allie dashing down the aisle last night out of his head. Why did she think running away was the answer to everything? So what if her family embarrassed her? Yeah, they were pretty bad, he wouldn't lie. And being surrounded by a crowd of people kissing, in the very church they were supposed to have gotten married in, had to be emotionally draining for her. He knew, because he'd felt it too.

But they could have been one of those kissing couples. They *were* one of them, just days before in Zach's kitchen. What had happened?

She'd reappeared, like a ghost from Christmas past, at the rehearsal dinner, face stoic and eyes averted, dutifully serving his sister as maid of honor yet clearly a thousand miles away in her head. She didn't want to be there.

All he'd ever wanted was to be by Allie's side—and she kept running away.

From him.

He might still be in love, but he wasn't stupid.

"Here." He slapped the rings on the counter with a clink, trying to ignore the ache deep in his chest. "How much for these?"

Bert grunted and squinted over the top of his magazine, eyed Marcus with suspicion, then went for his magnifying glass.

He looked up in surprise.

Marcus nodded. "I know, man. They're real." All too real. And too useless. He swallowed and gripped the edge of the counter with his fingers. "How much?"

Bert named a figure well under what the rings had cost, but Marcus nodded without argument. "Sold."

No more looking back.

Allie had chosen.

~

Red eyeliner was never appropriate for a wedding.

Unfortunately, Allie's makeup-free face boasted exactly that very look.

She rubbed at the bags under her eyes and stared dejectedly into the bathroom mirror, adjusting the tie on her fuzzy turquoise robe. Accusations screamed back at her teary, rumpled morning reflection. *Heartbreaker. User. Hypocrite.*

She could only imagine what Marcus must think of her right now, bolting from the church—again—and ignoring his panicked texts and phone calls the rest of the evening. She wasn't sure what was worse—the incessant phone calls and message chimes, or the silence that hovered when they stopped.

She was more than a little ashamed of herself.

Maybe she'd taken the coward's way out by running.

But in running, she'd saved Marcus from another near-mistake. She wouldn't have been able to reject him to his face. Not after that kiss, not after the connection they'd resurrected.

Not after feeling those few moments of hope.

At least she'd left one final message, something she'd

never gotten the chance to do last time. Maybe it would help—or make things incredibly worse.

Guess she'd find out.

The doorbell rang, and her heart jerked in a violent twist. If it was Marcus, she wouldn't open the door. Not only because of her disheveled appearance, but because if he looked at her with anything other than pure anger in his eyes, she'd melt like a cherry Popsicle.

She peered through the peephole, her heart sinking in an odd mixture of relief and disappointment. Not Marcus.

It was his mother.

What was Mrs. Hall doing here when Hannah's wedding was that very night? She should be getting ready or puttering around the church with last-minute preparations. Allie would be doing the same, as soon as she figured out how to get her makeup to cover the consequences of crying all night long.

She took a deep breath and pulled open the door. "Julie—I mean, Mrs. Hall."

"It's still Julie." Marcus's mom bustled inside, as if she knew Allie might close the door at any minute. A garment bag was draped over one arm. "I've brought your dress."

An even stronger wave of shame and embarrassment washed over Allie. "I didn't want Hannah to ask you to do that. It didn't seem right. But . . . thank you." She reached for the bag, but Julie held it out of reach.

"First things first." She pointed toward the living room, and Allie followed willingly, like a child desperately needing instruction. Something about Julie's take-charge yet kind demeanor was like chicken soup to her sick heart. "Sit."

Allie sat.

Julie perched on the edge of the couch, two cushions away, close enough to talk intimately but not so close that Allie felt pressured to run again. "Now I'm going to talk, and I want you to listen. Not apologize. Not explain yourself. Just listen."

She began to unzip the garment bag, and Allie braced herself to see the dress that always tore up her insides. At least the rip would be fixed now, and she could give the dress to her mother as expected and avoid that pending headache.

But the dress Julie pulled from the bag wasn't the Andrews' family wedding dress.

"What is that?" Allie leaned closer, then drew back as reality sank in. It was her dress. Completely remade.

Horror began a slow creep up her chest. Her mother was going to kill her. Actually, there'd be a line to kill her, starting with her grandmother, who treated that gown like some sort of ancient family heirloom. It *was* an ancient family heirloom.

Ancient family curse, too, but she was clearly the only one who cared.

"I took some liberties."

Julie held her hand to stop the words she probably assumed were about to flow out of Allie, but there was no danger of that. Allie couldn't speak if she tried. Her tongue felt glued to the roof of her mouth.

"But I felt like it had to be done." She paused, as if gathering her thoughts, and Allie couldn't tear her eyes away from the material that used to be what she considered one of the ugliest dresses in the history of wedding dresses.

This gown, this shorter, stylish, tailored gown, was nothing short of a masterpiece.

It looked exactly like her. Right down to the thin straps and the turquoise sash knotted around the waist.

"Allie, I've been a mother a long time." Julie reached across the couch and took Allie's hand in hers, her manicured fingers cool, yet her touch warm all at once. Exactly like a mom's should be. Allie squeezed back as if clutching a lifeline. "And I've watched you around my son. You love him. You never stopped."

Tears—how could she possibly have any left?—pressed behind Allie's eyes, setting off another headache pounding in her temples. She fought to draw a ragged breath as she nodded her confirmation.

"So I've been trying to figure out what went wrong last fall, since clearly you still have the same feelings for Marcus you've always had." Julie hesitated, the silence illuminated only by the ticking of the antique wall clock.

Twin tears dripped into Allie's lap as she waited for the slice of the guillotine.

"You're believing lies, Allie." Julie took her chin and demanded her gaze. "And it's time to stop."

"What lies?" Silly question. If she could plug in her brain, she could hit Print and let Julie and the rest of the world just see for themselves. Except the thoughts didn't feel like lies. They looked a lot like truth. Like a bunch of unnecessary baggage for someone like Marcus to carry.

"You are not defined by your family, sweet girl. You're not destined to repeat their mistakes." Julie leaned closer, her gaze serious. "But you're making your own because of trying so hard to avoid theirs."

Now *that* sounded like truth, and pricked like it too.

Was she guilty of that? Had Allie somehow, in trying so desperately to avoid being like her family, done the exact same thing? Pushed men away in order to avoid getting hurt? In this case, she'd pushed Marcus away to prevent hurting *him*.

Same premise. Same consequences. Same end result.

Heartache.

Before Allie could fully process the possibility, Julie picked up the dress and draped it over the back of the couch between them. "You and Marcus have always had something special in common. You both like to restore things."

Allie thought of the message she'd left on Marcus's porch, and grief knotted in her stomach. She nodded through the tears. He'd been the one to convince her to believe in her gift and open her own shop, while she'd been the one always propped beside him and an open hood, fascinated by his ability to turn uselessness into value.

"Instead of furniture and cars, why not make your next project something more worthwhile?" Julie fingered the short hem of the remade dress, then smoothed the silky sash. "There's beauty in everything, Allie. There's a time to tear and a time to mend."

Allie risked a glance fully into her almost mother-in-law's eyes, and read for herself the love and acceptance inside. If Julie could forgive and forget the hurt Allie had caused their entire family—twice—was there a chance Marcus could do the same?

Was it even fair to ask?

Doubts tickled her conscience, and her hope wavered. She ran her hands lightly over the dress, then stood up, pulling it off the couch and holding it up against her body. It would fit perfectly, she could already tell. The hem fell just to her knees, though it dipped longer in the back. The once-lacy sleeves had been cut into thin straps that would highlight her collarbone and narrow shoulders, while the waist tapered into the low-slung turquoise sash. Modern, with a classic flare.

Exactly the kind of dress she would have chosen for herself.

Exactly the kind of dress she would love for Marcus to see her in.

And exactly the kind of dress that could allow her to be a new creation, once and for all. Maybe she could do it—redeem the dress. Redeem her relationship with Marcus.

Redeem herself.

"Don't be afraid to mend, Allie. Don't be afraid to heal." Julie smiled, as if sensing the direction of her thoughts. "I think it's time. Don't you?"

Allie began to tug the dress off the hanger in response, a faint image of hope urging her on.

And a brief vision of the look on Marcus's face when he realized that this time she wasn't running anywhere.

~

Marcus should have felt lighter without the weight of those two gold bands in his pocket, but an anvil sat on his chest and refused to budge. He turned off his truck, shot a glance at the garage hiding the car he'd labored over so painstakingly, and trudged toward the porch.

A tall, polished wooden workbench sat in front of his door.

He blinked, then ran his hand over the sturdy shelves. The entire piece was beautiful, down to the carved details on the back and the sleekness of the legs. Where had it come from? He needed one, for sure, but this wasn't the kind of bench to stick in a garage. This was more like a keepsake.

A closer look revealed deep scuffing under the stain, hinting at a long history of prior use. The screws on the back of the bench attaching the shelves were new. A lot of effort had gone into this restoration.

And he only knew one person with a touch like that.

The same person whose handwriting adorned the front of a white envelope resting under a rock on the shiny restored seat.

Anticipation and dread warring for placement in his heart, Marcus sank slowly to the bench and opened the envelope, pulling out several pieces of paper lined with Allie's familiar scrawl.

Marcus,

Hannah said you were considering moving to Texas. I wouldn't really blame you, because some days I'd escape me too, if I could. Like last night. I know what my running out of the church must have done to you, but I couldn't seem to get my heart and my feet on the same page. I'm sorry I hurt you. Again.

But in hurting you, I'm only trying to save you. Save you from ending up worse, later, with me. You know my family, you know where I come from. Who I am. You're better off, Marcus. Please believe me. It has nothing to do with you, and everything to do with me.

I wanted you to have this bench, this reminder that there's a lot of good that can come from old. A lot of use that can come from worn.

That's what Mrs. Hawkins told me when she brought this bench into the store, nearly falling apart in her nephews' hands.

I wish restoring the past were as simple as restoring this bench. If it were, I'd buy stock in stain and sandpaper and give it all I had. But I'm afraid some things weren't meant to be mended.

Sort of like my family's wedding dress, the one I'm so grateful you never saw me in. It was awful, for so many reasons, most of them having nothing to do with vanity at all, but rather, with what that ridiculous gown represented. Decades of failed marriages. Broken promises.

When I found a rip in the sleeve in the bridal room before our ceremony started, it was like a sign, a symbol urging me to tear myself away for your own good.

I've never been good at mending lace.

And all I can do now is ask for your forgiveness and wish you the best. Because you're a treasure, Marcus.

And you deserve the same.

Love always,
Allie

Marcus folded the papers, then turned them over and over in his hand. A treasure. Did Allie have no idea how *he* saw *her*? Had he failed that miserably as a friend, a boyfriend, a fiancé, over the past several years, that she was clueless to her own value? A value that had nothing to do with family trees and genealogy and cursed dresses.

Rather, a value that shone *because* of who she was. Her experiences and family, crazy as they were, had shaped her into the woman she was.

The woman he loved.

A swell of hope shoved the anvil off his heart, and he

stood, pocketing the letter and grabbing for his keys. Allie might have burned him twice, but it'd take three times before he'd learn his lesson. Maybe four. It didn't matter.

He checked his watch, then quickened his pace toward his truck. He had about six hours until the wedding—four, really, until he needed to be at the church for pictures.

He'd have to hurry. He shot a glance at the garage and made a quick detour. First to the garage.

Then to the pawn shop.

~

Allie adjusted the turquoise tie on her dress for the tenth time as she paced outside the bridal suite, waiting for Hannah to finish talking to her father in private. She'd called her friend on the way to the church several hours prior for pictures and received permission to execute her crazy plan. She hadn't wanted to steal the show on her friend's big day, but Hannah was so excited that she didn't mind in the least.

Allie wore her bridesmaid gown for the group pictures, then donned her new wedding dress with shaky hands, determined to be proactive for once in her life.

At least if she ran this time, she wouldn't have to hike up the hem.

No, no running. For the first time in a long time, peace flooded her heart. She had to try. Marcus deserved her best, and while the flutters in her stomach had yet to be convinced that her plan had even a chance of working, she remained determined to stick it out.

"It's time." Hannah and her father walked out of the bridal suite, and a chorus of nerves burst into anthem in Allie's heart. It was time. Now or never.

She really, really didn't want it to be never.

She gripped her friend's hand. "You look amazing."

"So do you." Hannah leaned in close as she adjusted her bouquet and grinned. "You ready?"

"Let's do this." They slapped a high five, and Allie went to join the processional line in front of Hannah and her dad.

Julie, who had been keeping Marcus at bay all afternoon with bogus tasks, darted around the corner of the long hallway and shot a thumbs-up sign to Allie.

Go time.

Her stomach flipped. She was crazy. What if this didn't even work? What if he couldn't forgive her?

What if *he* ran?

She joined the end of the line in the foyer outside the double doors of the church and waited for Marcus to file in beside her, looking heart-stoppingly amazing in his tuxedo. He slipped into place as the music started inside and the elderly family members began to be escorted into the church.

"Finally. I've been trying to talk to you all afternoon. I wanted to tell you thank you—" He stopped and did a double take. "Did you change your dress after the pictures?"

"Yes." Her voice came out barely above a whisper, so not what she had practiced. But it was hard to concentrate with that white collar setting off his brown eyes, and the way his hair curled slightly over the sides of it.

"It's beautiful." His gaze flickered over her dress, then back to her eyes.

Suddenly the hallway felt much too crowded.

She pulled Marcus a few feet away, ignoring the look she could feel Hannah shooting her from the far side of the processional line. The music changed to Pachelbel's Canon in D. She only had a few minutes to get Marcus's answer.

"Thank you for the bench. And the letter." Marcus reached out and cupped her arm, grazing his fingers from her elbow to her hand. His touch sent shock waves of electricity up her arm, but did he mean to? Or was he just being friendly?

"You're welcome, but you deserve a better explanation than that." She swallowed and gathered her nerve. She could do this, had to do this. Marcus was worth it. And she wasn't the old Allie anymore. She wasn't a victim. She wasn't trapped in an old life.

She was a new creation. Just like her dress.

Just like she and Marcus could be, if she could just get the words out without crying.

The music surged onward, and her heart rate tripled. The speech she'd planned, all the careful words she'd written that afternoon, fled her memory, and all she could blurt out was the deepest desire of her heart. "Marry me, Marcus."

His eyes widened. With shock? Grief? Regret? Hope? She couldn't tell.

But it was almost their turn down the aisle, and she didn't know if her February wedding had a groom.

"I'm a mess, and so is my family. I don't know what's going to change, or if I'll ever really get over everything I've believed all my life." Allie hesitated, wringing her fingers together, wishing she had more eloquent words to express her heart. "But I want to try. You make me want to try." She reached for him, then stopped, as she still had no idea what was going on behind his piercing gaze. "I just know that when I saw what your mom did to this dress, saw how it could be restored and made new, I had hope—real hope—that maybe we could be too." She tugged at her sash, self-conscious. "So . . . will you? Marry me?"

Marcus shook his head, and her heart fell into her high-heeled shoes.

"I understand."

Who had she been kidding? Of course it couldn't be that easy. After all she'd put him through . . . yet now they had to walk down the aisle together as if nothing was wrong. As if her bleeding heart wasn't leaving a trail right down her dress. As if her future hadn't just been knocked away by a wrecking ball once again.

"I can't say yes, because I have my own question." Marcus took her hands and knelt before her. "Will *you* marry *me*?"

Gladness bubbled from deep inside, seeping out through the edges and bursting free in a joyous laugh like she hadn't experienced in years. "Yes. Yes!"

Canon in D swelled as Marcus stood, and she pressed her lips against his to seal the promise. His arms locked against her waist, and her head spun as he lifted her slightly off the ground. She was home.

She was with family.

"There's just one more detail to that question I asked you." She nudged him in the side with her elbow, giddiness filling her spirit. He was going to freak out. "It's only good for today. A double wedding."

They didn't have a marriage license, of course, but the ceremony would seal their commitment, and they could take care of the legalities as soon as the courthouse opened back up.

"What? *Today?*" Marcus feigned what was clearly pretend shock before he grinned. "Let me show you something." He pulled her a few more feet toward the outside doors, and bumped one open with his hip. Then he tugged her to his side and wrapped his arms around her from behind. "See anything familiar?"

No. She looked away, confused about why he wasn't more surprised, and why she was staring at a parking lot.

Then, yes. A Mustang. A 1973 Mach 1, if she wasn't mistaken, parked under the awning at the side of the reception hall. Was that—

She blinked, then swallowed, then blinked again, pulling slowly out of Marcus's arms to get a closer view. "Is that my car? I thought you sold it." She couldn't believe it—though yes, on second thought, she could. Typical Marcus.

And the turquoise racing stripe down the front was all her.

"Anything can be restored, Allie." Marcus brushed escaped tendrils of hair back from her cheeks, leaning in close to steal another kiss. His voice drifted to a lazy whisper. "A time to tear . . ."

"And a time to mend."

She wasn't afraid of mending anymore. Or tearing. Because a little bit of both just made her that much stronger.

Made love that much stronger.

They kissed again as the music inside the sanctuary changed to the traditional wedding march.

"I believe that's our cue." Marcus held out his arm, and she fit her hand neatly into his elbow. In front of them, Hannah shot a wink and a grin as she marched down the aisle beside her father.

Then it was their turn.

Allie's stomach twisted as rows and rows of heads turned to stare at the second bride walking down the aisle. But her feet remained firmly in place, routed forward to the altar, and her arm remained tucked safely into Marcus's. She wasn't running anywhere.

Except straight into her very own February wedding.

1. Allie took a Biblical truth about generational cursing and applied it to her life in a defeated way, rather than seeking to use her faith in God to break the destructive cycle in her family. Have you ever misunderstood or misapplied a Biblical truth in your life? What was the result?
2. Marcus was torn about accepting the job offer in Texas after his breakup with Allie because he wasn't ready for that official Next Step, that final nail in the coffin. Have you ever hesitated to move on after a life change for fear of the unknown? What did you decide and what was the consequence?
3. Allie and Marcus both loved each other unconditionally, yet in trying to do what was best for the other, ended up pushing each other away. Have you ever pushed away someone in your life whom you loved for good reason? Was the result beneficial or heartbreaking? What did you learn from the experience?

4. Hannah's wedding plans and parties threw Allie and Marcus together many times. Do you think those painful reminders of their own wedding season helped bring Allie and Marcus back together or caused more drama between them? Why?
5. Restoring old things and making them new is something both Marcus and Allie are naturally drawn to. How was this symbolic to their love story?
6. Hannah and Allie's friendship survived a significant road bump after Allie left Hannah's brother at the altar. Have you ever had a friend forgive you or show you grace after a hard decision or mistake? What did that teach you about the friendship? Have you ever had to show grace to a friend in a similar manner?
7. Allie and Marcus both desired to give the other a significant gift to remind them of their feelings for each other. Have you ever used a gift to show someone your love or care for them? What did you give and what was their response?

Special thanks to Becky Philpott, editor extraordinaire, for her heart, vision, and friendship. And to the entire team at Zondervan Fiction, for their hard work and dedication in putting out a product that entertains and inspires. Novel writing is such a team effort!

A graceful curtsey in the general direction of my fellow "bridesmaids" in A Year of Weddings collection—you ladies know how to make weddings look good! I am so blessed to be in this series with all of you.

As always, thanks to my super-agent team, Tamela Hancock Murray and Steve Laube, for their support, advice, and unceasing cheerleading. "Y'all rock!"

Thanks also to my good friend, who offered his expertise in all things cars, to make a few scenes in this story jive. And just for the record, my Camaro can still beat your Mustang. (I'm just saying.)

I couldn't have made this story happen without my girl Kim! Thanks for dropping everything to respond to my SOS at Barnes & Noble. I owe you a mocha, a brainstorming session, and probably a nap. You are such a gift.

Photo by Ken Raney

Betsy St. Amant is one Good Girl who enjoys writing about reformed Bad Boys in her romance novels. Southern gal by both choice and default, Betsy grew up in Louisiana and has an adorable preschooler who is already giving Mama a run for her money in storytelling. When Betsy isn't writing, she can often be found consuming massive amounts of Pickle Pringles and singing along to the *Tangled* soundtrack with her daughter. An avid reader who is constantly wondering where Mr. Darcy went, Betsy holds a B.A. in Christian Communications, is a freelance journalist, multi-published fiction writer, and nonfiction contributor. She enjoys speaking and teaching on the craft of writing and sharing the good news of God's grace through her stories.

9780310338284-B

Hope is used to creating the perfect setting for others' nuptials at her aunt's Victorian inn and charming rustic barn. But when someone from her past comes back into her life, will she end up walking down the aisle herself?

Available in e-book only November 2014

9780310338741-A

A Year of Weddings

ZONDERVAN®

9780310338741-A